The Revelat
Yahushua the

GW01019298

A Clear, Common-Sense Commentary
for Those who Embrace the Hebraic Roots of their Faith

"Come out of her, My People" – Revelation 18:4

"Hypocrites! You know how to discern the face of the sky, but you cannot discern the signs of the times." - Yahushua

**Infuriating to Many
Terrifying to Some
But Thrilling to the Few who are Open to the Truth, Enlightened
by it, Take it to Heart, and Act on it**

**By Watchman Bob
Last Trump Ministries**

Cover design by Estela Jia Ceyril Redulla

ISBN-13: 978-1490554471
ISBN-10: 1490554475

Last Trump Ministries

www.RevelationUnderstoodCommentary.com
WatchmanBob@gmail.com

Table of Contents

Important Terms and Concepts

This commentary is written from the perspective of a Messianic Believer (a "Christian" who embraces the Hebraic roots of his faith). Why? . . . simply because it is impossible to fully understand the *Bible* without understanding the Hebraic perspective from which it was written. Also, there are over 200 references to the Hebrew Scriptures in the Revelation. For the sake of faithfulness to the original language of the Scriptures (Hebrew), which is often distorted by English translations from Greek manuscripts, numerous Hebrew terms like Yahuah ("God"), Yahushua ("Jesus"), and Messiah (a transliteration of Mashiach) are used in this commentary. Several terms and concepts are used that may be somewhat unfamiliar to most Christians. So, for the purpose of effective communication, the following explanations are provided:

Y-H-W-H—the closest English approximation of the Hebrew letters that represent the name of the god of Abraham, Isaac, and Jacob (Israel). Written Scriptural Hebrew (in the earliest extant manuscripts) contains no vowels—just marks that indicate what vowels should be used in pronouncing words. And because of prohibitions against speaking the name of the Creator, scribes of the earliest extant Hebrew Scriptures refused to include a mark for the second vowel in His name. However, at least one expositor[1], who has thoroughly researched the spelling and pronunciation of the name of the Most High God, explains that the correct pronunciation of *YHWH* is "Yahuah," which means "The Self-Existent One, Who is the Beginning and the End." Actually, the earliest extant Hebrew manuscripts spell the Name *YHVH*. But research has also revealed that, in ancient, pre-Solomon Paleo-Hebrew, there was no such letter as *v*, and the third letter of the name is *w* (*waw)*, pronounced "uu." The poetic short form of the Name is *Yah*, pronounced "Yah" (as in "yawn"). Historically, the Jews, in their hesitancy to speak the name represented by the letters Y-H-W-H, have substituted *Adonai* ("Lord"). But, contrary to the practice of most Jews and many Messianic Believers, if we have an intimate, Renewed

---

[1]For an excellent exposition of the Names of the Father (represented by *YHWH)* and the Son, visit www.MyHolyName.com.

Covenant relationship with our loving heavenly Father, He delights in hearing His Children speak His name, imperfect though our attempts to do so may be. *YHWH* actually occurs more than 6,800 times in the earliest extant Hebrew manuscripts. Moses, to whom the name of the God of his fathers had first been revealed (Exodus 3:15), openly proclaimed His name (Deuteronomy 32:3). Yahuah's People are exhorted to take oaths in His name (Deuteronomy 6:13; 10:20), exalt His name (Psalm 34:3), give thanks to His name (Psalm 122:4), praise His name (Psalm 113:1, 3; 135:1), bless His name (Deuteronomy 10:8; Psalm 145:21), minister in His name (Deuteronomy 18:5), serve in His name (Deuteronomy 18:7), call upon His name (Isaiah 12:4), and glorify His name (Isaiah 24:15). King David sang praises to His name (Psalm 18:49), declared that he would wait on His name (Psalm 52:9) and make His name to be remembered (Psalm 45:17), appealed to Yahuah to save him by His name (Psalm 54:1), and prophesied that all the earth would sing praises to His name (Psalm 66:4) and all nations would glorify His name (Psalm 86:9). Finally, Solomon asked, "What is His name, and what is His Son's name? Surely you know!" (Proverbs 30:4) Indeed, how are we going to make the distinct name of our God known to the world without speaking it? *Jahovah* is an Anglicized corruption of the name represented by YHWH, formed by changing the *Y* to *J*, the *W* to *v*, and combining the letters J-H-V-H with the vowels of Adonai. But, as with *v* there is no *j* in ancient Hebrew. The terms *LORD* and *GOD* as used in most Greek (Gentile) translations of the Scripture (including the New King James Version, which is quoted in this commentary) in the place of *Yahuah,* are not proper names of the God of Israel and should not be used as such. They are descriptive titles. So, unless otherwise indicated, *the Lord,* as used in this commentary, refers to a title of the God of Israel and not to His name. Also, the Hebrew plural term *'elohiym* (English: *Elohim)* is frequently translated *God* in Scripture (e.g., Genesis 1:1), but is a title referring to Yahuah's divine, omnipotent, triune nature rather than to His proper name. *Elohim* is also used in Scripture to refer to created or spiritual off-spring of Yahuah or even to other gods (cf. Exodus 22:19; Psalm 8:5; John 10:35), so may be confusing when used as a title of Yahuah. Although *God* is commonly used in referring to Yahuah by Christians, Jews and Messianic Believers, its meaning must be determined by context, and will be used in this commentary only when quoting the Hebrew text.

Yahushua—which means "The Self-Existent One, Who is Salvation," is the Hebrew name of Israel's Messiah. Note that the name of the incarnation of Yahuah, to reflect His divinity, actually contains the name of the God of Israel. "Jesus" is a Greek (Gentile) corruption of the name of the Messiah, actually, some say, having been derived from a variation of the name of the Greek god Zeus ("Y'Zeus" or "Ie-Zeus"), so it may actually represent an attempt to replace the name of the Hebrew Messiah with the name of a pagan god. "The Lord" may be a title of either Yahuah the Father or Yahushua the Son - or both - depending on the context.

Messiah—an English transliteration of the Hebrew title *Maschiach,* meaning "Anointed One." The Greek or Gentile version is "Christ" (from the Greek: *Khristos)* which also means "anointed one" and is combined with "Jesus" in most English translations of the *Bible* to form the alleged full name of the Messiah—"Jesus Christ" or "Christ Jesus." However, *Khristos* was a title the Greeks used for several of their pagan Gods, so neither "Jesus" nor "Christ" will be used in this commentary as the name of the Messiah.

BCE (**B**efore the **C**ommon **E**ra) and **CE** (the **C**ommon **E**ra)— refer to events or times before or after Yahushua's birth. The usual terms BC (Before Christ) and AD (*Anno Domini* – in the year of the Lord) are misleading because they, in a subtle way, undermine the deity of the Messiah, implying that He did not exist before His birth. They also play into the hands of the replacement theologians who teach that Christians have replaced Israel as Yahuah's chosen People. The alternative terms BCE (Before the Common Era, Christian Era, or Current Era) and CE (the Common Era, Current Era, or Christian Era) are also misleading because they are ambiguous terms developed by Jews and secularists to deny that the coming of the Messiah Yahushua to Earth was the turning point of world history and, indeed, to deny the Son of the Father Yahuah's existence altogether. Also, they are inaccurate, because astronomical and historical evidence have shown that Yahushua was born in 3 BC or BCE. However, for the sake of communication and the lack of a better alternative, the neutral terms BCE and CE will be used in this commentary to designate calendar dates.

The *Tanakh* and the *B'rit Hadashah*—commonly referred to as the Old Testament and the New Testament, respectively. However, "Old Testament" and "New Testament" are misleading terms, giving the impression that Scripture given before the time of Yahushua is outdated or has been replaced by Scripture given after the time of Yahushua.

But the apostle Paul stated, *"All Scripture* [referring especially to the *Tanakh*, because the *B'rit Hadashah* had not yet been compiled] *is given by the inspiration of* [Yahuah] . . ." (2 Timothy 3:16). *"Tanakh"* is an acronym made from the first letters of the three main divisions of the Hebrew Bible: *Torah* (the "Law" or "instructions" of Yahuah), *Nevi'im* (Prophets) and *K'tuvim* (writings). *"B'rit Hadashah"* is a Hebrew term meaning "new covenant," and is used for Scripture written after the birth of Yahushua because He established the New Covenant, which is the *Torah* written on Believers' hearts, with the sacrifice of Himself for our sins (cf. Matthew 26:28).

Israel or **the Hebrews**—refers to the descendants of Jacob (natural or proselytized). "True Israel," as distinguished by the apostle Paul (cf. Romans 9:6), looks forward in faith to the coming of the Messiah, whether or not they have yet recognized that He is Yahushua (cf. Romans 11:25). Although "Hebrews" referred originally to the descendants of Abraham, the two terms came to be used interchangeably in referring to the descendants of Jacob.

Jews—originally and technically referred to members of one of the tribes of Israel - the tribe of Judah. But after the Northern Kingdom (Israel or Ephraim) divided from the Southern Kingdom, "Jews" referred to subjects of the Southern Kingdom because of its dominant tribe, Judah. However, after the Northern Kingdom was destroyed by the Assyrians in 722 BCE and many thousands of subjects of the tribes of the Northern Kingdom fled to the Southern Kingdom, intermingling all twelve tribes, "Jews" came to refer to the entire nation of Israel. And that is how the term was used by the apostle Paul, himself an Israelite of the tribe of Benjamin (Romans 11:1), who, in explaining his own Jewishness, clearly stated that the Jews were citizens of "my own nation" (Israel) and members of "all our twelve tribes" (Acts 26:4-7). Then, throughout His letter to the Romans, Paul used the terms "Israel" and "Jews" interchangeably.

The Saints, the Redeemed, or **the Elect**—Yahuah's ancient People Israel who, in faith, anticipated the Messiah, His current People the Jews who look forward in faith to the coming Messiah, and the Disciples of Yahushua are all, in both the *Tanakh* and the *B'rit Hadashah*, referred to as the *"called,"* the *"chosen,"* the *"elect,"* the *"redeemed,"* and the *"saints."* Indeed, as the apostle Paul explains, *"There is neither Jew nor Greek, there is neither slave nor free, there is neither* *male nor female; for you are all one in [the Messiah Yahushua]"* (Galatians 3:28). Whether "the Saints," "the Redeemed," or "the Elect" are referring to those Hebrews who look forward in faith to the coming Messiah, to the ones who have already accepted Yahushua as their Messiah, or to both must be determined by context.

Disciples of, Followers of, or **Believers in Yahushua (the Messiah)**—commonly referred to in Gentile translations of the *B'rit Hadashah* as "Christians." However, "Christian" is a misleading term coined by Greek-speaking Gentiles, giving the impression that the Hebrews who believe in the coming Messiah but have not yet recognized that He is Yahushua are separate from and have been relegated to an inferior status or replaced by the Christian Church, when, in fact, the People of Yahuah, including ancient Israel, have believed in, interacted with, and followed the Messiah throughout their history. See "Appendix 3—Who are the People of Yahuah"—for details.

Life in the Messiah—commonly referred to as "Christianity."

Yahuah's People, the Messianic Community, or **the Assembly of, the Congregation of, the Community of** or **the Body of Believers in Yahushua**—commonly referred to in Greek translations of the *B'rit Hadashah* as the "Church" (Greek: *ekklesia*—a gathering of citizens called out from their homes to some public place of assembly). "Church" is a Greek term that has taken on misleading connotations because it gives the false impression that Yahuah's People Israel or the Jews are separate from His People the Church. However, in both the *Tanakh* and the *B'rit Hadashah*, the *"assembly,"* the *"congregation,"* and the *"bride"* refer to the corporate People of Yahuah. And the apostle Paul explains that Gentiles who become Disciples of Yahushua are *"grafted into"* the *"commonwealth of Israel,"* which makes them *"fellow citizens with the saints* [Israel]" (cf. Romans 11:24; Ephesians 2:12, 19). In the Kingdom of Yahuah, there is no distinction between those of ancient Israel who looked forward in faith to the coming Messiah, the modern-day Jews who anticipate in faith His coming, and the present-day Disciples of Yahushua. Also, etymological studies have shown that the original root of the word "church" is the name of the Greek witch, sorceress, and goddess Circe, the daughter of the sun god Helios. So, in this commentary, in most cases, the term "assembly" will be used rather than "church."

5

Antimessiah—commonly referred to as "Antichrist" (1 John 4:3). Although many have the anti-messiah spirit, at the End of the Age, there will be a man (Revelation 13:18), the incarnation of Satan, the false messiah who, for a short time (42 months) will rule the world.

Note: When terms are substituted for original terms in quotations, they are enclosed by [brackets].

Introduction

The Lord Yahuah reveals, in an astonishing way through His prophetic Word, as explained in this crystal clear, common-sense Revelation commentary, what is happening in the world, what will soon happen, and what His People need to be doing about it, before it is too late. But . . .

Warning! This Revelation commentary may be hazardous to your complacency.

Yahushua did not come to Earth to perpetuate the status quo. His message was radical, using Scripture to expose the spiritual bankruptcy of the religious establishment. He was not one to mince words as He vilified the religious leaders with, "*Hypocrites! You know how to discern the face of the sky, but you cannot discern the signs of the times*" (Luke 12:56).

I, Watchman Bob, testify to you from personal experience (see "About the Author," page 303), sadly because I am one, that the majority of Christians today have exactly the same attitude toward the Truth and will "crucify" anyone who tries to share it with them.

However, if you will suspend any preconceived, church-taught docrines and conceptions of the "End of the Age" long enough to read this commentary with your mind and heart open to the Truth of Yahuah's Word, you will be amazed at how clearly current events in the light of *Bible* prophecy come into focus. And you will know the answers to all kinds of vexing questions like: Who is modern, prophetic Babylon? Who, really, are Yahuah's People? Who is Antimessiah ("Antichrist")? When is the Rapture? What is the Day of the Lord? What is True Christianity? Does the *Bible* really teach eternal torment for the unsaved? How can Yahuah's Wrath be avoided? How do I need to be living my life in the light of the Lord's Revelation? and, Did you know that there is incredible good news in the end for those who believe the Truth?

Then, best of all, if you will submit to the Lord's will, as revealed in His Revelation, you will find that His spiritual peace, love, joy, and hope will fill your heart, dissolving any of the dread that most people will increasingly experience as times get more trying and the Day of the Lord approaches.

So, get ready!

Fasten your seat belt and get ready for the ride of your life (if you have the courage to face up to reality), because, although this Revelation commentary is exegetically correct and the result of many years of diligent study, it is not the typical dry, doctrinally-heavy, detached-from-real-life Sunday school or seminary study. As Yahuah's Word, correctly understood and taken to heart, has always done, it will rock your churchianity boat and demand your faithful action, *if* you want to successfully navigate the perilous days ahead.

Signs of the Times

Natural and man-made calamities are increasing at an astonishing rate, are seriously shaking the economies and social stability of the whole world, and are showing no signs of letting up. In 2010 ethnic conflicts in Kyrgyzstan caused over 100,000 to flee that troubled land; massive volcanic eruptions in Iceland inundated Europe with volcanic ash, shut down airlines, and pummeled the European Union economy; the impending collapse of the economy of Greece and riots in that country forced her bailout by the EU, further destabilizing the economy and social order of Europe. In 2011 numerous other nations were on the verge of bankruptcy. Uprisings, the destabilization of governments, and the threat of all-out war in the Middle East continue to ravage that part of the world. Hurricanes, floods, earthquakes, and other natural disasters continued to increase in number and magnitude, killing hundreds of thousands all over the world. A massive earthquake and tsunami in Japan caused deadly damage to a nuclear power facility and terrible destruction and loss of life to the nation as a whole. According to a 2011 U.N. report, approximately 17,000 children (not including adults) were dying of starvation daily. Violence in general was increasing globally. In 2012, nothing changed for the better. Natural disasters, wars and rumors of wars, and economic distress continued to increase globally. The secular governments of one nation after another in the Middle East fell and were replaced, with the approval and support of the U.S. and other NATO nations, by Islamist regimes. The threat to the security of Israel, and indeed its very existence, increased dramatically as Iran continued to utter warnings of Israel's annihilation and to develop nuclear weapons, and Israel's surrounding Arab neighbors and terrorist groups continued to amass armaments near Israel's borders and even, from Gaza, to fire thousands of rockets into Israel. In 2013, all the above trends continued unabated and even accelerated—wars and rumors of wars, devastating natural disasters, famines and hunger, hoarding of the wealth by the top .1% while the masses sank into poverty and indentured servitude. And now, in 2014, global natural, social and spiritual disintegration have continued to accelerate, rapidly approaching meltdown. For example, in perfect fulfillment of *Bible* prophecy (Zechariah 12:3; 14:2, et. al), the Obama-led U.S. government, in a complete about-face from being (allegedly) Israel's staunchest ally, is now siding with Russia in supporting Iran, Israel's arch-enemy, in taking the role of the dominant, lead nation of the Middle East.

And America, on her home soil, is not exempt from these escalating calamities. Since the "Great Recession" began in the U.S. in 2008, because of corporations downsizing and offshoring jobs, millions have lost their employment and homes in this nation. In 2010, the eruption of an oil gusher in the Gulf of Mexico severely damaged the ecology and economy of the Gulf Coast of the U.S.A. In 2011, unprecedented destruction by tornadoes, floods, fires, and drought killed hundreds and drove thousands from their homes and further crippled the economy of the U.S. The Wealthy Elite continued to get richer as they placed trillions of dollars in off-shore accounts, eroding the tax base, and the government continued to bail them out, while everyone else sank toward poverty and servitude. Mass protests, as in Europe, the Middle East, North Africa, and other parts of the world, were held in the U.S. before they were squelched by brutal police force. In 2012, increasingly devastating natural disasters, including Hurricane Sandy and a severe drought affecting over 60% of the states—especially the agricultural states—with no end in sight, hammered America. At year's end, Americans were apprehensive as the "fiscal cliff"—the end of stimulus money that had been pumped into the economy during the Bush and Obama administrations and a significant offsetting raise in taxes approached at the beginning of 2013. In 2013 unseasonably bad weather (freezing temperatures and paralyzing snow storms in late spring in parts of the nation, in other parts floods, tornados, searing heat and droughts) continued to take a toll. Through censorship of the news and intrusive surveillance of phone and email records, Internet usage and bank statements (under the Patriot Act and other Presidential and Congressional enactments and in the guise of the "War on Terror"), the U.S.A. is becoming more and more a police state with government agencies and police forces invasively and oppressively infringing on the rights of America's citizens. "Obamacare"—the mandatory health care plan sponsored by the President—was showing signs of increasing tremendously the tax burden on the middle class and ruining many small businesses. Over 60% of 2012 college graduates, many with large student loans to pay off, had still, in 2013, not found jobs in the professions for which they had college degrees. At the end of the year, fifteen percent of the U.S. population—over 47 million— were on foodstamps.   And now, in 2014, the combination of Obamacare and the unlimited, unsustainable U.S. debt ceiling is seri- ously threatening to collapse the American economy, which will result in riots, looting, bloodshed, martial law and a police state, which, in turn, will cause a chain reaction of the same sequence of events hap- pening in nations worldwide.[2]

What does it all mean?

So, what is the meaning of all this continually increasing turmoil? Is it just the natural, normal course of events, or does it have pro- phetic significance?   What is going to happen in the immediate and distant future? Is there any real hope for relief? Is the downward des- tiny of humanity inevitable, beyond our control? Or will we be able to turn things around and make something good out of this mess in which we increasingly find ourselves?

Trends analysts like Gerald Celente (renowned for the accuracy of his political and economic forecasts) are predicting global disasters (e.g., "The Greatest Depression" and "The Greatest World War") in the short term.   But most of the trends prognosticators are trying to maintain a positive long-range outlook, saying that the ones who are prepared will survive the terrible tribulations of the next few years, turn things around, and make the world a better place than ever in which to live (a veiled survival-of-the-fittest philosophy).

Do you believe them? I am going to state this bluntly, because cor- rectly forecasting what is going to happen in the near future is not just a matter of idle speculation or trends analysis; it is a matter of "eter- nal"[3] life or death necessity: Actually, trends analysts and other self- proclaimed prophets **do not have a clue** about what is going to happen past a year or two in the future! Their sophisticated trends research

---

[2]Please visit RevelationUnderstoodCommentary.com   for updates on im- portant current events prophesied in the *Bible* that you may not see published by the mainline media.

[3]Note that, throughout this Revelation commentary, "eternal," "forever," and related terms are placed in quote marks when those terms apply to the millennial Kingdom of Yahuah or to "eternal" torment in Hell. Please see "Appendix 8—How long is 'Forever' in the *Bible*"—to see why.

tools or "prophetic" insights may get part—even a large part—of what is going to happen correct—a few months or even a year or two ahead; but beyond that, they **do not have a clue**! And **you are a fool** if you believe them and stake any part of your future on what they say.

Only One Source of Truth

But, there is good news. There *is* one (and only one) source of information about the future that is totally, 100% reliable, on which every one of us can stake his or her future and can have the very real expectation of a glorious, joyful, and wonderful eternal life in Paradise: the inspired Word of Yahuah, specifically Yahuah's prophetic Word, and most especially the Revelation of the Lord. All the turmoil that is happening in the world today was exactly and completely predicted 2,000 years ago by Yahushua when He was speaking to His disciples (c.f., Matthew 24; Mark 13; Luke 21) and in His Revelation, by other *B'rit Hadashah* ("New Testament") writers, and hundreds of years earlier by BCE prophets. But, unlike what secular forecasters are able to even begin to do accurately, the prophetic Scripture tells us exactly what will happen in the future—all the way into eternity—and what we need to be doing about it.

Father Yahuah does not want His children to be in the dark about what is happening in the world in these last days. He wants us, like Israel's tribe Issachar, to understand the times in which we live so that we will know what to do (1Chronicles12:32).

That is why He gave us His Revelation. The Revelation, when rightly understood, casts startling light on current events, explaining not only exactly what is happening in the world today but where it is all headed, how it is going to end, and how we need to be living our lives in the knowledge of that reality.

Why the Confusion?

So, why is there so much confusion and disagreement about the meaning and practical implications of the Revelation? Why do so many say that they do not understand it?

The reason is that the Christian Church, especially in the United States of America, is being led by blind guides. And that is not because the Revelation of the Lord is difficult to understand: Ministers, *Bible* scholars, and teachers in the Christian Church, especially the American Church, are selectively ignoring certain key truths given to us in the *Bible*.

And one of the most important keys for unlocking the meaning of the Revelation (that is being ignored) is that it, like every other book of the *Bible*, is written from a Hebraic perspective. Very few Christian *Bible* expositors acknowledge the critical importance of understanding the Hebrew language, idioms, modes of thought, and culture in correctly interpreting both the "Old Testament" (the *Tanakh)* and the "New Testament" (the *B'rit Hadashah)*. Very few of them recognize that **all** of Scripture, including the Revelation, was given by the Lord to **all** of His People, including the Jews who have not yet (but will) recognize that Yahushua is the Messiah and the Believers in Yahushua at the present time ("Christians"). Very few of them recognize the absolutely essential necessity of thoroughly knowing and understanding the *Tanakh* in correctly interpreting the Scripture written and compiled after the first coming of Yahushua. This is especially true of the Revelation, which contains far more quotes (31) from and references (over 200) to the *Tanakh* than any other *B'rit Hadashah* book of the *Bible.* Indeed, the Revelation is the completion of the revelation to Daniel—the revelation of the contents of the scroll that Daniel was told to seal until *"the time of the end"* (Daniel12:4).

Also, one of the most important keys for unlocking the meaning of the Revelation that is being ignored is the identity of modern, prophetic, "mystery" Babylon. Of the twenty-two chapters of Revelation, two entire chapters plus parts of other chapters are devoted to Babylon. The final exultation of the multitude in Heaven at the end of the Final Seven Years is over the destruction of Babylon. Modern Babylon is not named in the *Bible* because she did not exist when the Revelation, the last book of the *Bible*, was written. But there are over sixty indicators in over 250 verses of Scripture that tell us very clearly who she is. When it came time for Babylon to take her place on the world stage among the nations of the world, Yahuah obviously intended for there to be no doubt as to who she is.

So, why do we not know? Why is there so much disagreement among *Bible* scholars and Christians as to the identity of Babylon? Again, the Body of Believers in Yahushua (the "Church") is closing her eyes to that reality because it is just too painful and threatening to face. That is why this commentator has not yet found even one Christian leader, minister, teacher, theologian, or author to endorse this book. And that is not because none agree with it—some do. They just will not put their reputations and positions in Christiandom and in the community on the line for the plain Truth of Yahuah's prophetic Word. And that is exactly why Yahushua told the religious leaders who asked

Him for a "sign from Heaven" to prove Himself, "*Hypocrites! You know how to discern the face of the sky* [to predict the weather], *but you cannot discern the signs of the times*" (Matthew 16:1, 3). They were ignoring the hundreds of prophecies that clearly told who He was and of His coming.

Time is short. Act now!

The second coming of the prophesied Messiah and all the awesome events that will accompany His coming will occur soon—very soon. And it is the prayer of this commentator that if this Revelation Commentary is distributed widely enough, the Lord will use it to open the eyes of some to the critically-important true meaning and practical implications of His Revelation. And it is my prayer that many true Believers will visit the Last Trump Ministries page of the RevelationUnderstoodCommentary.com website, and some will join us in this watchmen's ministry. Yes, I pray that it will be as in the days of Elijah, when he cried out to the Lord, "*I alone am left, and they seek to take my life*," to which the Lord replied, "*I have reserved seven thousand in Israel . . . all whose knees have not bowed to Baal . . .*" (1 Kings 19:14, 18). I pray that there are at least seven thousand among the Followers of Yahushua who have not bowed to the god of Babylon (Satan) and who want to join us in warning our loved ones to "*Come out of her, my people, lest you share in her sins, and lest you receive of her plagues*" (Revelation 18:4), before it is too late.

Meanwhile, please judge for yourself. Read this *Revelation of Yahushua the Messiah* commentary, and if the Spirit of Yahuah witnesses to your spirit that what you are reading is the Truth, please let me know. Every positive response is a life-sustaining breath of fresh air and drink of pure, cool water in this suffocating, scorching spiritual desert called Babylon the Great.

And once we do look at Yahuah's prophetic Word through the eyes of those who put it into writing and accept the true identity of modern, prophetic Babylon, it is amazing how the meaning of the whole book of Revelation slides seamlessly and with crystal clarity into place. All those vexing questions about the timing of the "Rapture," the role of the anti-messiah, how Yahuah is going to deal with Jews and the Community of Believers in Yahushua during the Final Seven Years, and so forth are easily answered by studying the Revelation in the same literal, common-sense manner that we study any other book of the *Bible*. And that kind of study is what this Revelation commentary offers.

What You Get

Included in this Revelation commentary (which is more than just a commentary) is a brief, common-sense guide to understanding *Bible* prophecy (not that difficult if a few simple study principles are followed); a short narrative of how the Final Seven Years may very well play out; the verse-by-verse commentary; an essay that gives historical and scriptural, irrefutable proof as to the identity of modern, prophetic Babylon; how we can be saved from the Wrath of Yahuah; who the People of Yahuah really are; the real difference between a True Christian and a phony "Christian"; the timing of the "Rapture"; fantastic Good News for those Believers in Yahushua who remain faithful to The End; the debatable doctrine of "eternal" torment; and Yahuah's ultimate plan for the restoration of His entire Creation, including fallen heavenly and human beings, to Himself.

The verse-by-verse commentary part of this volume is concise. That means that it does not go into a lot of detail or provide a lot of documentation for many of its assertions and interpretations. However, that does not mean that those assertions or interpretations are "off the wall" or unsubstantiated. The idea is to be **clear**, not to bog the reader down with unnecessary technical details or confusing references to various, often contradictory interpretations the way most commentaries do. Please remember that a major premise of this Revelation commentary is that **the *Bible* is its own best interpreter**. Plenty of Scriptural cross-references are provided to back up the interpretations and observations in this volume. Please read those. Then, if you still have doubts or questions about any point made, please contact me. Many years of diligent, prayerful study have gone into this work, and I will be glad to discuss and provide additional documentation or explanation for any part of it.

May the Lord bless your study!

I just pray that the Lord Yahuah will speak to your heart through *The Revelation of Yahushua the Messiah* because, as is indicated by current events in the light of His prophetic Word, the awesome, terrible, fantastic, and wonderful events of the Revelation could start literally any day now. And those who do not understand what is happening and submit to how the Lord tells us to deal with the Final Seven Years (which is clearly revealed in His Revelation) will be lost.

So please keep reading. I promise that the true message of the Revelation of the Lord will not be boring or difficult to understand. Even if it does infuriate you or terrify you, it will, in going far, far be-

14

yond what any Nostradamus or trends analyst can tell you, be very enlightening. And if you will believe it, take it to heart, place your life in the hands of the Messiah Yahushua the Lord, and trust Him to show you what to do, you will be filled with joy and thrilled beyond measure as you anticipate the very-soon-to-come Day of the Lord!

May the Lord use this book to open more than ever the eyes of your understanding to the true meaning of His magnificent Revelation. And through correctly discerning the "signs of the times" and acting in faith on that understanding, may you be one of the very few (cf. Matthew 7:14) who, rather than fearful or angry because of the terrible circumstances of this tumultuous, rapidly deteriorating, disintegrating world, are filled with the joy of His salvation in anticipation of the awesome events *"which must shortly take place"* (Revelation 1:1).

How to Understand *Bible* Prophecy

A Common-Sense Guide

The three basic messages of the *Bible* are simple. Any infant or mentally handicapped person who does not even know human language can understand them because they are best communicated through nonverbal actions. They are: (1) the pure, unselfish love of Yahuah, (2) the absolute necessity of total trust in the One who takes care of us, and (3) the essential importance of perfect obedience in submission to the One who created us and sustains us. Understanding and yielding our lives to those three messages will save us from the main consequence of sin (separation from Yahuah) and from spiritual impotence and misery in this life. In fact, acceptance and submission to those three messages will fill our hearts with spiritual peace, love, joy and hope that transcend all understanding and carry us through any circumstance in which we may find ourselves.

However, if we want more understanding of what Yahuah tells us about the past, present or future, then we need to dig into Scripture and study it diligently. But it is still not that difficult. We do not have to have a seminary education or even to know the original Biblical languages (primarily Hebrew and Greek) to understand Scripture just as well as any minister, *Bible* teacher, seminary professor, or even the Pope. Did you know that? Yahuah did not design the *Bible* to be read and understood only by the highly intelligent or highly educated. He designed it to be understood by the average person, if that person is enlightened by His Spirit. Studies have shown that most of the *King James Bible*, even with its outdated Old English language, can be understood by the average fifth grader. To me, that is good news.

I personally prefer and recommend the *Hebraic Roots Version* (HRV), translated from Aramaic and Hebrew manuscripts and with an abundance of explanatory footnotes and cross-references, because the *Bible* was originally written from a Hebrew cultural context using many Hebrew terms, idioms and modes of thought that are not clearly or, in many instances, even accurately translated in other versions of the *Bible*. Virtually all other translations of the *Bible*, particularly of the *B'rit Hadashah* (including the *Complete Jewish Bible*) are translated from corrupted Greek manuscripts and cast a Greek/Gentile (anti-Semitic) slant on Yahuah's Word. But that is not to say that the HRV is perfect, because one of Satan's favorite ploys to mislead Yahuah's

17

People is to corrupt His Word, and many distortions have crept into **all** versions of the Scriptures through the centuries. I use the HRV as my basic study text but also compare it with other translations. That is easy to do with a computer program like *e-Sword,* in which several versions can be lined up side-by-side. By the way, *e-Sword* is absolutely **free** and can be downloaded at www.e-sword.net. Another excellent free program is *Bible Analyzer,* which can be downloaded at *www.bibleanalyzer.com.*

Commentaries (including this one) can help throw light on the meaning of Scripture, but their interpretations must always be confirmed by our own prayerful, Holy Spirit-led *Bible* study. The Berean Believers in Yahushua were commended for checking out for themselves in the Scripture what even the Apostle Paul, who wrote much of the *B'rit Hadashah,* taught them (Acts 17:11). Again (we cannot emphasize it enough), just remember one important point: **The *Bible* is its own best interpreter!** If we will just dig into it—learning what it says; comparing related words, statements, and sections; asking Yahuah to reveal its meaning to us—it will start to make sense to our minds and come to life in our hearts until we know that we know that the *Bible* is truly Yahuah's inspired Word of Truth! "The proof of the pudding is in the eating." If there are some words we do not understand, locations of places we do not know, or if we want to compare how words or concepts are used in different parts of the *Bible,* plenty of study aids like dictionaries, atlases, and concordances are available. In fact, on the Internet we can find all the help we need. And computer software like *e-Sword, Bible Analyzer,* or *BibleWorks* places all those kinds of helps right in front of our eyes and at our fingertips.

About one-third of the *Bible* is prophetic. This commentator knows that there are all kinds of attitudes toward and interpretations of the prophetic parts of the *Bible.* Some believe that the *Bible* is just a collection of myths. Some believe that its prophecies are just allegorical—symbolically portraying the universal conflict between good and evil, or something. Some believe that the prophecies of Scripture are literally true but have virtually all been fulfilled. Others believe in some combination of allegorical and literal fulfillment of Biblical prophecies. Many volumes have been published extolling each point of view. So, we are not going to wade into that debate; it is far beyond the scope of this little essay. I am just going to share with you what I believe that Yahuah has shown me through His prophetic Word that impacts every human being on Earth at the present time and will impact every person in the near future, based on a lifetime (69 years) of being taught the *Bible* and studying it for myself.

I believe that Yahuah is real and communicates through His inspired Word, the *Bible*, to those whose minds, hearts, and spirits are open to Him. I also believe that the *Bible* is literally true. When it says, "*In the beginning,* [Elohim] *created the heavens and the earth,*" I believe that is exactly, literally what happened. When it says that Yahushua, Yahuah the Father's only begotten Son, was crucified on a Roman cross and was resurrected from the dead on the third day after His crucifixion, I believe that is exactly, literally what happened. When Scripture says that someday soon, the Savior will return to give those who have believed in Him and dedicated their lives to Him glorified bodies and take them to a place He has prepared for them in Heaven, I believe that is exactly, literally what will happen. When the *Bible* says there will be a man it calls the anti-messiah (among other names) who will deceive the whole world into following him as their (false) messiah, I believe that is exactly, literally what will happen. Of course, as in many great works of literature, the *Bible* uses symbolism, especially in the poetic and prophetic parts. But it is not difficult to tell from the context which characters, events, places, and so forth are symbolic and which are literal. And this commentator has found that when he reads the *Bible* in this common-sense way, taking it at face value, asking the Lord to reveal the Truth of His Word to him, then it really comes to life, helping him to understand history, what is happening in the world around him at the present time, what is going to happen in the near future, and what he needs to be doing about it—exactly how he needs to be living his life.

In addition to the above assumptions, there are six principles of interpretation of Biblical prophecy that may be helpful in understanding those prophecies:

- **The events of *Bible* history that impact Yahuah's People repeat themselves over and over until they reach their final fulfillment during the Final Seven Years and the Millennium.** Western Gentiles have a Greek mindset and linear concept of history in which all events occur sequentially. However, the inspired writers of the Scriptures, the Hebrews, had a circular view of history in which events repeat themselves in different ways over and over. Solomon (the wisest man in history) said, *"What has been is what will be, what has been done is what will be done, and there is nothing new under the* *sun"* (Ecclesiastes 1:9). Then, he repeated the truism by stating, *"That which is has already been; and what is to be has already been"* (Ecclesiastes 3:15). And the apostle Paul wrote that everything that happened to ancient Israel has implications for those living in the present (cf. 1 Corinthians 10:6, 11). In other words, by studying the history of Israel and the nations that impacted Israel in the past, we can know the future of Israel and the nations that will impact her at that time (all the nations of the world).

For example, Yahuah's People Israel exited from Egypt and the bondage of Pharaoh, and the army of Pharaoh was destroyed. Then, after 40 years, they were led into the Promised Land by Yahuah. But, in 722 and 586 BCE, the twelve tribes of Israel were taken into captivity by the Assyrians and Babylonians, respectively, and during the following centuries, especially in 70 and 135 CE (the Roman dispersions) were scattered throughout the world. Then, exactly as was prophesied, a remnant of the Jews returned from the nations of the world to re-establish the nation of Israel in 1948. In the near future, they will again escape into the wilderness from the tyranny of Antimessiah, and just as Pharaoh's was, his army will be destroyed. Finally, at the end of the Final Seven Years, *"all Israel will be saved"*—brought back into the Promised Land by the Messiah, where they will be established as His kingdom Saints throughout His millennial reign (cf. Ezekiel 37:21; Romans 11:26). In the same way, Yahuah's People the Believers in Yahushua are, at the present time, scattered among the nations of the world, but will, when He returns to *"gather His elect from the four winds"* (Matthew 24:31), take them to dwell in and to reign with Him from New Jerusalem. See the commentary on Chapters 7 and 20 for details.

Another example of Israel's history repeating itself is the prophesied War of Gog and Magog (Ezekiel 38), in which multiple nations of the world come against Israel. A partial fulfillment of that prophecy occurred when nations of the Middle East and North Africa came against Israel when her people returned to the Land in 1948, then attacked her again in 1967 and 1973. A more complete fulfillment will probably occur at the beginning of the Final Seven Years, at which time the armies of the nations that come against Israel will be destroyed and the anti-messiah will enact a peace treaty with Israel that he will later treacherously abolish when he attempts to destroy Yahuah's people (cf. Ezekiel 38:19-22; Daniel 9:27; Isaiah 28:15). Then, at the end of the Final Seven Years, the armies of many nations will come against the Messiah in Jerusalem. Then, the final War of Gog and Magog will occur when the armies of all nations gather against the Lord's People and New Jerusalem at the end of the Millennium. See the commentary on Chapters 19 and 20 for details.

A third example is the rise of many prototypes of the anti-messiah—Nimrod, Pharaoh, Haman, Antiochus Epiphanes, Herod the Great, the Roman general Titus, Constantine, Hitler, et al.—throughout history, which will culminate in the final false messiah (the incarnation of Satan) arising to rule the world. See the commentary on Chapter 13 for details.

A fourth example is the fall of Babylon, which has actually already occurred twice. The ancient city of Babylon founded by Nimrod/Sargon, the ruler of the world's first empire, the Akkadian Empire, fell very quickly when a comet impacted the earth with the force of dozens of nuclear bombs only about 125 miles from the capital city of Akkad and nearby Babylon, killing the residents of that part of the empire and scattering survivors far and wide. Then, the Babylonian Empire ruled by Nebuchadnezzar also fell quickly—in a surprise infiltration and overthrow in one evening—to Cyrus, King of Persia. Very similar to ancient Babylon, especially Nimrod's Babylon, all natural life in modern Babylon the Great will very quickly, in "one hour," be annihilated by fire, probably near the midpoint of the Final Seven Years, setting the stage for the rise of the anti-messiah. Then, Babylon will be totally physically annihilated at the end of the Final Seven Years. See the commentary on Chapters 17 and 18 and "Appendix 1—Who is Modern Babylon?" for details.

- *Bible* **prophecies are fulfilled literally, specifically, and without fail.** For example, the prophet Daniel foretold in about 538 BCE, when the Jews were still in captivity in Babylon, that an order would be issued for them to restore and rebuild Jerusalem (which had been destroyed by Nebuchadnez-zar) and that it would be 483 years from the time that command was issued until the arrival of *"Messiah the Prince"* (Daniel 9:25). According to Biblical and historical records and astronomical calculations, from the time the Persian king Artaxerxes issued the order on Aviv 1 (on the Jewish calendar), 457 BCE, to rebuild Jerusalem (cf. Nehemiah 2:7-9), it was exactly 173,880 days (483 prophetic years of 360 days, to the day) until Yahushua was identified by John the Baptist as the "Lamb of Yahuah," the Messiah, on Aviv 1, 27 CE.[4] Uncanny, is it not? And there are hundreds of other specific *Bible* prophecies that have been fulfilled with 100% accuracy, while **none** have been proven to be false.

- **Both the Jews and the Followers of Yahushua are the People of Yahuah.** Yahuah's ancient People Israel who have looked forward in faith to the coming Messiah (including Joseph, Moses, David, Elijah and all the other *Tanakh* Saints plus present-day Jewish people of faith), although they have not yet recognized that Yahushua is their Messiah, are just as much the People of Yahuah as are those who have already accepted Yahushua as their Savior and Lord. They have just been **temporarily** blinded to who their Messiah is until all the Gentiles who are being saved have been "grafted into" the Kingdom of Yahuah and made "fellow citizens" in the "commonwealth of Israel." In fact, it is more correct to affirm that Gentiles who have come to faith in Yahushua are now Israelites (in a spiritual sense) than it is to state that Jews who have come to faith in Yahushua are now Christians. A very important key to understanding the prophetic Scripture—all of it, including the Revelation—is understanding that it was written by Hebrews, the caretakers of Yahuah's Word, for **all** of Yahuah's People—Jews and Believers in Yahushua. See "Appendix 3—Who are the People of Yahuah"—for more details.

---

[4]For a complete discussion of how Biblical dates are accurately determined, get the DVD *The Creator's Calendar and the Restoration of all Things* at www.michaelrood.tv or view the YouTube video by the same name.

- *Bible* **prophecy applies to Yahuah's People the Jews in a physical sense and to His People the Disciples of Yahushua in a spiritual sense.** For example, Revelation 18:4 states, *"Come out of her* [Babylon], *my people, lest you share in her sins, and lest you receive of her plagues."* The correct interpretation is that Yahuah's People the Jews who believe in the coming Messiah but who have not yet accepted Yahushua as their Messiah should come out of literal Babylon and return to the land of Israel, and Yahuah's People the Followers of Yahushua, who are already partakers of the indwelling Spirit of Yahuah under the Renewed Covenant, should repent of ("come out of") Babylon's sins and take refuge in the righteousness of the Messiah.

- **Nothing is prophesied in the book of Revelation that was not previously foretold, usually several times and in various ways, in other books of the *Bible*, and in the events, traditions, and festivals of Israel.** The *Bible* states, *"The* [Lord Yahuah] *does nothing unless He reveals His secret to His servants the prophets"* (Amos 3:7). And no *B'rit Hadashah* book of Scripture quotes the *Tanakh* more than the Revelation. So, for a clear understanding of the meaning of the Revelation and what will happen in the near future, knowledge of other *Bible* Scripture, especially the *Tanakh*, and most especially the book of Daniel, is absolutely essential. Also, the Spring feasts or festivals prescribed by Yahuah (Leviticus 23)—Pesach (Passover), Hag haMatzah (Unleavened Bread), First Fruits of the Barley Harvest, and Shavuot (Pentecost)—were "dress rehearsals" for the Messiah's first coming, accurately foretelling to the very day and, in some instances, the very hour of His first advent: His arrival in Jerusalem being proclaimed the Messiah (Matthew 21:9), His being nailed to the cross and His crucifixion (Luke 23:44-46), His resurrection (Luke 24:1), and the outpouring of His Spirit on His followers (Acts 2:1-18). And although the Lord's End Times timetable for His People the Followers of Yahushua is a little different than for His physical nation of people Israel (see "Appendix 6 - When is the 'Rapture'"), in the same way, the Fall Feasts - Yom Teruah (the Feast of Trumpets), Yom Kippur (the Feast of Atonement), and Sukkot (the Feast of Tabernacles) - accurately foretell the events of the Messiah's second advent, including His return as King of kings and Lord of lords, the destruction of His enemies at "Armageddon," the final outpouring of the Wrath of Yahuah on the earth, the separation of the "sheep and the goats" among His People Israel and the nations who are still on Earth, and the establishment of His millennial kingdom. So, a knowledge, not only of prophetic Scripture, but of the historical events, traditions, and feasts of Israel prescribed by Yahuah are essential to fully understanding the sequence and timing of the events of the Revelation.

- **Time and sequence must be interpreted correctly.** There is much confusion among Bible expositors regarding the timing and sequence of events of the Revelation. The text must be studied carefully for clues regarding the correct interpretation. One helpful principle is that after chapter 3 when John is told to *"Come up here"* (4:1) the view is from Heaven. And the view from Heaven is panoramic—more like looking at a mural than a strict time-line sequence of events. For example, the revelation of the first six trumpet judgments is given in chapters 8 and 9. Then, chapters 10 and 11:1-13 interrupt the narrative to give more details about what is happening during the execution of the Lord's judgments. Then, 11:14-19 briefly describes the execution of the seventh trumpet judgment. Next, chapters 12-14 interrupt the narrative again to reveal more details of what happens during the last half of the "Final Seven Years." And finally, chapters 15 and 16 reveal what happens in Heaven and on Earth when the six bowls of the Wrath of Yahuah are poured out on Earth. Actually, a careful analysis of the text reveals that even the apparent sequence of the events of these chapters (the trumpet judgments followed by the bowl judgments) is not necessarily the way it happens—the trumpet and bowl judgments apparently occur simultaneously, as will be explained in the commentary.

On the other hand, some definite time markers are given and should be interpreted literally, unless the context indicates otherwise. As examples, several events are identified as happening during the last 42 months, 1260 days or three and one-half years of the "Final Seven Years": the pursuit of "the woman" (Israel) into the wilderness, where she is provided for and protected from "the serpent" (Satan) 1260 days (Revelation 12:6); the "beast" (Antimessiah) declaring himself to be "god" (2 Thessalonians 2:4) at the midpoint of the seven years (cf. Daniel 9:27) and ruling over Earth, causing the "Great Tribulation," for 42 months (Revelation 13:5); and the "two witnesses" prophesying during this same period of time (Revelation 11:3). These specific time markers are very helpful in determining the timing and sequence of events of the Revelation, as will be clarified in the commentary.

If you can agree with the above simple assumptions and principles, then Yahuah may use this book to cause the Revelation to come to life for you. The insights that are going to be shared from Yahuah's Word in this commentary may not only astonish you but may save your (eternal) life. If you do not agree about how *Bible* prophecy should be interpreted, then I pray that you will read on anyway, because you may see that there is more—a whole lot more—to the *Bible* in throwing light on what is happening in the world than you thought.

The "Tribulation"

Before we get to the verse-by-verse commentary, please bear with me as I suggest a scenario for what I am calling the Final Seven Years of world history—what many call the "Tribulation Period." I have come to realize that many have trouble digesting detailed study, but prefer parables and narratives. And that is fine, because that is the way Yahushua ("Jesus") taught. So I pray that the following "story" will heighten your interest so that you will really want to get into the Word to see for yourself if these things are true. This narrative is based on a common-sense, face-value, literal interpretation of Scripture, which I believe is the way our Heavenly Father wants His Word to be understood. I, Watchman Bob, do **not** claim to be a prophet or that all the events are in exactly the correct sequence or that their timing is precisely accurate. Although I have been studying current events in the light of Bible prophecy many years, I am simply a teacher who presents my understanding of what Scripture says is happening at the present time and will happen in the near future the best I can. And the identification of future characters, dates and circumstances in the following scenario should be evaluated by Scripture references given to determine if they are reasonably possible. If any of those future characters, dates and events turn out to be inaccurate, they will be changed in revisions to this narrative as the Lord gives further insight. On the other hand, the following narrative is not just a figment of the author's imagination. It is based on over 20 years of study of current events in the light of *Bible* prophecy. And I do believe that the interpretations on which it is based are as solidly based on Scripture as any out there. The current events portrayed (as of 2014) are actual. And please note especially that every future character, place and event that is included in the following narrative does occur in Scripture and **could** happen very much as portrayed. Again, the reader is encouraged to verify the feasibility of the following narrative by studying the Scriptures referenced and especially the commentary on the Scriptures in the book of the Revelation referenced. Also, three recently published, eye-opening books—*The Comets of God* by scientist Jeffrey Goodman, the New York Times Best Seller *The Harbinger* by Jonathan Cahn, and *The 9/11 Prophecy by James Fitzgerald*—have provided additional, powerful support for "The Final Seven Years." For more details and documentation, the reader is encouraged to read those three books. Plus, for thorough details concerning the exact identity and soon-coming triple destiny of the United States of America according to *Bible* prophecy, visit www.TheTenthHarbinger.com.

The Final Seven Years

A Quasi-Fictional End-of-the-Age Scenario

The Kingdom of Heaven

Yahushua is, at the present time, establishing the Kingdom of Yahuah ("God") in Heaven (*"I go to prepare a place for you . . ."*— John 14:2), in the hearts of His regenerated People, His Disciples (Luke 17:21), and in its various spiritual manifestations on Earth (Matthew 12:28). But His People (His "Bride") will not **physically** dwell there until He comes to change them into glorified, heavenly beings, gather them to Himself, and take them there (*"that where I am, there you may be also"*—John 14:3). Then, later, after the wedding ceremony and feast in Heaven (Revelation 19:7-9), He will return with His heavenly armies (glorified Saints and angels—Revelation 17:14; 19:8, 14; Matthew 16:27; 2 Thessalonians 1:7) to defeat his enemies on Earth and set up His millennial kingdom here (Revelation 19:11-20:4; Luke 13:29).

Meanwhile, while the Bride (the Congregation of Followers of Yahushua) is in her new home in Heaven (specifically, New Jerusalem), what is happening on Earth? Well, all Heaven is breaking forth, that is what. The final execution of the Wrath of the Lord is being poured out on Earth, big time (Revelation 16:16-21). But, to get the whole picture, let us back up a few years.

The Setup—The First Three and One-Half Years

For years, the United States of America—the world's only remaining "superpower" nation after the fall of the Soviet Union in 1989—had been gaining more and more global hegemony through subverting one government after another and converting them into "client states" with puppet leaders. In 2009 her only serious rival for dominance of the world's economy was the European Union. But then, in 2010, several of the EU's member nations—Portugal, Italy, Ireland, Greece, and Spain—having greatly overextended their credit and having accrued tremendous deficits that they could not service, got into serious financial trouble. Greece was on the verge of collapse; riots were breaking out. So, other EU member states bit the bullet and bailed her out, further weakening the stability of the whole Union. But then, by October 2011, Greece's bailout had failed, causing massive protests and rioting, threatening bankruptcy of the nation and a calamitous domino effect in other European nations. And the United States,

29

having accrued more that sixteen trillion dollars in debt, which was owed at home and abroad and was growing rapidly because of having to fund natural disaster recovery efforts in the homeland and constant involvement in foreign wars, was in no position to help the ailing nations although they were dependent on her as by far the largest consumer of their commodities and services. If the economy of the U.S.A. collapsed, the economies of the whole world would collapse. In fact, in spite of assurances of the government through the mainline media to the contrary, the stability of the U.S. economy was quite precarious. One major national catastrophe could cause it to collapse.

Then, in 2014, reality overtook America's worst fears. First, because of the economic stress caused by full implementation of the national health care plan ("Obamacare") and increased taxation resulting from the unsustainable national debt ceiling, nations around the world, beginning with China, France and Russia, began to abandon the U.S. dollar as their medium of exchange and it was devalued and replaced as the global reserve currency. This caused widespread panic, riots and looting in the U.S. Martial law was declared and a police state was established, making the President a virtual dictator.

Then, the following year, 2015, exactly as prophesied (Isaiah 9:10; Jeremiah 51:8, 27-28), there was a massive terrorist attack on America from within and outside her borders. For many years, Muslims had been freely allowed into the U.S.A., and thousands of them had been clandestinely developing hundreds of Jihad terrorist cells around the country. A confederation of Muslim nations led by Iran and Turkey had been funding, training and coordinating the terrorist cells and was also planning to attack U.S. military installations and ships abroad. The attack was meticulously planned and coordinated because the aggressors knew that if the U.S. military, with its awesome fighting capabilities, was allowed to respond in a cohesive way they would not succeed. And the attack went exactly as planned! Simultaneously, all over the nation, thousands of bombs, including suitcase nuclear devices, were detonated—mainly in large population centers including Washington D.C. and New York City. And, because there was no plan to counter such a devastating and widespread attack from within the nation (the U.S. Defense establishment was almost totally set up to respond to attacks from outside the borders of the U.S.), the whole nation was thrown into total chaos. National Guard units could not be called up and activated instantly and police departments were not logistically prepared to counter the multi-faceted, massive attack. There were some joint police-military anti-terrorist units and plans in place, but strangely, no orders came from the President to activate them. So, Americans, in their panic, were sitting ducks for the armed, trained and coordinated terrorists, and all who resisted were mowed down in the streets and in their homes. The terrorists also took over all National Guard and police units around the country and bombed and forced the surrender of military installions, which were totally unprepared for such an attack, especially with no directions coming from Washington. Meanwhile, simultaneously, air, ground and missile attacks were being carried out on U.S. military installations, troops and ships all over the world—especially in the Near East. And also, having no directions from Washington, which was totally occupied with the attack at home, those installations, troops and ships could mount no coordinated response, were either destroyed or immobilized, and were taken over by the Muslim forces. In fact, the attacks at home and abroad were so effective that, within just a few hours, the government of the United States of America was in the hands of radical Islamists.

Then, the confederation of anti-Israel, anti-America nations from the Near East and North Africa (Jeremiah 51:27-28; Psalm 83:2-8; Ezekiel 38:2-6) that had caused the downfall of America, with the USA out of the way, immediately turned their attention to Israel—to invade and annihilate that tiny nation. Mobilizing rapidly, they set up support facilities all around Israel and came like a vast, menacing pack of wolves through the mountains of northern Israel. Surrounded by the anti-aircraft and anti-missile weaponry of her enemies and without the support of the U.S.A., there was virtually nothing the Israelis could do to retaliate. But then, an amazing thing happened: All kinds of natural calamities began to occur in and around Israel, focused, incredibly, on the invading armies of her enemies: Comet fragments rained from the sky on them. The impact of a large fragment caused a tremendous earthquake, like the world had never seen, and collapsed the cliffs of the mountains on those armies; torrential rains flooded their camps; ten-pound comet fragments destroyed their equipment and killed large numbers of personnel; and even volcanic eruptions caused by comet fragments penetrating the earth's crust burned camps and covered them with lava. Then, in total panic and confusion, what was left of Israel's enemy forces attacked and destroyed one another (Ezekiel 38:20-22)!

Of course, in the aftermath of the attacks on the U.S. and Israel, the economies of all nations had immediately collapsed and the whole world was in chaos.

But there was a man, Kurtarici Mesih, the new head of the Turkish branch of PNB Paribas, the largest global banking organization in

31

the world, who had been rapidly garnering a reputation as being an incredibly persuasive, charismatic leader, and many said that he was a financial genius. In his first few months as head of PNB Paribas Turkey, Mesih had been able to develop powerful financial ties with some of the wealthiest investors from all points east and west of Turkey—from China to Paris (the location of the main bank and headquarters of PNB Paribas). The leaders of the EuroMed Partnership (a consortium of 44 European, North African, Middle Eastern, and Balkan nations formed in 1995 to promote mutual economic support and development) had started to tout Mesih as the potential leader of the EMP because Turkey was a key, centrally-located member with strong political and economic ties to both Europe and the Mediterranean Basin nations as well as being the leading nation, financially and militarily, of the trans-EuroMed area. Also, Turkey (together with Iran) had led the Islamist nations in their attacks on the U.S. and Israel, and Mesih emerged as the primary leader of those who were already executing plans to re-establish the (former) U.S.A. (but now under Islamist control) as the anchor and stabilizer of the global economy. So when, in an emergency meeting in Barcelona, the leaders of the EMP frantically stormed their brains for a solution to their dilemma (economic chaos), one name dominated their thoughts—Kurtarici Mesih. They called him and asked him to meet with them. Much to their relief, he agreed. And the next day, in Barcelona, Kurtarici Mesih, by consensus acclamation, was named President of the EuroMed Partnership.

Then, the EMP, with Mesih as its President, working closely with other Muslim leaders who had been involved in the attack on the U.S.A., took over all the U.S.A.'s domestic and foreign political, industrial, commercial and economic institutions and her military installations, quickly (re-) establishing that nation as the "superpower" of the world. Also, in recognition of her new, Near Eastern rulers and of the many characteristics she uncannily had in common with ancient Babylon (cf. "Appendix 1—Who is Modern Babylon?"), the former United States of America was re-named New Babylon. And with New Babylon now established as the main sustainer of the economies of virtually all of the world's nations, and either by persuasion, political intrigue, violent force or economic coercion—to even greater an extent than the U.S.A. had accomplished before her fall—all the nations of the world were made "client states" of New Babylon.

Meanwhile, although most of her own people had survived the destruction of the armies of her enemies, the land of Israel was devastated. She was left without the wherewithal to sustain or to protect herself if her enemies should regroup and attack her again or if another enemy (e.g., Russia or China) should attack her. So, Israel's leaders were very happy when the EuroMed Partnership (of which Israel was also a member), although many of their forces had been destroyed in "the War of Gog and Magog" (cf. Ezekiel 38), offered to come to her aid. Representing the EMP as its leader, Kurtarici Mesih signed a military peace treaty with Israel, agreeing to protect her from further invasion or attack (cf. Isaiah 28:18; Daniel 9:27a). Mesih and the EMP also agreed to restore total sovereignty over her land to Israel, to help her clean up the mess left by the destruction of her enemies, and to allow her to re-establish all the religious practices of ancient Israel. And after Mesih's peace treaty with the leaders of Israel was signed, making Israel an (apparent) safe harbor for Jews, millions of other Jews from around the world (the vast majority of the world's Jews), with the assistance of the EMP, immediately migrated to the land of Israel. So, although the fall of the U.S.A. and the economies of all the other nations caused global desperation, chaos and violence, there was "peace" in Israel, allowing the Jews to start rebuilding their nation and their Temple.

Nevertheless, wars, bloodshed, food shortages, unsanitary conditions, disease, and death continued all over the world, resulting in about a quarter of the world's population dying during the next few years (Revelation 6:3-8).

But, with his charismatic personality, dynamic persuasive powers, and amazing organizational skills, Mesih was being more and more recognized as the de facto leader of the world and the solver of the world's problems. Conformity in government, commerce, and religion were mandated. All the world's religions were brought under the banner of Islam. Dissidents were persecuted, even martyred. (Strangely, the Israelis, who were allowed to practice their own religion, were the exception.) And some semblance of world order was maintained.

But then, approximately three years after the peace treaty with Israel had been signed, the greatest catastrophe in history, since the Great Flood, occurred. A large comet exploded in the atmosphere above North America totally annihilating all life in New Babylon and in much of the neighboring nations Canada and Mexico, in exactly the same way ancient Sodom and Gomorrah had been destroyed (cf. Isaiah 13:19, 20; Jeremiah 49:18; 50:40; Revelation 17:16; 18:8). And again, the whole world was thrown into chaos as the nations looked on in horror as the smoke of New Babylon and it's "great city," New York City, that had sustained their economies, rose into the sky (Revelation 18:9-19).

But Kurturaci Mesih rose to the occasion. He immediately mobilized the EMP's worldwide military forces and economic institutions and, over the next six months, again restored order to a devastated world. And he expanded and established his headquarters in Istanbul as the headquarters of the New World Order. Having so quickly restored order to the world after the annihilation of all life in New Babylon, and now as leader of, by far, the most powerful global empire in world history, Mesih garnered the wonder of the whole world. Many were even suggesting that he was the true Messiah—the god-man anticipated by all the world's religions.

The Takeover and the Great Tribulation

And Mesih seized the moment. He stood in the Most Holy Place of the Temple and, filled with the spirit of His spiritual father, Satan, declared himself to be the messiah—"god" incarnate (Daniel 7:25; 8:23-25; 11:36-37; 2 Thessalonians 2:4; Revelation 13:6-8). And virtually all the people of the world pledged their allegiance to him and worshiped him (Revelation 13:3-4). Then Mesih immediately brought in his top aides, military commanders and 100,000 elite military forces from Turkey and, with the full cooperation of the Israelis, who also accepted him as the long-anticipated messiah who would establish his throne in Jerusalem from where he would rule all the nations of the world (cf. Isaiah 9:6, 7), he took over the Knesset building and other Israeli government facilities as well as all of Israel's military installations, making Jerusalem his new global headquarters. And all the leaders of the world, as though they were mesmerized, rallied around him and quickly formed a ten-region global government and economic system under martial law (Revelation 17:12, 17).

The man who had been the head of religion of the EMP now took center stage as Mesih's Chief of Religion and World Order. He was also empowered by Satan, working all kinds of supernatural signs and wonders to deceive the world into worshiping Mesih. He even somehow developed a lifelike image of Mesih that could be made to appear all over the earth. And he set up a system in which every person, in order to participate in the global economy, had to take an oath of allegiance to worship the "Messiah Mesih" as "Lord of the World" and receive an identification chip under the skin of their hand or forehead. Immediate execution was the consequence of failure to take Mesih's mark or to worship his image. (Revelation 13:15-16)

But prior to the fall of the U.S.A. to the Muslims, 144,000 Jewish men, including 12,000 orthodox Jews (Revelation 7:4), and their families had left the U.S.A. and migrated to Israel, being convinced that somehow the Lord's command, *"Come out of her, my people"* (Jeremiah 51:45), applied to them. And when they saw Mesih standing in the Temple proclaiming himself to be "god," the 144,000 remembered the words of Daniel and what he had spoken about the diabolical *"prince who is to come,"* the abominations and desolation the evil prince would cause (Daniel 9:26, 27), plus the prophecies about the coming time of *"Jacob's trouble"* (Jeremiah 30:7; Daniel 12:1), and they refused to take the mark or to worship Mesih. And the 144,000 and the Messianic Believers in Jerusalem and throughout Israel who remembered the words of Yahushua (Matthew 24:15-21) immediately fled to hiding places in the mountains of Israel and the wilderness area east of the Dead Sea, where they were led by the Lord to places of safe refuge and sustenance (cf. Isaiah 16:3-4; Revelation 12:6). Also, about one-third of the Jews in Jerusalem and Israel who did not flee refused to take Messih's mark and to worship him. But, rather than have them executed, Mesih stripped all Jews who refused to take his mark of ownership of their property, gave them bare, subsistence provisions, and subjected them to the harshest of slave labor conditions. Many of them died daily under those conditions.

Then, as if to add more aggravation to the escape of the Jews and Messianic Believers, an angel was seen streaking through the sky proclaiming,

> *Fear [Yahuah] and give glory to Him, for the hour of His judgment has come; and worship Him who made heaven and earth, the sea and springs of water.* (Revelation 14:7)

And another angel followed, saying,

> *Babylon is fallen, is fallen, that great city, because she has made all nations drink of the wine of the wrath of her fornication.* (Revelation 14:8)

Then, a third angel followed, saying with a loud voice,

> *If anyone worships the beast and his image, and receives his mark on his forehead or on his hand, he himself shall also drink of the wine of the wrath of [Yahuah], which is poured out full strength into the cup of His indignation. He shall be tormented with fire and brimstone in the pres-*

ence of the holy angels and in the presence of the Lamb. And the smoke of their torment ascends "forever" and ever; and they have no rest day or night, who worship the beast and his image, and whoever receives the mark of his name. (Revelation 14:9-11)

Finally, something else was happening that was a continual annoyance and distraction to Mesih. There were two men with appearances like ancient prophets, dressed in sackcloth (the Jews said they were Moses and Elijah), who appeared and were warning everyone in Jerusalem and the surrounding area not to accept Mesih as "Lord of the World" and were proclaiming that they needed to repent and accept Yahushua, whom they crucified, as their true Messiah. Mesih sent some of his commandos to kill them, but the two "witnesses" (Revelation 11:3) seemed to have supernatural powers that created all kinds of disasters and havoc, and they were not able to succeed.

Mesih, being enraged by all these events, made a terrible and treacherous proclamation that no Jew would be allowed to take the mark and participate in the global economy. Just as in Hitler's Third Reich, all Jews in Israel were required to wear special identification badges. Those who resisted were to be executed. The Israeli Jews were then given a bare subsistence allotment of food, clothing and shelter and were subjected to excruciatingly hard labor in maintenance, support and production work in the land and government facilities of Israel. The elderly Jews and others in failing health or who were disabled, unable to serve some useful purpose in Israel, were executed. Mesih also ordered his followers worldwide to report any they spotted who had not taken the mark and bowed to his image, especially Jews and Followers of Yahushua, and that they be killed on the spot (Revelation 12:17; 13:15-17).

This was a time of great tribulation (Matthew 24:21; Revelation 7:14) and carnage for Jews who had not migrated to Israel and Believers in the true Messiah Yahushua. During the next 42 months, almost all of them, except the ones who had escaped into the wilderness, were killed. And the millions of Jews in Jerusalem and Israel who had been subjected to virtual slavery by Mesih were also under great tribulation and hardship, thousands of them dying daily from the terrible conditions to which they were subjected.

As he tightened his grip on the global control that his father Satan had given him (Revelation 13:4, 7), Mesih was totally convinced that he was indeed Lord of the World. Because of advanced surveillance technology, his "eyes" all over the world, and supernatural reconnaissance, it seemed obvious that his enemies, those despicable Jews and

Disciples of Yahushua, would not be able for long to escape their inevitable end.

The Day of Yahuah Begins

But then, about a year into the "Great Tribulation," all Heaven broke forth—what the prophets had frequently referred to as the "*Day of [Yahuah]*" (cf. Joel 2:1, et al.). Exactly as foretold (Joel 2:10, 11; 3:4; Matthew 24:29; Revelation 6:12-13), fragments of comets showered the earth with the force of thousands of nuclear bombs, the sun and moon were darkened because of clouds of smoke and debri produced by the commentary impacts; the stars disappeared; the sky looked like it was being rolled up like a scroll as the atmosphere was largely evaporated by heat from the explosions; and there was a violent, world-wide earthquake, moving every mountain and island out of its place. It was like the whole cosmos was being shaken. People everywhere were crying out in terror to be hidden from or even to be killed to escape the Wrath of the One who was doing this, because it was obvious that an awesome supernatural power was in control. Then, as suddenly as it had begun, it ended. The sun, moon, and stars once again gave their light, though dimly through the dense haze. The whole earth was in disarray and traumatized; millions had lost their lives. But compared to the awesome events that had just transpired, it was eerily quiet, like a spooky calm in the midst of a great storm. The wind was not even blowing (Revelation 7:1).

Mesih was trying to gather his wits and his lieutenants to deal with the situation. Then, the 144,000 who had fled into the wilderness a year earlier were seen marching into Jerusalem from the direction of Petra! They all had a peculiar seal on their foreheads. And they were being led by the true Messiah— Yahushua! They marched right up to the top of Mount Zion, the highest peak in Jerusalem, and they were standing there with Yahushua, singing a serenely beautiful song that apparently only they could understand (Revelation 14:1-3). Mesih was told about the 144,000, but just as he was attempting to marshal his forces against them, terrifying, surreal noises, like those who had been murdered crying out for vengeance (Revelation 6:10), were heard; deafening claps of thunder and blinding flashes of lightning came out of the darkened sky! Then, another great earthquake shook the whole earth, causing many buildings to tumble (Revelation 8:5). Mesih forgot about the 144,000 as reports of great damage poured in from all over the world. He blamed the disasters on the two witnesses who were still walking the streets of Jerusalem boldly proclaiming gloom and doom on those who took the mark of the false messiah and destroying, with amazing personal powers and control of the forces of nature, all those who opposed them.

For the next two and one-half years, the same cycle of events continued, but with increasing intensity. Mesih continued to seek out and kill any he could find who had not taken his mark or who failed to worship his image, and to attempt to kill Moses and Elijah. But, as time went on, he was more and more preoccupied with disaster management. And the two witnesses continued to prophesy while Yahuah sent a series of plagues of increasing intensity on the world in the following order: giant, burning "hailstones" (comet fragments) exploded in the atmosphere causing a third of the trees and all green grass to be burned and released toxic substances which caused great, foul-smelling, pus-filled, oozing sores to appear on the humans (although, amazingly, those who had not accepted the "mark of the beast" were not affected) (cf. Revelation 8:7; 16:2); a great, burning "mountain" (a large comet) "thrown" into the sea causing a third of the ships to be destroyed and a third of the world's salt water to turn blood red from the reactions of the comet's toxic chemical radicals with the sea water, which in turn caused a third of all living creatures in the sea to die (cf. Revelation 8:8-9; 16:3); fragments from a large, disintegrated, toxic comet contaminated a band of rivers and lakes around the earth's northern hemisphere, including the Great Lakes of North America and Lake Baikal in Siberian Russian—sources of over one-third of the earth's fresh water—causing close to a third of the world's remaining human population to die (cf. Revelation 8:10-11; 16:4); then, the light and heat from the sun, moon and stars were affected by all the cometary explosions so that one-third less light reached the earth and temperatures plummeted around the globe an average of 40 degrees Farenheit, but also much of the ozone layer protecting the earth from ultraviolet radiation was destroyed, so at the same time people were chilled by the cold, their skin was being scorched by the ultraviolet radiation (cf. Revelation 8:12; 16:8-9).

But, as terrible as the first four plagues of the Wrath of Yahuah were, the last three ("woes") were much more dreadful. First, another giant "star" (comet) fell from "heaven" (outer space—the Oort Cloud of billions of comets that surround the earth's solar system), causing a "bottomless" crater (one that penetrates the earth's crust) and releasing a huge plume of deadly bacteria-filled smoke that darkened the sky. (When magnified, these bacteria exactly resembled bizarre-looking locusts with horse-like heads and tails like those of scorpions.) This plague, with these bacteria which caused horrible, unbearable sores and skin diseases, lasted an agonizing five months. (cf. Revelation 9:1-10; 16:10-11). Next, four large comet fragments impacted the Euphrates River, drying it up, while simultaneously spraying millions of small comet fragments high into the atmosphere from where they were scattered all over the earth, killing all people (about one-third of the remaining world's human population) with whom the intense heat of the burning sulfur in the fragments came in contact (cf. Revelation 9:14-19; 16:6-12).

From the time the Day of the Wrath of the Lord began until the end of the seven years, **all** of Earth's inhabitants (except for about one-third of the Jews in Israel [cf. Zechariah 13:8] and several million Gentiles who had helped the Jews and who had not taken the "mark of the beast" during the "Great Tribulation" of the previous 42 months) suffered tremendously from the first six sets of plagues of the Wrath of Yahuah. And more than five and one-half billion or two-thirds of Earth's inhabitants had died violent, painful deaths. During these plagues of the Wrath of Yahuah, the people who dwelt on Earth would cry out in terror for mercy, but as soon as the destruction stopped, they would refuse to repent and would blaspheme Yahuah (Revelation 9:20-21; 16:11).

At the end of the seven years and six sets of plagues of the Wrath of Yahuah, Mesih's global kingdom was greatly decimated and devastated and, for all practical purposes, was at an end. However, Yahuah had another exercise in humiliation in store for him.

Moses and Elijah had openly walked the streets of Jerusalem every day since Mesih had stood in the Most Holy Place of the Temple and declared himself to be "god." They constantly spoke out against him, proclaiming that he was the false messiah, telling people not to take his mark or to worship his image, but to worship the true Messiah, Yahushua of Nazareth. And they performed all kinds of signs and wonders, exactly as had Moses and Elijah of ancient Israel, and destroyed all who attempted to attack them. But then, three and one-half years after Mesih had stood in the Most Holy Place of the Temple and declared himself to be "Lord of the World," it seemed that the two witnesses had lost their supernatural powers! Fire no longer came from their mouths to consume those who got in their way. They were no longer calling forth the plagues that tormented their enemies. A glimmer of hope that the tide of death and destruction caused by his two nemeses was about to turn rose in Mesih's evil heart. And he, at the head of all that was left of the armies of the kings of the earth who

39

ruled under him, came into Jerusalem and personally shot the two witnesses dead. Then, as they lay in the streets of Jerusalem for all the world to see and gloat over, and to demonstrate Mesih's power and sovereignty, the armies of the kings of the earth ransacked Jerusalem, ravished the women, and took half of the residents captive (Zechariah 14:2). But then, to the total amazement and consternation of everyone and the dismay of Mesih, three and one-half days after they had been killed, Moses and Elijah revived and ascended into Heaven! Immediately, there was an earthquake in Jerusalem, the city was divided into three parts, and 7,000 of the enemies of the Jews were killed. Mesih and his followers were terrified, but the Jews in Jerusalem recognized the hand of the Lord and glorified Him. (Revelation 11:3-13)

Then, suddenly, there was a brilliant flash of light, like lightning flashing from horizon to horizon, and the glorified Messiah, Yahushua, appeared in totally white, luminous clouds, descending out of Heaven (Matthew 24:27, 30)! And there was the overwhelmingly loud sound of a great shofar (Jewish trumpet), and gleaming white angelic beings appeared and flew to every part of the sky all around the earth; and other glorified beings from all over the earth, under the earth, and even from within the seas flew up to meet them, from where they were instantly taken to meet the Messiah in the air (Matthew 24:31; 1 Thessalonians 4:16, 17). Then, the Messiah, the angels, and the "raptured" ones all vanished into Heaven.

And that seventh and final trumpet sounding also announced the third "woe"—the final set of plagues of the Wrath of Yahuah. And because the reign of Antimessiah on Earth had ended, a loud chorus of voices was heard shouting from Heaven, *"The kingdoms of this world have become the kingdoms of our Lord and of His* [Messiah], *and He shall reign forever and ever!"* (Revelation 11:15)

Then, all Heaven broke forth in a series of catastrophes that, for the next ten days, demolished the whole planet: A great, global earthquake caused every island to disappear and every mountain (except the mountains in and near Jerusalem—Mount Zion, Mount Moriah and the Mount of Olives) to collapse. The earthquake shook the earth so violently that it also caused all the buildings of all the world's cities to collapse (except Jerusalem which, although it was split into three sections, remained standing). Then, a giant comet fell on the now lifeless, barren former U.S.A. and New Babylon (which was now inhabited only by evil spirit beings—Revelation 18:2), sinking that land and much of North America beneath the waves of the sea. Finally, hundreds of millions of 100-pound, flaming "hailstones" (comet fragments) rained down on the earth, killing virtually all of the planet's remaining inhabitants (except those supernaturally protected by the Lord and the remaining armies of the kings of the earth in and around Jerusalem). (cf. Revelation 11:15-10; 16:17-21; 18:20-21).

The Final Showdown

After that, a great multitude in Heaven was heard proclaiming with a loud voice,

> *'Alleluia! Salvation and glory and honor and power belong to* [Yahuah] *our God. For true and righteous are His judgments, because He has judged the great harlot who corrupted the earth with her fornication; and He has avenged on her the blood of His servants shed by her.' Again they said, 'Allelujah! Her smoke rises up forever and ever!' And the twenty-four elders and the four living creatures fell down and worshiped* [Yahuah] *who sat on the throne, saying, 'Amen! Allelujah!' Then a voice came from the throne, saying, 'Praise our God, all you His servants and those who fear Him, both small and great!' And it was heard, as it were, the voice of a great multitude, as the sound of many waters and as the sound of mighty thundering, saying, 'Alleluia! for the Lord* [Yahuah] *Omnipotent reigns!'* (Revelation 19:1-6)

Finally, the Messiah Yahushua —the King of Kings and Lord of Lords—was seen streaking through the heavens from the east, riding a great and powerful, gleaming white horse and wearing a crimson garment, followed by a great host of angels and glorified saints wearing pure white linen garments and also riding white horses. The Lord Yahushua then stood at the peak of the Mount of Olives, which split from the west to the east forming a valley that ran all the way to the north end of the Dead Sea. All the Jewish inhabitants of Jerusalem who remained in the city and who had not taken the mark of the beast then fled through the valley to the east. Mesih sent his army (what was left of it after all the plagues of the Wrath of Yahuah) after them like a flood, but, incredibly, the earth opened up, forming a huge crevasse that swallowed his army. Then a white light like a great laser sword came from the mouth of the Messiah, slaying all the armies of the kings of the earth who had gathered against Jerusalem (cf. Revelation 16:13-14). The Messiah then took Kurturaci Mesih and his Chief of Religion and cast them alive into the Dead Sea which had filled with blazing bitumen from the great rift in the earth that had swallowed Mesih's army. (cf. Zechariah 14:3-5; Revelation 19:11-21).

41

The Beginning

Of course, that is not the end of the story, which, for those who understand and believe it and who believe in the One who authored it all, is thrilling indeed. Revelation goes on to describe the binding of Satan for 1,000 years; the millennial Kingdom of Yahuah; the new heavens, new earth, and New Jerusalem: who will be there, who will not, and what will happen there; the final war of Gog and Magog; the Final Judgment; and a peek at eternity in the glorious presence of the Lord Yahuah. But, hopefully, this has given you a taste of what the Revelation is all about.

And, hopefully, this narrative has whetted your appetite to get into the Scripture for yourself to get all the details and to find out for yourself what Yahuah's plan is for "the End of the Age," how you can avoid being sucked into the doomed, global "new world order" of the false messiah, and how you can be sure that you are a citizen of the unimaginably wonderful, eternal Paradise of Yahuah.

And to help you do that, Yahuah has given us the following detailed, crystal-clear commentary on the book of the Revelation. I also want to invite you to visit my ministry website, www.RevelationUnderstoodCommentary.com, where I share with anyone who has "eyes that see and ears that hear" all about what is happening in the world right now in the light of *Bible* prophecy, what it means to be a True Follower of Yahushua in today's confusing, tumultuous world that is rapidly plummeting toward The End, and how you can be involved in helping others get off this sinking ship called Planet Earth into the lifeboat called Yahushua, before it is too late.

Revelation Understood!

A Clear, Concise, Common-Sense Commentary
on the Revelation of Yahushua ("Jesus") the Messiah

Contrary to what most people think, the book of the Revelation, the last book of the *Bible*, is **not** difficult to understand if we will take a simple, face-value, common-sense approach to interpreting it. It is only when we start to over-allegorize it or to force its interpretation according to our pre-conceived ideas or doctrines about the *"End of the Age"* and the World to Come that it gets indecipherable.

The *Bible* is Yahuah's ("God's") inspired, written Word. We are not going to get into the many arguments and evidences for the inspiration of the *Bible*. That fact is assumed in this commentary. Anyone who reads the *Bible* with an open mind and heart, enlightened by the Holy Spirit, will know that it is no mere human composition. There have been errors in human translation and transmission of the *Bible*, but nothing that affects the basic *Bible* doctrines, which include: There is one, true God who created and sustains the universe and everything in it; Yahuah's creation is doomed for destruction; and the only way to be saved from that destruction and to live "forever" in union with Yahuah is through a personal, spiritual relationship with Yahuah incarnate, Yahushua the Messiah. Also, it is assumed that there are no errors in translation and transmission of Scripture that cannot be resolved through diligent prayer and study because, as Yahushua said, *"Heaven and earth shall pass away, but My words shall not pass away"* (Matthew 24:35).

It is clear that Yahuah intends for His written Word to be understood by the average person. For many centuries, it was kept from the general public by church clergy who communicated the Scripture only in languages (e.g., Latin) which were unfamiliar to the masses. Today, there are still many ministers and *Bible* teachers who pretend to be the ultimate authorities on *Bible* interpretation and application; they do not encourage their followers or students to get into the Word for themselves, prayerfully trusting Yahuah to reveal its meaning to them. However, Yahuah says, through the apostle Paul, *"Be diligent to present yourself approved to [Yahuah], a worker who does not need to be ashamed, rightly dividing* [interpreting and applying] *the word of truth"* (2 Timothy 2:15). It is kind of hard to see how we can correctly interpret Scripture unless we study it for ourselves, is it not? As was mentioned before, the Believers in Yahushua in Berea were commended—considered more "noble" than other congregations—because they studied the *Bible* to see if what Paul taught them was accurate (Acts 17:11). Yahushua said, *"Search the Scriptures; for in them you think you have eternal life: and they are they which testify of Me"* (John 5:39). Now, why would He tell us to do that if the *Bible* cannot be understood by the average person?

Also, as was mentioned before, there are many approaches to *Bible* interpretation, particularly prophetic Scripture. This has resulted in much confusion in the understanding of the Scriptures. But "[Yahuah] *is not the author of confusion"* (1Corinthians 14:33). So, this commentary takes a literal, face-value, common-sense approach. There are many symbolic images in *Bible* prophecy, but it is clear from the context of each which is to be taken as literal and which as symbolic. And **every symbol can be understood** if we will simply compare Scripture with Scripture, allowing the *Bible* to be its own interpreter.

Finally, the apostle Peter wrote, *". . . no prophecy of Scripture is of any private interpretation"* (2 Peter 1:20). That means that no individual can claim exclusive discernment of the correct interpretation of any *Bible* passage, term, or image because every correct interpretation must be revealed by the Holy Spirit (cf. 2 Peter 1:21). So, the writer of this commentary certainly does not claim to know the correct meaning of every word of the *Bible*, specifically the Revelation. Therefore, he will endeavor, by the Grace of Yahuah, to be honest in his comments—noting areas of uncertainty when there are those and possible alternative understandings when there are those. Then, the reader is encouraged to dig into the Word, like the Bereans, asking Yahuah to reveal its true meaning. And, with enough diligence and patience, waiting on the Lord, that meaning will be revealed, because Yahuah promised those who have real faith, *"Seek and you shall find"* (Matthew 7:7), and, *". . . when he, the Spirit of truth, is come, he will guide you into all truth"* (John 16:13).

One last word: This commentary is not the text of a debate. Much study and contemplation of various insights, interpretations, definitions, descriptions, and commentary of others has gone into it; but, except for some possible alternative interpretations when in doubt, only what the writer believes the Lord has shown him, personally, will be presented. And although he has had no seminary training—does not even know the original languages (mainly Hebrew and Greek)—the writer believes that, after years of prayerful, diligent study, looking up the meanings of various terms in *Bible* dictionaries and lexicons (which any literate person can do), Father Yahuah, in His wonderful grace, has given him a pretty clear understanding of the Revelation of the Lord and related Scriptures. So, more than anything, it is the writer's prayer that all you "average" lovers of the Truth will take heart in the confidence that **you *can* understand Yahuah's prophetic Word**, understand the critical End Times in which we live in the light of that Truth, and know what our Heavenly Father wants us to do about it, before it is too late—which is a main purpose of the Revelation.

A Brief Background

In the Beginning, Yahuah created the universe (the "*heavens and the earth*") and all that is in them, including human beings created in His own image (Genesis 1:1-27). And He gave man the power to reproduce others in Yahuah's image and to have dominion over Earth— to rule over it and take care of it (Genesis 1:28).

But there was a period of probation in a specific part of the earth, the Garden of Eden. In the Garden, Adam and Eve, the first humans, were given a choice: eat of the Tree of Life and live forever, or eat of the Tree of the Knowledge of Good and Evil and die (Genesis 2:9, 17). No doubt, if they had chosen to eat of the Tree of Life, Adam and Eve would have fulfilled Yahuah's original plan for them and lived forever, reigning over the earth in perfect unity with Yahuah the Son, by whom all things were created (Hebrews 1:2). But, the brightest angel, Lucifer, who aspired to supplant Yahuah (Isaiah 14:13), was also in the Garden in the form of a serpent. And he appealed to Adam and Eve through something beautiful ("*the lust of the eyes*") and that tasted good ("*the lust of the flesh*") and through telling them, "*You shall be like* [Yahuah]" ("*the pride of life*"), to rebel against Yahuah and do what He had told them not to do (Genesis 3:1-6; 1 John 2:16). And they fell for it.

And through their sin, Adam and Eve allowed Satan to get a foothold in Yahuah's creation and to usurp their (and through them, Yahushuah's) dominion over the earth. And it has been downhill since that time, both for Yahuah's natural creation and for man, because it is the basic nature of Satan to kill, not to give life, and to destroy, not to create or maintain Yahuah's creation (John 10:10).

But Yahuah has a plan for taking Earth back, placing it under the direct dominion of Yahuah the Son, Yahushua (the second, life-giving Adam—1 Corinthians 15:45)! At the present time, Yahuah is preparing a special, chosen people, a remnant of the nation of Israel who are followers of Yahushua, to rule with Him over the new, restored Earth (Revelation 2:27). Then, during the last seven years of the dominion of Satan over Earth, Yahuah will set the adversary up to make a spectacle of him by allowing his incarnation, the "beast" (anti-messiah), to think that he truly is Lord of the World (cf. Revelation 13:5-7). But then, Yahuah will totally destroy the beast's global dominion. Finally, in the greatest showdown in world history, the Lord Yahushua will return with the armies of Heaven to totally defeat the false messiah and the armies of the kings of the earth. He will then restore the earth to its original Edenic state and rule over it with His Redeemed Ones for 1,000 years (the millennial Kingdom of the Lord).

After that, the heavens and the earth will be destroyed, Final Judgment of all those who have followed Satan in rebellion against Yahuah throughout history will occur, they will be cast into the "Lake of Fire" along with Satan and his spirit-being followers, and eternity in perfect unity in the Spirit with Yahuah the Father and Yahuah the Son will begin for the Redeemed of the Lord.

And that is what the Revelation is all about—the "Final Seven Years" of world history, as we have known it all our lives, and the events to follow. And it truly is a magnificent story—far greater than any movie ever made or science fiction story ever written. And it is all the more fantastic because it is absolutely true!

Verse-by-Verse Commentary

Chapter 1—John's Assignment

1:1, 2   *The* (a) *Revelation* (b) *of [Yahushua the Messiah], which [Yahuah] gave Him to show* (c) *His servants—things which must* (d) *shortly take place. And He sent and* (e) *signified it by* (f) *His angel to* (g) *His servant John, who* (h) *bore witness to the word of [Yahuah], and to the testimony of [Yahushua the Messiah], to all things that he saw.*

a.   The word "*revelation*" in the original Greek is *apokalupsis* or, literally, "uncovering" or "unveiling." The Revelation is an uncovering of events that had been previously hidden or "sealed" from human knowledge that will happen during, as we shall see, the last seven years of the reign of Satan over Yahuah's ("God's") creation and the events following those seven years.

b.   This is not the "Revelation of John," as some translations state. It is the Revelation of Yahushua ("Jesus") the Messiah, Yahuah the Son, given to Him by Yahuah the Father. John wrote what was shown and told to him by Yahushua and other heavenly beings.

c.   The purpose of the Revelation is to show the "*servants*" of Yahuah things which will occur in the future. Both ancient Israel (Deuteronomy 9:27; 2 Chronicles 6:23; Psalm 79:2; et al.), and the Disciples of Yahushua (John 18:36; Acts 4:29; et al.) are referred to in the *Bible* as the Lord's servants. The Revelation was given to **both** the Jews and the Followers of Yahushua.

d.   "*Shortly*" could have any of several meanings. The Greek words, *en tachos*, can mean "soon to come" or "in quick succession." It may mean soon to come from Heaven's point of view, where "*a thousand years is as one day*" (2 Peter 3:8). It may mean that the events of Revelation are the next to occur in Yahuah's agenda of significant scene changes in the drama of the history of the world. It may mean that, considering how short life is, for any individual the events will come very soon. Or, it may mean that once the events of the Revelation begin, they will all occur in rapid order. Whatever the specific meaning of "*shortly*," it would appear that a sense of constant watchfulness and expectancy is meant to be conveyed, which was the attitude Yahushua told His Disciples to have (Matthew 25:13).

e. The Greek word for *"signified"* (*semaino*) can mean either to give a sign/to indicate, or to communicate/make known. In this context, it would appear to mean to communicate or make known. Although Revelation contains a lot of symbolism, it is not, as a whole, an allegory. The events of Revelation will actually, literally occur.

f. The Greek word translated *"angel"* (*aggelos*) literally means "messenger," especially one sent from Yahuah. The Greek construction of this sentence seems to indicate that this is a special angel or messenger. Yahuah often assigns specific jobs or tasks to angels. Although John is spoken to by others and hears others speak, it appears that this angel is with him throughout the Revelation. It seems that he is assigned the task of making sure John gets the message revealed to him by the Lord and gets it written down (cf. 19:9-10; 22:8, 9).

g. Conservative *Bible* scholars are almost universally agreed that this is John the apostle—the one *"[Yahushua] loved"* (John 19:26), who also wrote the gospel of John and the first, second, and third letters of John.

h. The Revelation is not hearsay or a product of John's imagination. It is the record of what he personally heard and saw.

1:3 (a) *Blessed is he who* (b) *reads and those who hear the words of this* (c) *prophecy, and* (d) *keep those things which are written in it; for* (e) *the time is near.*

a. As Yahushua promised, while He was on the earth, blessings to those who keep His commandments (cf. Matthew 5:3-12), He promises blessings to those who read, hear, and keep the things written in His Revelation.

b. The Revelation is intended for everyone—both those who read and those who hear.

c. The Revelation is a prophetic book (like numerous books in the *Tanakh*). As the last book of the *Bible*, continuing where the book of Daniel in the *Tanakh* left off (cf. Daniel 12:9), it foretells the final events of world history.

d. The blessings are not for those who are passive, merely reading or hearing the Revelation. The Revelation is a book of **action**, not just prophecy. It is a how-to manual for dealing with the terrible, yet wonderful (depending on ones' point of view) times soon to come. As James wrote, *". . . be doers of the Word, and not hearers only, deceiving yourselves"* (in thinking that you will receive any

48

benefits by being passive) (James 1:22). For faithful obedience (Revelation 22:7), steadfastness (Revelation 2:25), alertness, spiritual purity (Revelation 16:15), victorious spiritual warfare (Revelation 21:7), and remaining united with the Lord to the end (Revelation 14:13), numerous blessings or benefits are promised, including: eternal life; freedom from all sorrow, weeping, or pain (Revelation 21:4); reigning with the Lord over all nations in His millennial kingdom on Earth; and reigning with Him forever after that in His eternal kingdom (cf. 2 Timothy 2:12; Revelation 2:26, 27; 5:10; 20:6; 22:5).

e. The sense of urgency and expectancy is reinforced. Even though, from Earth's perspective, it has been close to 2,000 years since the Revelation was written, from Heaven's perspective there is no difference between one day and a thousand years. Yahuah transcends time. All of history is like a giant mural in His view. Something that will happen a thousand years from now, from Earth's point of view, will happen very soon from the perspective of eternity. A key to understanding the Revelation is to see its events from Yahuah's heavenly perspective.

1:4-6 *John, to the* (a) *seven [assemblies of Believers in Yahushua] which are in Asia: Grace to you and peace from* (b) *Him who is and who was and who is to come, and from* (c) *the seven Spirits who are before His throne, and from* (d) *[Yahushua the Messiah], the faithful witness, the firstborn from the dead, and the ruler over the kings of the earth. To Him who loved us and washed us from our sins in His own blood, and has made us kings and priests to His God and Father, to* (e) *Him be glory and dominion forever and ever. Amen.*

a. Some say that the Revelation was written just to the seven assemblies of Asia Minor that are addressed in Chapters 2 and 3. But there are several indications that it was intended not only for the Lord's People the Believers in Yahushua, in general, but also for His People the Jews: (1) There were more than seven assemblies of Believers in Asia Minor. The distinctly different characteristics of the seven from one another seem to indicate that they are representative of all assemblies. (2) Seven is the number of completeness in the Revelation: seven spirits before the throne (1:4), seven candlesticks (1:12), seven stars (1:16), seven lamps (4:5), seven seals (5:1), seven horns (5:6), seven eyes (5:6), seven angels standing before Yahuah (8:2), seven trumpets (8:2), seven thunders

(10:3), seven thousand people killed (11:13), seven heads (12:3), seven crowns (12:3), seven angels (15:1), seven plagues (15:1), seven bowls (15:7), seven mountains (17:9), and seven kings (17:10). So, since the Revelation is the prophecy of the completion of all things and what will occur during the final seven years of history, it would seem that the seven assemblies represent different aspects or different types of congregations of the Followers of Yahushua in general throughout history. (3) Revelation was written not only to the seven assemblies, but to the **angels** of the seven assemblies (2:1, 8, 12, 18; 3:1, 7, 14). Addressing the Revelation to the angels, just as it was addressed to the seven assemblies, would seem to indicate that angels are responsible for doing something with it besides getting it to the seven, literal assemblies. Would not this special, important assignment be getting the Revelation to Yahuah's People in general, just as an angel was responsible for communicating it to John (1:1)? In fact, Revelation 22:6 indicates that the mission of Yahuah's angel was more than to just show the Revelation to John, but to His People in general. And that would seem to indicate that the Revelation was intended for more than the seven literal churches in Asia Minor. (4) There are numerous prophecies about the Jews in the Revelation. If it is written just to the seven assemblies, why would they be concerned about what will happen to the Jews? (5) The language used by John appears to be directed to both Yahuah's People the Disciples of Yahushua and to Yahuah's People the Jews. For example, he points out that the dragon of Chapter 12 is ". . . *that serpent of old, called the devil and Satan*" (12:9). "Serpent" is the language of Yahuah's BCE People Israel. In the *Tanakh*, the adversary of the Lord is called the "*serpent*" 34 times and "*Satan*" (Hebrew for "adversary") 14 times, but never, of course, the "*devil*," which is from a Greek (Gentile) word (*diabolos*). In the *B'rit Hadashah*, he is called "*Satan*" 36 times and "*devil*" 35 times, but "*serpent*" only seven times. And two of those seven occurrences are in reference to his activities in BCE times. The other five are all in the book of Revelation. Therefore, it appears that John intended for his readers to be both the Followers of Yahushua and the Jews. So, why was John told to write to the seven assemblies rather than to the Jews (1:4)? That is obvious if we understand how Yahuah is dealing with the Jews (those of His People who have not yet recognized that Yahushua is the Messiah) at the present time: They have been **temporarily** blinded to the Gospel until the "*fullness of the Gen-*

50

tiles has come in" (when the Assembly of Yahuah's People will be complete) (Romans 11:25). Meanwhile, it is the Assembly's job to preach the Gospel, including the Revelation, to the whole world, **especially** to the Jews (cf. Romans 1:16). Then, when the Jews see all these things coming to pass, their eyes will be opened to the Truth that Yahushua is their Messiah, and ". . . *all Israel* [as a literal nation] *will be saved"* (Romans 11:26).

b. This phrase refers to Yahuah the Father, but also, as is clarified in 1:8, it refers to Yahuah the Son. Again, Yahushua *is* Yahuah!

c. Some have conjectured that these are seven angels, but nowhere in Revelation does it explicitly state that the seven spirits are seven angels. In fact, note that in 3:2 the seven spirits of Yahuah and the seven stars (which are identified as angels in 1:20) are separate entities from one another. Some say they are the seven-fold Spirit of Yahuah (the Holy Spirit), but the term "spirits" (plural) is used in the *Bible* to refer to various entities, positive and negative, including familiar spirits (Leviticus 19:31), the four spirits of Heaven (Zechariah 6:5), unclean spirits (Matthew 10:1), evil spirits (Luke 7:21), the spirits of the prophets (1 Corinthians 14:32), angels (Hebrews 1:14), and the spirits of demons (Revelation 16:14). Also, the seven spirits are before Yahuah's throne rather than emanating from it, as are the seven angels of 8:1, suggesting a position of submission and readiness to carry out the will of Yahuah. So, this commentator believes that the *"seven Spirits of* [Yahuah]" simply represent the various manifestations of the Holy Spirit, the executor of Yahuah's will on Earth, whether through angels or otherwise, in perfectly and completely bringing about the end of the dominion of Satan on Earth during the Final Seven Years.

d. Yahushua is seen in His divine attributes as Savior and Messiah— the witness to Himself, the Truth (John 8:14, 18); *"firstfruits"* of the resurrection (1 Corinthians 15:23); King of Kings (Revelation 19:16); and Redeemer (Titus 2:14)—making us a royal priesthood (1 Peter 2:9) who minister to Yahuah (cf. Joel 2:17).

e. Why? —so that the Lord will receive glory and dominion over His creation "forever" (Revelation 19:1, 6, 7).

1:7 *Behold,* (a) *He is coming with clouds, and* (b) *every eye will see Him,* (c) *even they who pierced Him. And all the tribes of the earth will mourn because of Him. Even so, Amen.*

a. The "second coming" of the Messiah (initiating the "Day of Yahuah") is the key, focal event, the central theme, of Revelation. After Yahushua's apostles watched Him ascend toward Heaven enveloped in a cloud, *"two men [angels] stood by them in white apparel,"* and told them, *"... this same [Yahushua] who was taken up from you into heaven, will so come in like manner as you saw him go into heaven"* (Acts 1:9, 10, 11).

b. And it will not be a private, "secret" event; the whole world will see him. Other books of the *Bible* give us more details. Yahushua Himself told His Disciples,

> *As the lightning comes from the east and flashes to the west, so also will the coming of the Son of Man be. . . . Immediately after the tribulation of those days the sun will be darkened, and the moon will not give its light; the stars will fall from heaven, and the powers of the heavens will be shaken. Then the sign of the Son of Man will appear in heaven, and then all the tribes of the earth will mourn, and they will see the Son of Man coming on the clouds of heaven with power and great glory. And He will send His angels with a great sound of a trumpet, and they will gather together His elect from the four winds, from one end of heaven to the other* [the 'Rapture']. (Matthew 24:27, 29-31)

Then, the apostle Paul, in his second letter to the Thessalonians, gives us a few more details of the second coming:

> *The Lord [Yahushua] Himself will descend from heaven with a shout, with the voice of an archangel, and with the trumpet of [Yahuah]. And the dead in [the Messiah] will rise first* [the resurrection of the Redeemed]. *Then we who are alive and remain shall be caught up together with them in the clouds to meet the Lord [Yahushua] in the air* [the 'Rapture']. *And thus we shall always be with the Lord [Yahushua].* (1 Thessalonians 4:16-17)

This will also be the fulfillment of the BCE prophecy of Daniel 7:13-14. What an awesome event—the "Blessed Hope" of the Believers! As we go through the Revelation, many more details concerning the second coming, including when it occurs in the sequence of events of the seven years, will be filled in. And, as you will see, Yahuah does not want us to be confused about what is going to happen; it will all be very clear.

c. Although everyone on Earth will witness the spectacular return of the Messiah, among those who witness His return will be *"those who pierced* [crucified] *Him*" and who will *"mourn because of Him."* Who this includes is easy to determine because this is a direct reference, a quote, from Zechariah 12:10. And Zechariah 12:10, according to Hebrew scholars, is talking about Israel—not just Judah, but all twelve tribes of Israel, who, at the present time are scattered all over the world, "hidden" among the nations of the world. The word translated *"tribes"* (Greek: *phule*) in verse 7 can mean clans or families, as in the families or tribes of Israel, rather than nations or peoples in general. And the word translated *"earth"* (Greek: *ge*) in most translations can refer to "land," or a specific nation. Apparently, in this verse, the people who *"mourn him as they mourn an only son"* (Zechariah 12:10) are the Jews. In other words, the eyes of the Jews (those who are the true Remnant of Israel, who really believe in the coming Messiah—cf. Romans 9:6), whose temporary blindness (cf. Romans 11:25) has been removed, will recognize that He is their Messiah when He returns and will mourn because they have rejected and crucified Him. (The words translated *"mourn"* in Zechariah and Revelation mean mourning in sorrow for what has happened to another, not in dismay for what has happened to oneself.) And then, they will repent and, as a nation, be saved (Romans 11:26-27). How the salvation of the Jews fits together with the salvation of the Followers of Yahushua is a magnificent story of Yahuah's amazing providence and grace and will become very clear as we proceed through the Revelation. And understanding that, in the end, *"all of Israel will be saved"* is a very important key to understanding how the Final Seven Years will play out on Earth and in Heaven.

1:8 *"I am the Alpha and the Omega, the Beginning and the End,"* says *[Yahuah], "who is and who was and who is to come, the Almighty."*

See verses 4, 11, 2:8, and 22:13. In the context of 1:7, this is referring to the Messiah, Yahuah the Son—the One who *"is to come."* But it also refers to Yahuah the Father—*"the Alpha and the Omega, the Beginning and the End, the First and the Last"* (22:13), *"the Almighty"* (cf. Genesis 17:1). Also, note that the Son is called the *"mighty God"* in Isaiah 9:6. Again, Yahushua *is* Yahuah!

1:9 *I, John, both* (a) *your brother and companion in the tribulation and kingdom and patience of [Yahushua the Messiah],* (b) *was on the*

53

island that is called Patmos for the word of [Yahuah] and for the testimony of [Yahushua the Messiah].

a. Life in the Kingdom of Yahuah was not a cakewalk for John. He described it as being *"in the tribulation and patience of [Yahushua the Messiah]."* In other words, like the apostle Paul, he was sharing in the Messiah's sufferings (2 Corinthians 1:5). Life in the Messiah in this present life on Earth, contrary to the worldly-minded thinking of many, is not the life of a conquering crusader, dominionist, or materially successful and prosperous person. It is the life of, like Yahushua when He was on Earth, the suffering servant. The joy is spiritual. This understanding is very important in the interpretation of the Revelation, which is all about the *"tribulation"* of Yahuah's People at the *"End of the Age"* (Matthew 24:3), Yahuah's People the Disciples of Yahushua are taken "out of here," and Yahuah's People the Jews are protected in hiding until the King of Kings returns, in person, to reclaim His dominion on Earth. The sequence of all these events and many more in the fantastic "showdown" between Yahuah and Satan in the Final Seven Years, contrary to the opinion of many, are made very clear in the Revelation of the Lord.

b. Patmos, off the coast of Asia Minor about 60 miles southwest of Ephesus, was an island to where criminals and enemies of Rome were exiled by the emperor Domitian, who ruled from 81-96 CE, at the time Revelation was written (about 95 CE). Victorinus, a 2nd Century Christian writer, wrote:

> When John saw these things [the visions of the Revelation], he was on the Isle of Patmos, condemned to the mines by Caesar Domitian. There he saw the Apocalypse; and when at length grown old, he thought that he should receive his release by suffering; but Domitian being killed, he was liberated. (*Introduction to the New Testament*, Everett P. Harrison, page 473)

Like Paul, who wrote his most joyful letter, to the Philippians, while imprisoned in Rome, John saw every situation as an opportunity to spread the Word of Yahuah and the testimony of Yahushua the Messiah.

1:10-11 I was (a) in the Spirit (b) on the Lord's Day, and I heard behind me a (c) loud voice, as of a trumpet, saying, (d) "I am the Alpha and the Omega, the First and the Last," and, "What you see (e) write in a book and send it to (f) *the seven* [assemblies] *which are in Asia: to Ephesus, to Smyrna, to Pergamos, to Thyatira, to Sardis, to Philadelphia, and to Laodicea."*

a. *"In the Spirit"* indicates that John was not physically present in the situations described in Revelation. It was like he was in a trance, dream, or "out of body" experience, but it was more than that: It was a vivid vision supernaturally revealed to him by the Spirit of Yahuah.

b. The Greek word translated *"Lord's"* (*kuriakos*) is used in only one other place in the *Bible* (1 Corinthians 11:20), in referring to the *"Lord's supper."* Contrary to popular opinion, in the absence of any other references to this day in the *Bible*, it would appear in this context to be one, solitary day chosen by Yahuah for a special purpose—the Revelation of the Day of Yahuah (in Hebrew, there are no possessive contractions like "Lord's"). In other words, John is being transported, in visions, to view the events leading up to and including the Day of Yahuah (cf. Joel 2:1, 11; 3:14, et al.). *"Lord's Day"* is definitely not a reference to the Sunday "Sabbath" or Sunday "Lord's Day," Replacement Theology's substitute for the seventh-day Sabbath.

c. *"A loud voice"* compared to a trumpet blast, a peal of thunder, or the sound of roaring water is used 22 times in Revelation, where it always indicates a significant message from an angel or divine being.

d. See the notes on 1:8.

e. John was instructed to write what he saw in a book, so it was meant to be read and heard in the assemblies (cf. 1:3).

f. The seven assemblies were in cities in western Asia Minor, east of Greece, across the Aegean Sea from Greece. They were all within a half-circle arc radiating out about 70 miles from Smyrna, the location of one of the assemblies, a city on the west coast of Asia Minor. So, it was only a journey of one to three days by foot between the assemblies. There was a road connecting the cities, and the assemblies are listed here and in Revelation 2 and 3 in the order in which they may have been visited by the apostles.

1:12-16 *And I turned to the voice that spoke with me. And having turned I saw (a) seven golden lampstands, and in the midst of the seven lampstands (b) One like the Son of Man, clothed with a garment about the chest with a golden band. His head and hair were white like wool, as white as snow, and His eyes like a flame of fire; His feet were like* *fine brass, as if refined in a furnace, and His voice as the sound of many waters; He had in His right hand* (c) *seven stars, out of His mouth went a sharp two-edged sword, and His countenance was like the sun shining in its strength.*

a. The lampstands are identified in verse 20.
b. "Son of Man," in referring to the Messiah, occurs only in Daniel (7:13-14) in the *Tanakh*, but 89 times in the *B'rit Hadashah*. Yahushua frequently used the title in referring to Himself. Some may object that *"**like** the Son of Man"* indicates that this person or being is not Yahushua, but the description in Daniel, which is very similar, refers to the Messiah. Also, the Greek term *huios*, translated *"**the** Son"* in this verse, is more correctly translated "**a** son." In John's vision, He looked "like" a man but was much, much more than that. Just because He resembled a man does not mean that He was not Yahuah the Son. Also, verses 17 and 18 of this chapter confirm His identity. One *"like the Son of Man"* appears again in Chapter 14, reaping the harvest of human souls. But in that context, he is an angel who represents the Messiah, and again, *"the"* should be "a" and the "s" on *"son"* and the "m" on *"man"* should not be capitalized.
c. The seven stars are also identified in verse 20.

1:17-18 *And when I saw Him,* (a) *I fell at His feet as dead. But He laid His right hand on me, saying to me, "Do not be afraid; I am the First and the Last.* (b) *I am He who lives, and was dead, and behold, I am alive "forevermore."* (c) *Amen. And* (d) *I have the keys of Hades and of Death.*

a. This is an appropriate response to such an awesome sight: the King of kings and Lord of lords (19:16), Yahuah the Son glorified. The Revelation is all about His Day, when He will return to Earth to claim, glorify, and take to Heaven those who belong to Him, His People the Assembly of Followers of Yahushua, and hide His People the Jews in protective seclusion until He has finished pouring out His Wrath (6:16) on the earth, destroying the global kingdom of Satan and Satan's incarnation, the anti-messiah. Then finally, He will return the earth to its original, magnificent, Eden-like beauty and rule over it with His redeemed Saints. This whole scenario constitutes the long- and often-prophesied Day of Yahuah. And, as we shall see as we proceed through this commentary, its

56

sequence of events is crystal clear to those who read the Revelation in the same common sense, literal manner that every book of the *Bible* should be read.

b. Compare and contrast this description with 17:8, which is a description of the beast, the false (counterfeit) messiah.

c. "*Amen*" is a word of finality or emphasis, meaning "So be it."

d. Death separates one from life. Hades is a waiting place for souls until the time of their final dispensation. The Lord Yahushua has the keys—controls who is subjected to Death and Hades (cf. Matthew 16:18).

1:19 "*Write* (a) *the things which you have seen, and* (b) *the things which are, and* (c) *the things which will take place after this.*

a. These are the things John has seen up to this point (Chapter 1).

b. These are the things happening at the present time on Earth and in Heaven (Chapters 2-5).

c. These are things that will occur in the future (Chapters 6-22).

1:20 "*The* (a) *mystery of the seven stars which you saw in my right hand, and the seven lampstands: The* (b) *seven stars are the angels of the seven* [assemblies]*, and the* (c) *seven lampstands which you saw are the seven* [assemblies]*."*

a. A mystery is knowledge that has not previously been revealed. But the meanings of the stars and the lampstands are about to be revealed.

b. Some have argued that the seven "angels" are human beings— messengers to or leaders of the seven assemblies. And indeed, in Jewish synagogues and early assemblies of Believers in Yahushua, the leading elder, who read messages to the assembly, was called "the messenger of the assembly." But, the term "angels" in this verse apparently carries a double meaning. Just as the seven assemblies are types of assemblies throughout history, and the Greek term *aggelos* can refer to either messengers or angels, these human messengers of the seven assemblies may be types of messenger angels to the universal Assembly of Believers in Yahushua throughout history, just as it is an angel through whom the Revelation was given to John. There are several references in the Revelation to seven stars or angels who are assigned various tasks during the Final Seven Years. There are literal stars (e.g., in 8:12),

57

angels in Heaven, and fallen angels (e.g., in 12:4, 9). Another indication that the seven *"angels"* are not merely human beings but are supernatural beings is that they are seen in the Lord's right hand (ready to carry out His will) (2:1), just as groups of seven angels carry out His will in other situations (cf. 8:2, 15:2, 16:1).

c. The Hebrew word translated *"lampstand"* in the *Tanakh* is *menorah*—a seven-branched lampstand. There were ten of these in Israel's Tabernacle and Temple. But the Greek word translated *"lampstands"* here in the Revelation (*luchnos*) often means single candlesticks. So, these *"lampstands,"* although they are seen as separate, with the Lord Yahushua walking among them (2:1), may also refer to the single candleholders on a menorah, indicating that these seven assemblies are parts of the single universal Assembly of the Lord Yahushua the Messiah, representing different aspects or types of the Assembly of Believers.

Chapter 2—Letters to the Assemblies at Ephesus, Smyrna, Pergamos, and Thyatira

2:1-3 *"To the (a) angel of the [assembly] of (b) Ephesus write, 'These things says He who holds the seven stars in His right hand, who walks in the midst of the seven golden lampstands: I know (c) your patience, and that (d) you cannot bear those who are evil. And you have tested those who say they are apostles and are not, and have found them liars; and you have persevered and have patience, and (e) have labored for My name's sake and have not become weary.*

a. Again (cf. 1:20), "angel" (Greek: *aggelos*) may carry a double meaning, referring to both the leading elder (the "messenger") of the assembly and to an angel who is charged with getting the message to the types of assemblies represented by the assembly at Ephesus throughout history.
b. Ephesus, an opulent seaport city of about 500,000 on the western coast of Asia Minor, across the Aegean Sea almost directly east of Athens, Greece, was the political capital of the Roman province of Asia and also a prominent cultural, commercial, and religious center. It was famous for its fabulous temple of the goddess Artemis, or Diana—one of the seven wonders of the ancient world. Paul's teachings caused a life-threatening uproar among those who practiced false religion there (cf. Acts 19:23-31). He lived in Ephesus, establishing the church there, for about three years, and one of his *B'rit Hadashah* letters was written to the church at Ephesus. Later, Paul's disciple and close companion, Timothy, was the leader of the assembly at Ephesus. The apostle John was the "resident apostle" there during the last years of his life—about 90-100 CE. According to historians, he died there. John wrote his gospel while he lived at Ephesus which was not far from the Isle of Patmos where he received the Revelation.
c. There was much persecution of the Assembly in that part of the world—from Rome, the pagan religions, and the Jews. The assembly at Ephesus was commended by the Lord for her patience in the face of much opposition.
d. The Believers at Ephesus were also commended for their strong stand against "evil" people and false teachers and leaders in the assembly.
e. And they were diligent and tireless in their efforts to maintain doctrinal purity and right living in the assembly.

2:4-5 '*Nevertheless I have this against you, that* (a) *you have left your first love. Remember therefore from where you have fallen; repent and* (b) *do the first works, or else* (c) *I will come to you quickly and remove your lampstand from its place – unless you repent.*

a. Regardless of her patience, perseverance, tireless good works, intolerance of evil people, and diligence to maintain doctrinal correctness, there was something fundamentally wrong with the assembly at Ephesus—she had fallen out of the love of Yahuah which she had in the beginning. She had neglected the "first and great commandment": "*You shall love* [Yahuah] *your God with all your heart, with all your soul, and with all your mind,*" and the second great commandment: "*You shall love your neighbor as yourself*" (Matthew 22:37-39).
b. What was the solution?—remembering her loving relationship with Yahuah, repenting (turning away from) her loveless form of life in the Messiah, and doing the "*first works*" (works done in love).
c. What were the consequences of continuing in her present ways?— Yahuah would remove her light, her Gospel witness, in the world.

2:6 (a) '*But this you have, that you hate the deeds of the Nicolaitans, which I also hate.*'" (b)

a. It was said by various writers at the time that the Nicolaitan "Christian" sect encouraged idolatrous worship, denied that Yahuah was the Creator of the world, and was morally licentious. Also, rooted in Gnostic heresy, the Nicolaitan clergy exercised dominion over the laity and claimed exclusive power to correctly interpret Scripture.
b. In conclusion, the assembly at Ephesus represents those asemblies who are spiritually dead or close to death because they maintain the outward form of life in the Messiah—doctrinal fidelity, right living, and intolerance of conspicuous evil in their midst—but they are just going through the motions, having neglected the Spirit of Yahuah's love in which they began.

2:7 "(a) *He who has an ear, let him hear what* (b) *the Spirit says to* (c) *the [assemblies].* (d) *To him* (e) *who overcomes I will give to eat from* (f) *the tree of life, which is in the midst of the Paradise of [Yahuah].*"

a. Notice that the final exhortation: *"He who has an ear, let him hear what the Spirit says to the* [assemblies]. *To him who overcomes . . .,"* is exactly the same for each of the seven assemblies (cf. 2:11, 17, 26, 29; 3:5, 6, 12, 13, 21, 22).

b. Although the message of each assembly may be delivered by the written or spoken word, or by an angel, ultimately it is from Yahuah the Spirit.

c. The message to each assembly is for all assemblies—the universal Assembly—not just the seven assemblies.

d. And ultimately the message to each of the seven assemblies is for the individual believers in all assemblies.

e. Just hearing the Word is not enough; there must be a victorious response in the love of Yahuah.

f. The ultimate reward for faithful, victorious obedience is, by eating of the Tree of Life, eternal life in Paradise. (By rebelling against Yahuah, Adam and Eve forfeited the opportunity to eat of the Tree of Life and live forever in Paradise [cf. Genesis 2:9; 3:26].)

2:8-9 *"And to the angel of the* [assembly] *in* (a) *Smyrna write, 'These things says* (b) *the First and the Last, who was dead, and came to life: I know your* (c) *works, tribulation, and poverty (but you are rich); and I know* (d) *the blasphemy of those who say they are Jews and are not, but are a synagogue of Satan.*

a. Smyrna, the main commercial center of western Asia Minor, was a very prosperous and beautiful city 40 miles north of Ephesus. Persecution of the assembly was severe there. Polycarp, a disciple of the apostle John and an early "Church father," was martyred in Smyrna in 156 CE.

b. Reinforces that the One who dictated the letters to the assemblies to John was not only Yahuah, but specifically Yahuah the Son, Yahushua the Messiah.

c. Tribulation and poverty, probably resulting from persecution, were the circumstances of the assembly at Smyrna; but they were spiritually *"rich."*

d. Part of the persecution in Smyrna apparently came from Jews who were Jews by birth but not truly Jews spiritually (cf. Romans 2:28-29)—actually called *"a synagogue of Satan"* by the Lord because of their blasphemy.

2:10 (a) *'Do not fear any of those things which you are about to suffer. Indeed, (b) the devil is about to throw some of you into prison, that you may be tested, and you will have (c) tribulation (d) ten days. (e) Be faithful until death, and I will give you the crown of life.'* (f)

a. About 60 years earlier, Yahushua had warned his Disciples that, *"Then* [at the *"End of the Age"*] *they will deliver you up to tribulation and kill you, and you will be hated by all nations for My name's sake"* (Matthew 24:9). But He also comforted them with, *"Do not fear, little flock, for it is your Father's good pleasure to give you the kingdom"* (Luke 12:32). He is just repeating that warning and that consolation to the assembly at Smyrna.
b. Here, the name *"devil"* is used because the assembly at Smyrna was primarily a Gentile, Greek-speaking congregation. Satan is behind all persecution of the Disciples of Yahushua.
c. The term *"tribulation"* (Greek: *thlipsis*—pressure, distress, oppression, affliction) is used throughout the *B'rit Hadashah* to refer to the suffering, at the hands of the wicked, of those who follow Yahushua. Some call the entire seven years at the End of the Age, foretold in the Revelation, the "Tribulation." However, as we shall see, the "Great Tribulation" (7:14) is a limited period of time within the Final Seven Years which are nowhere called "the tribulation."
d. In Daniel (cf. 7:7-24) and in Revelation, the number 10 seems to refer to the complete wickedness of the world. In other words, all of the world's wickedness would come against the assembly at Smyrna for a limited period of time.
e. Again, the promise of eternal life is not to those who are passive in their faith, but to those who *"endure to the end,"* even if that means martyrdom.
f. Please notice that in contrast to the assembly at Ephesus, who was sound in doctrine and *"good works"* but lacking in love, and the churches that were compromised in some other way, the Lord had nothing negative to say to the poor, persecuted assembly at Smyrna, but just encouraged her to hang in there until she received her reward.

2:11 *"He who has an ear to hear, let him hear what the Spirit says to the [assemblies]. He who overcomes shall not be hurt by the second death."*

Same exhortation and promise as to the assembly at Ephesus, except to these Believers who were likely facing martyrdom, the promise is phrased in such a way as to comfort them in the face of death, as Yahushua had previously comforted and exhorted His Disciples with, "Do *not fear those who kill the body but cannot kill the soul. But rather fear Him who is able to destroy both soul and body in hell* [the '*second death*']" (Matthew 10:28).

2:12-13 *"And to the angel of the [assembly] in* (a) *Pergamos write, 'These things says* (b) *He who has the sharp two-edged sword:* *"I know your works, and where you dwell,* (c) *where Satan's thone is. And* (d) *you hold fast to My name, and did not deny My faith even in the days in which Antipas was My faithful martyr, who was killed among you,* (c) *where Satan dwells.*

a. Pergamos (Pergamum), about 70 miles north of Smyrna, was the main religious center and, with a vast library of 200,000 volumes, literary center of Asia Minor. The city was addicted to idolatry and was filled with statues and altars to pagan gods, including Zeus (from whose name "Jesus" (Je-Zeus) may have been derived). So, religious persecution in Pergamum was great.
b. The sharp two-edged sword is symbolic of the Word of Yahuah, personified in Yahushua. It (He) is capable of distinguishing the physical from the spiritual and discerning the thoughts and intents of the heart. (cf. Hebrews 4:12)
c. No doubt due to the dominion of powerful spiritual forces of idolatrous religion in the city, the Lord called Pergamum the location where Satan dwelled and of his throne. It is interesting that the Hebrew name "*Satan*" is used here, perhaps indicating a strong Jewish element in the assembly at Pergamum.
d. The assembly at Pergamos was commended for "*holding fast*" to the name of Yahushua and not denying that He was their Lord and Savior, even when faced with the possibility of being killed for doing so, as one of their members, Antipas, was.

2:14-15 *'But I have a few things against you, because you have there those who hold* (a) *the doctrine of Balaam, who taught Balak to put a stumbling block before the children of Israel, to eat things sacrificed to idols, and to commit sexual immorality. Thus you also have those who hold* (b) *the doctrine of the Nicolaitans, which thing I hate.*

a. The pagan king of the Moabites, Balak, tried to get the false prophet Balaam to prophesy against Israel, but Balaam refused to do so. However, he counseled Balak to subvert and overcome Israel by getting her involved in pagan idolatry and sexual immorality, which happened (cf. Numbers 22-25). The apostle James, leader of the assembly at Jerusalem, had advised the assembly there, which was comprised entirely of Messianic Jews, to write to the Gentiles who had turned to faith in Yahushua, warning them to avoid involvement in practices which, to the Jews, were even symbolic of idolatry and sexual immorality (cf. Acts 15:13-20). But some in the assembly at Pergamos had given in to the pressure of the powerful pagan spirit of the city and gotten involved in the *"doctrine of Balaam."*

b. The doctrine of the Nicolaitans, as was noted in the commentary on the assembly at Ephesus, was essentially the same as the Doctrine of Balaam. But, unlike the assembly at Ephesus, which, like the Lord, hated the deeds (false worship and immorality) of the Nicolaitans, some in the assembly at Pergamum compromised and adopted those practices.

2:16-17 (a) *'Repent, or else I will come to you quickly and will* (b) *fight against them with the sword of My mouth. He who has an ear, let him hear what the Spirit says to the [assemblies]. To him who overcomes I will give some of* (c) *the hidden manna to eat. And I will give him a white stone, and on the stone a new name written which no one knows except him who receives it.'"* (d)

a. The solution? Those who had adopted the doctrines of Balaam and the Nicolaitans needed to turn away from those doctrines.

b. The consequences? If they did not repent, the Lord Himself would fight against them with His Word, which is capable of destroying false doctrines and those who hold them (cf. 2 Corinthians 10:4-5).

c. The rewards for spiritual victory?—hidden manna (Manna was food miraculously given to Israel to sustain her in the Sinai wilderness. For Believers in Yahushua the Messiah, the *"hidden"* manna is the *"Bread of Life,"* spiritual sustenance, the Lord Yahushua Himself in us.); a white stone (The defendant in Hebrew trials, if found innocent, was given a white stone; if found guilty, was given a black stone.); and a new name (As *"new creations"* in the Messiah, all things are new, including our heavenly names and the song that we sing—cf. 2 Corinthians 5:17; Revelation 14:3).

64

d. The assembly at Pergamos was compromised because some of her members had adopted pagan doctrines that led to idolatry and sexual immorality.

2:18-19 *"And to the angel of the [assembly] in* (a) *Thyatira write, 'These things says the* (b) *Son of [Yahuah], who has eyes like a flame of fire, and His feet like fine brass: "I know* (c) *your works, love, service, faith, and your patience; and as for your works, the last are more than the first.*

a. Thyatira, 45 miles southeast of Pergamum, was originally a Macedonian colony during the Greek empire of Alexander the Great. It was famous for its purple and scarlet dyes. Lydia, a convert of the apostle Paul, is mentioned as a *"seller of purple fabrics"* from Thyatira (Acts 16:14). Idolatry was prevalent in Thyatira, as it was in all of Asia Minor. The principal deity of the city was Apollos, the sun god, although Artemis, the twin sister of Apollo in Greek mythology, is also mentioned in inscriptions found in Thyatira.
b. The speaker and the One dictating the letter to the assembly at Thyatira is explicitly identified here as the Son of Yahuah, and His description is exactly the same as in 1:14-15.
c. The good works, faith, and patience of the assembly at Thyatira equal or exceed, because her works have increased over time, those of the assemblies at Ephesus and Pergamum.

2:20-23 *"Nevertheless I have a few things against you, because* (a) *you allow that woman* (b) *Jezebel, who calls herself a prophetess, to teach and seduce My servants to commit sexual immorality and eat things sacrificed to idols. And* (c) *I gave her time to repent of her sexual immorality, and she did not repent. Indeed* (d) *I will cast her into a sickbed, and those who commit adultery with her into* (e) *great tribulation, unless they* (c) *repent of their deeds.* (f) *I will kill her children with death, and* (g) *all the [assemblies] shall know that I am He who searches the minds and hearts. And* (h) *I will give to each one of you according to your works.*

a. Notice again that being a Disciple of the Messiah is not a passive religion. The Believers at Thyatira were censured by the Lord because they put up with this evil woman in their midst.
b. The woman, a false prophetess (claiming to speak for Yahuah), was probably not actually named Jezebel, but was, in her teaching

and seducing others in the assembly into idolatry and sexual immorality, like the notorious Queen Jezebel, the wife of Israel's King Ahab (cf 1 Kings 16:31-21:25).

c. Again, the solution to sin is repentance, both for the teacher—the instigator and leader of iniquity—and the followers. But this "Jezebel" refused to repent.

d. One consequence of sin and rebellion against the Lord may be physical illness.

e. Another consequence is *"great tribulation,"* which may come in the form of various calamities or distress.

f. A third consequence of continuing in sin while refusing to repent is for Jezebel's (spiritual) children (those who follow her teachings and give in to her seductions) to be *"killed with death."* That seems redundant, but *"killed with death"* is a Hebrew idiom for "slain with a most sure and awful death" in the same way that the literal Jezebel and her children met their end.

g. Sometimes, what is going on in an assembly is not obvious, but when those in other congregations see terrible things happening to members of an assembly that do not seem related to their stand for righteousness or truth, it may be that the Lord, who *"searches the minds and hearts,"* is bringing the consequences of their secret unrepentant sin and rebellion on them.

h. Note that consequences are not just for the evil in their hearts but are for the evil works that manifest that spiritual evil. Their chastisement was not just because of lack of faith, which was not a flaw of the believers at Thyatira, but because of their unrepentant, evil deeds, for, *"Faith without* [good] *works is dead"* (James 2:20).

2:24-25 (a) *"Now to you I say, and to the rest in Thyatira, as many as do not have this doctrine, who have not known the depths of Satan, as they say, I will put on you no other burden. But hold fast what you have till I come.* (b)

a. The Lord consoles any in Thyatira who have not given in to the teachings or seductions of "Jezebel," which have dragged others into *"the depths of Satan,"* with the promise that He will put no other burden on them than to continue resisting her and to continue steadfastly in what they already have—good works, love, service, faith, and patience.

b. So, the assembly at Thyatira represents the overly tolerant assembly—putting up with, to her ultimate demise, false prophets (one in particular) with their devilish doctrines and immoral practices.

2:26-28 *"And he who overcomes, and keeps My works until the end, to him I will give power over the nations—"He shall rule them with a rod of iron; they shall be dashed to pieces like the potter's vessels"—as I also have received from My Father; and I will give him the morning star.""*

This is an incredible promise to those who remain faithful, overcoming and doing the works of the Lord until the end. But it is not, as some think, a promise that the Assembly of Believers in the Messiah will establish the Kingdom of Heaven on Earth independent of the Messiah or before He returns **in person** to do that. Look at the last part of verse 27 and verse 28: *"—as I also have received from my Father; and I will give him the morning star."* Who is doing the speaking here? Who is making the promise to *"he who overcomes"*? It is the Lord Yahushua, the One who is dictating these letters to the seven assemblies. And, to whom is He making the promise? It is to *"he* (singular) *who overcomes"*—the individual Believer in Yahushua, not the whole Assembly of Believers. And what is He promising to give to the individual believer who overcomes? It is what Yahushua has received from His Father: *"... power over the nations—'he shall rule them with a rod of iron; they shall be dashed to pieces like potters vessels'—**as I also received from my Father; and I will give him the Morning Star.**"* Notice that the part about ruling the nations with a rod of iron is a quote from Psalm 2:9. That promise was originally made to the Son of Yahuah, not to the Followers of the Messiah. And how the exact same promise to the Son will be kept is shown in 19:15 (*"**He Himself** will rule them with a rod of iron..."*). So, what is 2:26-28 really saying? Is it saying that the Assembly, by herself, will rule the nations with a rod of iron? No! It is saying that Yahushua the Messiah, as was promised to Him from the beginning, long before the Revelation was written, will be the One who rules the nations with a rod of iron, and the individual believers will rule the nations with a rod of iron only to the extent that they sit on His throne with Him and share His rule with Him. As Paul told Timothy, those (individual believers) who *"endure* (to The End) *shall reign with Him"* (2 Timothy 2:12). He will share with them **His** power to rule

67

the nations. And how will He do that? By also giving them **Himself, the Morning Star** (2Peter 1:19; Revelation 2:28; 22:16), so that it is no longer they who live (and rule), but the Messiah who lives and rules in them, with them, and through them (cf. Galatians 2:20). This totally negates the dominionist/kingdom-now doctrine that the Kingdom of Yahuah will be fully established on Earth before the King of Kings returns **in person** to do that.

2:29   *"He who has an ear, let him hear what the Spirit says to the [assemblies]."*

Chapter 3—Letters to the Assemblies at Sardis, Philadelphia, and Laodicea

3:1 *"And to the angel of the [assembly] in* (a) *Sardis write, 'These things says* (b) *He who has the seven Spirits of [Yahuah] and the seven stars:* (c) *"I know your works, that you have a name that you are alive, but you are dead.*

a. Sardis, about 39 miles south and slightly east of Thyatira and 50 miles east of Smyrna, was a very prosperous city located on important commercial routes. Some wealthy citizens were involved in mystery cults, and the general citizenry worshiped Greek deities like Artemis, to whom was dedicated a great temple in Sardis. There was also a Jewish synagogue there that was much larger than any found even in Judea.
b. Here the seven spirits of Yahuah and the seven stars (angels) are seen as being held by the Son as in 2:1. They are active in the communication and execution of the events of the Revelation.
c. The assembly at Sardis had a reputation as being an active, lively church, but the Lord declares that she is (spiritually) dead.

3:2-3 *"(a) Be watchful, and strengthen the things which remain, that are ready to die, for I have not found your works perfect before [Yahuah]. Remember therefore how you have received and heard; hold fast and repent. (b) Therefore if you will not watch, I will come upon you as a thief, and you will not know what hour I will come upon you.*

a. The Lord gives the Believers at Sardis a series of things to do to remedy their deathly spiritual condition: be vigilant (a command of the Lord to Followers of the Messiah); strengthen the few, emaciated, imperfect attributes or good works that remain; remember how they had at first received the new life in the Messiah and heard from Yahuah; hold fast to the little that they have left of what they had received from the Lord; and repent of their lethargy in the Spirit.
b. The consequence of not being watchful in the Spirit was that the Lord would come on them when they least expected it, and that was not to bless or reward them (cf. a similar warning in Matthew 24:43-44). Notice also that the warnings to *"chastise"* those who

69

fail to repent and mend their ways (2:5, 16, 23; 3:3) is to congregations of the Assembly of Believers, not to unbelievers.

3:4-5 *"You have (a) a few names even in Sardis who have not defiled their garments; and (b) they shall walk with me in white, for (c) they are worthy. He who overcomes shall be clothed in white garments, and (d) I will not blot out his name from the Book of Life; but (e) I will confess his name before My Father and (f) before His angels.""'* (g)

a.   Though, for all practical purposes, the assembly at Sardis was spiritually dead, there were a few individual members who had not been separated from Yahuah by the *"unclean spirit"* that defiled the assembly as a whole.
b.   Those few who overcome (continue in their faithfulness to the Lord) are given several promises: white garments—a symbol of the spiritual purity of the Redeemed in Heaven (cf. 6:11; 7:14); walking with the Lord in "eternity" (cf. 1 Thessalonians 4:17); and not having their names blotted out of the Book of Life.
c.   It is not that it is their own worthiness that will save them, but that they are clothed with the worthiness of the Lord (cf. Galatians 3:27).
d.   Some hold the doctrine of unconditional security (Once Saved Always Saved). But that doctrine is a little difficult to substantiate when the *Bible* says things like,

> *Brethren, **be ... diligent** to make your call and election sure, for **if** you do these things you will never stumble; for so an entrance will be supplied to you abundantly into the everlasting kingdom of our Lord and Savior [Yahushua the Messiah]* (2 Peter 1:10-11); *He that shall **endure to the end**, the same shall be saved* (Matthew 24:13); *He who **overcomes** shall be clothed in white garments, and I will not blot out his name from the Book of Life* (3:5).

The question for the OSAS advocates is: How can someone's name be blotted out of the Book of Life if it was never written there in the first place?

And the apostle Paul stated, *"I discipline my body and bring it into subjection, lest, when I have preached to others, I myself should **become disqualified*** (from receiving the *"imperishable crown"* of eternal life) (1 Corinthians 9:25, 27).

70

Please use me as a Book mark.

page 48 - women angels.
page 90 - giants
page 98 - Number 10 -?
page 102 - years is (are?)
page 103 - 16 -??
page 115 - Author's note
anemals is (are??)

Again, the question for the OSAS advocates is: Why would Paul be concerned about "becoming disqualified" from receiving eternal life if there was no possibility of him doing that? Paul also pointed out that those Believers in Yahushua who are grafted into the cultivated olive tree, making them *"fellow citizens"* in the *"commonwealth of Israel"*—will be cut off if they do not continue in the goodness of Yahuah (Romans 11:22; Ephesians 2:12, 19).

OSAS advocates respond with,

> *And I give them eternal life, and they shall never perish; neither shall anyone snatch them out of My hand* (John 10:28); *I am persuaded that neither death nor life, nor angels nor principalities nor powers, nor things present nor things to come, nor height nor depth, nor any other created thing, shall be able to separate us from the love of [Yahuah] which is in [the Messiah Yahushua] our Lord.* (Romans 8:38-39)

Notice though, that although those whose names are written in the Book of Life were chosen *"in Him [the Messiah] before the foundation of the world,"* and were *"predestined . . . to adoption as sons by [Yahushua the Messiah] to Himself"* (Ephesians 1:4, 5), none of these Scriptures state that one cannot, of his own volition, turn his back on Yahuah and reject the gift of salvation that he has been given, just as we can trash any gift we are given, do they? He still has a choice whether to remain faithful to the Lord, or to turn his back on Him. As the Lord Yahuah told His chosen People Israel, *"I have set before you life and death, blessing and cursing; therefore choose life, that both you and your descendants may live"* (Deuteronomy 30:19), the same applies to His People the Assembly of Followers of the Messiah regarding their eternal life in Him. Perhaps a solution is to understand that the salvation of the Lord is a process, not a once-for-all, done deal (cf. 1 Corinthians 1:18, Philippians 2:12), and although He wants us to be (subjectively) sure of our security in Him at any given point in time, nothing is more deceitful than the human heart (Jeremiah 17:9) and we should never take our eternal salvation for granted or turn our backs on it. Although Yahuah, in His omniscience, knows who will be saved in the end and He does not desire that anyone perish (2 Peter 3:9), we are given a choice all the way to the end, just as we were given a choice whether or not to choose Yahushua when we first came to Him. In our human understanding, we cannot fully grasp the apparent paradox of Yahuah's choosing us versus us choosing Him, but let us remember that His ways are infinitely beyond our comprehension (cf. Job 11:7-9) and that, in the end, faith trumps understanding.

e. Cf. Matthew 10:32

f. There is really no such thing as a "secret sin" or a "secret good deed," for we are surrounded by a great cloud of witnesses—all the heavenly host (cf. Hebrews 12:1). The angels look with great interest on how the Yahuah's People handle the trials and tribulations of life. And if we do not deny the Messiah before men, either by our words or by our actions, He will proclaim that we are His, not only before Yahuah the Father but before all the angels.

g. The assembly at Sardis represents the virtually spiritually dead Assembly.

3:6 *"He who has an ear, let him hear what the Spirit says to the [assemblies]."*

3:7-8 *"And to the angel of the [assembly] in* (a) *Philadelphia write, 'These things says* (b) *He who is holy, He who is true,* (c) *"He who has the key of David, He who opens and no one shuts, and shuts and no one opens:*

a. Philadelphia was a Roman-built city 28 miles southeast of Sardis and 100 miles east of Smyrna. The main "god" of the Romans was the emperor—Domitian at the time of the writing of the Revelation about 95 CE. Because they refused to worship him, the persecution of Believers in Yahushua was strong during the reign of Domitian. Hence, most expositors believe that John was on Patmos because he was banished there by the Emperor.

b. These are more identifiers of the Lord Yahushua: holy, true, having David's keys.

c. Since David was the King of Israel from whose throne the Messiah was prophesied to rule "forever" (cf. Jeremiah 33:17, et al.), these are the keys of the Kingdom, which the Messiah will open or close to whomever He pleases.

3:8-9 *"I know your works. See, I have set before you an open door, and no one can shut it; for you have a little strength, have kept My word, and have not denied My name. Indeed I will make those of the synagogue of Satan, who say they are Jews and are not, but lie—*

indeed I will make them come and worship before your feet, and to know I have loved you.

The church at Philadelphia is commended because, although she is weak, she has kept Yahushua's Word and has not denied His name although she probably has been under considerable persecution by both the Romans and the false Israelites (the *"synagogue of Satan,"* as in 2:9). So, He has opened a door to the Kingdom for her, where the persecuting Jews will have to worship at the Philadelphia believers' feet, admitting that they are the true People of Yahuah—the ones He has loved.

3:10 *"Because you have kept my command to persevere, I also will keep you from the hour of trial which shall come upon the whole world, to test those who dwell on the earth.*

This is a controversial verse. Let us see if, by the grace of Yahuah, we can sort it out.

The assembly at Philadelphia is also promised that, because she has persevered although she is weak, the Lord will *"keep* [her] *from the hour of trial."* Some expositors say this means that the Followers of Yahushua will be removed from Earth prior to the seven years of "tribulation." However, common sense protests that interpretation: Why are not the other assemblies, especially the poor, persecuted assembly at Smyrna about whom the Lord had nothing negative to say, given the same promise? Also, as will be shown later, the only part of the seven years that is described as a time of special tribulation for the Disciples of Yahushua is the Great Tribulation (cf. 7:14), which is a limited period of time within the seven years. And the Great Tribulation is the time of severe persecution of Yahuah's People, not of the whole world, as this verse states. Thirdly, this is the hour of temptation or testing (Greek: *peirasmos*) that will come on the world, not the tribulation (Greek: *thlipsis*), oppression, or affliction that will come on Yahuah's People. So, what the Lord is saying here is that because the members of the assembly at Philadelphia are persevering in the Lord, He will keep them (protect them) from giving in to (rather than take them out of) the temptation or testing that will come on the unsaved world. Yahushua never promised His Disciples that they would not suffer physically or that He would take them out of the world so that they would not have to suffer, but He did promise them that he would always be with them, comforting and protecting them spiritually (cf. Hebrews 13:5).

3:11 *"Behold, (a) I am coming quickly! Hold fast what you have, (b) that no one may take your crown. (c)*

a. Although you are weak, do not give up! Hold on. I am coming quickly! The Lord continues to encourage a sense of imminence. Although, from Earth's perspective, it may be thousands of years until His return, from Heaven's perspective, it is very soon, a puff of smoke compared to "eternity."
b. Although the Kingdom of Yahuah is not yet physically actualized, the true Assembly of Believers is seen by the Lord as royalty in the Kingdom (cf. 1:6). And He reassures the assembly at Philadelphia that if she will *"hold fast,"* He will personally return to see to it that no one takes her crown.
c. The assembly at Philadelphia is the inconspicuous, not very powerful assembly who, nevertheless, faithfully holds to the Truth and refuses to deny the name of Yahushua, even in the midst of persecution.

3:12 *"He who overcomes, I will make him a pillar in the temple of My God, and he shall go out no more. I will write on him the name of My God and the name of the city of My God, the New Jerusalem, which comes down out of heaven from [Yahuah]. And I will write on him My new name."'"*

This is a preview of the faithful believer's place in the ultimate, fantastic Kingdom of Yahuah /Kingdom of Heaven, where all becomes one in the Lord Yahushua. The new name that no one can understand except the one who receives it (2:17) is the unknown name of Yahuah. See Chapters 21 and 22 for more details about how the Redeemed are identified with the Temple and the New Jerusalem that come down out of Heaven.

3:13 *"He who has an ear, let him hear what the Spirit says to the [assemblies]."*

3:14 *"And to the angel of the [assembly] of the* (a) *Laodiceans write, 'These things say* (b) *the Amen, the Faithful and True Witness, the Beginning of the creation of [Yahuah]:*

a. Laodicea, 56 miles southeast of Philadelphia and about 90 miles east of Ephesus, was originally a Greek city named Diospolis, the "City of Zeus." Later, after being taken over by the Romans, it was on a major trade route between the Middle East and Ephesus, and was a very worldly, wealthy city. The assembly at Laodicea was one of the earliest to be established in Asia, probably because there was a large population of Jews there. The apostle Paul directed that his letter to the assembly at Colossae, which was only eleven miles from Laodicea, also be read in the assembly at Laodicea (Colossians 4:16).
b. The Lord Yahushua again (cf. 1:8) introduces Himself as the Beginning and the End—the final Word ("Amen") and the Beginning of Creation (cf. John 1:1-3)—and also as the True Witness (cf. John 8:14).

3:15-16 *"I know your works, that* (a) *you are neither cold nor hot. I could wish you were cold or hot. So then, because you are lukewarm, and neither cold nor hot,* (b) *I will vomit you out of my mouth.*

a. The Laodicean assembly was passionate neither for the truth and righteousness of the Lord nor against falsehood and evil. They were disgusting to the Lord.
b. This is the harshest sentence passed on any of the seven assemblies—total rejection by the Lord

3:17-19 *"Because you say,* (a) *'I am rich, have become wealthy, and have need of nothing' – and do not know that you are wretched, miserable, poor, blind, and naked – I counsel you to buy from Me gold* (b) *refined in the fire, that you may be rich; and white garments, that you may be clothed, that the shame of your nakedness may not be revealed; and anoint your eyes with eye salve, that you may see.* (c) *As many as I love, I rebuke and chasten. Therefore, be zealous and repent."'"* (d)

a. The contrast between material wealth and spiritual riches is striking in the assembly at Laodicea. The Laodicean assembly was affluent in the things of this world, so much so that she was blind to her spiritual poverty and insensitive to her own miserable condition, lacking the fruit of the Spirit—the peace, love, and joy of the Lord.

b. The Lord's solution was to *"buy from Me gold refined by fire,"* which simply means to give sacrificially and to suffer hardship for the sake of the Kingdom of Yahuah. For materially wealthy people, this has to be voluntary; it will not occur just because of the circumstances in which they are comfortable. The way Yahushua put it was, *"Deny [yourself], and take up [your] cross daily, and follow me"* (Luke 9:23). In other words, the Laodicean church had to release her grip on her possessions and dedicate them to the Gospel if she wanted a real, spiritually vibrant relationship with the Lord. Other solutions were to be clothed with the righteousness of the Lord so that her covetousness not be revealed, and to clear her vision with the Truth so that she could see her nauseating condition and what to do about it.

c. Finally, to avoid the loving chastening of her Heavenly Father (cf. Hebrews 12:6), the Laodicean assembly is exhorted to exercise the zeal that she lacks, in repenting of her insipid ways.

d. Please note that of all the seven assemblies, the assembly at Laodicea most typifies the American assembly.

3:20   *"Behold, I stand at the door and knock. If anyone hears My voice and opens the door, I will come into him and dine with him, and he with Me.*

This promise is directed to the individual members of the Assembly of the Disciples of Yahushua. It has been used in witnessing to the unsaved, but in context, it carries the sad implication that affluent, worldly, lukewarm believers, like those in Laodicea, have shut the Lord out of their lives. But because He loves them so much, He is still knocking at the door of their hearts, offering to come back in and fellowship with them in the Spirit if they will repent and open the door.

3:21-22   *"To him who overcomes I will grant to sit with Me on My throne, as I also overcame and sat down with My Father on His throne. He who has an ear, let him hear what the Spirit says to the [assemblies]."*

As with the letters to the other six assemblies, this final exhortation and promise is to the individual Believers in all assemblies of the

Messiah. And the promise to the Overcomers is a wonderful one: We will sit on His throne with Him and reign with Him (See the end of the Revelation—20:6; 22:5).

And again, as is emphasized over and over in the Revelation, life in the Messiah is not a passive religion. It is a religion for workers and overcomers, "*until the end,*" in the Kingdom of Yahuah. Yahushua does not say, "If you love Me, just sit still and wait for My return," does He? He says, "*If you love Me, keep my commandments*" (John 14:15). He does not say, "If you will just have faith, you will be saved," does He? He says that he who exercises patience and labors for His name's sake and does not become weary (2:3) and repents and does the first works (2:5) and hates the doctrines and deeds of the false teachers and prophets (1:6, 15) and holds fast to His name and does not deny His faith (2:13) and works and loves and serves (2:19) and holds fast to what he has (2:25; 3:11) and keeps His works until the end (2:26) and is watchful and strengthens the things that remain and is ready to die (3:2) and remembers how he has received and heard (3:3) and keeps His command to persevere (3:10) and buys from Him gold refined in the fire and white garments and eye salve (3:18) and is zealous (3:19) and hears His voice and opens the door (3:20) and finally, **overcomes** (2:7, 11, 17, 26; 3:5, 12, 21), to him, He will grant to sit with Him on His throne (3:21). Some may object, "But that's a work-your-way-to-Heaven religion," to whom the reply is, "You do not understand the grace of Yahuah and the relationship of the true Believer to Yahuah the Son, who said, '*I am the vine, you are the branches. He who abides in Me, and I in him, **bears much fruit**; for without Me you can do nothing*' (John 15:5)."

Chapter 4—The Throne Room of Yahuah in Heaven

4:1 (a) *After these things I looked, and behold, a door standing open in Heaven. And* (b) *the first voice I heard was like a trumpet speaking with me, saying,* (c) *"Come up here, and I will show you things which must take place after this."*

a. The Revelation was given to John in more than 40 individual visions and/or sounds that he saw and heard, in a series of six units. Those six units are separated by the phrase, *"After these things,"* which also occurs at 7:1, 7:9, 15:5, and 18:1. So, the first unit of revelation to John is contained in 1:1-3:22; the second unit is 4:1-7:8; the third unit is 7:1-7:8; the fourth unit is 7:9-15:4; the fifth unit is 15:5-17:18; and the sixth unit is 18:1-22:21. And a key to understanding Revelation is to know that each shift from one unit of revelation to the next does not necessarily indicate a change from one time period to the next, but indicates a change in point of view or subject matter. *"After these things"* combined with *"I looked,"* *"I saw,"* or *"I heard"* indicates a change in visions or perspectives whereas *"after these things"* or *"after this"* (as at the end of this verse or in 9:12) without the change of perspective addendum indicates a change in time periods. In other words, Revelation is presented more from Yahuah's point of view, which transcends time, than from man's point of view, which is bound by time. It is more like a giant mural than a time-line chart, and the reader is taken, in John's description, to various parts of the mural until a clear view of the whole painting is formed. There is a general time sequence portrayed in Revelation in the events of the seven seals, the seven trumpets/seven bowls of wrath (which occur simultaneously) and other events the timing of which is indicated by specific time markers, but many parts are not in strict chronological order and are included to fill in details in the time sequences. So, a key to understanding the Revelation is to know which parts are time sequences, which parts are parenthetical details, and how all the parts fit together. Some of this may be discovered by contextual clues, but a **major** key to putting the pieces of the mural puzzle together is to realize that many of the pieces are not found in the book of the Revelation; they are found in other Scriptures, especially the prophecies of Daniel and Yahushua. As we proceed through the Lord's Revelation, you will see what we mean. It is the prayer of this commentator that the reader will be helped in putting together the scenario painted by the Lord in His Revelation into a clear understanding of the *"things shortly to take place"* at the End of the Age, because it is indeed a breathtakingly magnificent mural.

b. A better translation of this phrase is that of the original King James Version: *"the first voice which I had heard,"* which refers the reader back to 1:10 and the voice of the Lord Yahushua.

c. This means, "Come up to Heaven," as is clarified in the next verse. Some have surmised that the phrase, *"after these things"* and the clause, *"come up here,"* in this verse refer to a time sequence of future events, beginning with the present "Church Age," after which is the "Rapture," then the "Tribulation." However, as was explained in (a) above, the reference is to a change in perspective rather than to prophetic time sequence. John is simply stating that after he was given the Word of the Lord regarding the assemblies, he was told to *"come up here"* for his next revelatory vision—of things in Heaven. Some teach that the Disciples of Yahushua are not present during the last seven years, and this verse is one of the few straws they can grasp at to support that view. However, this cannot be true, because there are numerous references to them being present during those seven years, e.g., the multitude who came *"out of the great tribulation"* (7:14), *"the rest of her offspring"* (12:17), and *"the saints"* (13:7). The "Church Age" will be coming to a close only when *"the fullness of the Gentiles has come in"* (Romans 11:25), at the end of the 42-month Great Tribulation (cf. 13:5) and the Final Seven Years. This sequence of events will be clarified as we continue through the Revelation.

4:2-3 *Immediately I was* (a) *in the Spirit; and behold, a throne set in Heaven, and* (b) *One sat on the throne. And He who sat there was (c) like a jasper and a sardius stone in appearance; and there was a rainbow around the throne, in appearance like an emerald.*

a. "In the spirit," as in 1:10, is a Hebrew idiom that means in a vision or trance, although, without a doubt, this is a special vision induced by the Holy Spirit.

b. There is only one other record in Scripture (Daniel 7:9-10) of Yahuah the Father seated on the throne, and that is for the Final Judgment at the End of the Age.

c. Besides the breathtaking beauty of the Lord, these precious gemstones probably represent more. When we search the *Tanakh*, we do find other significance for them. Each of the twelve tribes of Israel was represented by a gemstone. Reuben (which means "behold, a son"), Jacob's first-born son, was represented by the jasper (diamond?). Benjamin (which means "son of my right hand"), Jacob's twelfth son, was represented by the sardius, a beautiful red stone. So, the stones may represent Yahuah the Son in purity (the sparklingly clear jasper) and redemption (the blood-red sardius), the First and the Last, and the eternal King of Yahuah's People seated on the throne. And, *"around the throne"* is a beautiful emerald rainbow—the symbol of Yahuah's mercy in not destroying His chosen People.

4:4 *Around the throne were twenty-four thrones, and on the thrones I saw twenty-four elders sitting, clothed in white robes; and they had crowns of gold on their heads.*

The identification of the 24 elders has been the subject of endless debate, largely because of some confusion among *Bible* translations. In making the correct interpretation, it may help to remember that the Revelation is Yahuah's final Word to both the Jews and the Assembly of Believers. Because the 24 elders are wearing white robes (purity) and golden crowns (royalty), and are sitting on thrones (only Yahuah the Father, Yahuah the Son, and the Redeemed are seen in other parts of Scripture as sitting on thrones in the Kingdom of Heaven), they would appear *in some sense* to represent the Redeemed of the Lord. Also, there are twelve elders of ancient Israel (the twelve patriarchs) and twelve elders of the Assembly (the twelve apostles) whom Yahushua promised would sit on twelve thrones with Him judging the twelve tribes of Israel (Matthew 19:28). If the NKJV of 5:9-10 is correct, then it is clear that the 24 elders are the representative leaders of Yahuah's People. According to the NKJV, the new song sung by the 24 elders says,

> *You are worthy to take the scroll, and to open its seals; for You were slain, and have redeemed* ***us*** *to [Yahuah] by Your blood out of every tribe and tongue and people and nation, and have made* ***us*** *kings and priests to our God; and* ***we*** *shall reign on the earth.*

But the translation according to some early Greek manuscripts, as it is in the New American Standard Version (NASV), is,

81

*Worthy art Thou to take the book, and to break its seals; for Thou wast slain, and didst purchase for [Yahuah] with Thy blood **men** from every tribe and tongue and people and nation. And Thou hast made **them** to be a kingdom and priests to our God; and **they** will reign upon the earth.*

In the latter translation, the 24 elders are not necessarily including themselves among those who are redeemed, so, according to the NASV, it may be that the 24 elders are non-human heavenly beings who represent the Redeemed of Israel, rather than actually being the Redeemed. Another indication that the 24 elders may not literally be the Redeemed is the obvious fact that at the time John saw this vision, the Redeemed were not yet in Heaven in their glorified bodies, and, of course, John, one of the apostles, was not yet among them.

However, another intriguing possibility suggested by Michael Rood (www.aroodawakening.tv) is that the Saints who were resurrected immediately after the resurrection of Yahushua (Matthew 27:52) ascended into Heaven with the Messiah and are the 24 elders. This would make them the "firstfruits" (cf. James 1:18) of those resurrected who are dead in union with the Messiah (spiritual Israel), just as the 144,000 will be the "firstfruits" of those sealed as the Redeemed of Yahuah out of physical Israel (cf. 14:1, 4).

Whichever is the correct translation and interpretation, however, the 24 elders represent the redeemed People of Yahuah (including the grafted-in Believers in Yahushua).

4:5-8 *And from the throne proceeded* (a) *lightnings, thunderings, and voices.* (b) *Seven lamps of fire were burning before the throne, which are the seven Spirits of [Yahuah].* *Before the throne there was* (c) *a sea of glass, like crystal.* *And* (d) *in the midst of the throne, and around the throne, were four living creatures full of eyes in front and back.* (e) *The first living creature was like a lion, the second living creature like a calf, the third living creature had a face like a man, and the fourth living creature was like a flying eagle. The four living creatures, each having six wings, were full of eyes around and within.* (f) *And they do not rest day or night, saying: "Holy, holy, holy, [Yahuah] Almighty,* (g) *Who was and is and is to come!"*

a. Lightnings, thunderings, voices, and other ominous sounds are signs in Scripture of the awesome presence of Yahuah and something equally awe-inspiring about to happen. For example, there were lightnings, thunderings, and the sound of a trumpet so loud from Mount Sinai when the Law was given and Israel was established as a nation that all the millions of people in the camp at the base of the mountain trembled (Exodus 19:16).

b. Fire is a sign throughout Scripture of the Spirit of Yahuah active in the purification of His People and the destruction of His enemies. (See comments on 1:4.)

c. The floor of Yahuah's throne room. The only two references in the *Bible* to a *"sea of glass"* are here and in 15:2, so the symbolic meaning is not clear. A possible *Tanakh* parallel may be the bronze *"sea"* in the Temple (1 Kings 7:23)—a huge wash basin for the cleansing of priests. And in 15:2, the sea of glass is seen combined with fire, Yahuah's purifying agent. Also, the sea may be a symbol of multitudes of people (cf. 13:1; 17:15). So, when all these Scriptural references are combined, the sea of glass may symbolize the purification of Yahuah's redeemed People who are seen standing on it in 15:2.

d. Four creatures in the *"midst"* of the throne (cf. also 5:6 and 7:17) is a scene difficult to visualize. The Greek word (*mesos*) can also mean "amongst." Perhaps it means in the center of the throne room, in front of and around the throne. Or perhaps, in some mystical way, the throne occupies the whole scene. Other examples of mystical images in Revelation are in 3:12 and 21:2. Nor can we visualize how Yahuah the Father, Yahuah the Son, and Yahuah the Holy Spirit can be separate but One. Our limited human minds can comprehend only so much of ultimate reality, and human words are just not sufficient to describe it all.

e. There are numerous opinions regarding the significance of the four creatures. One that seems sensible is that they are manifestations of various attributes of Yahuah in relation to His natural creation: the lion, majesty and omnipotence; the calf (correctly translated "ox"), patience and power in labor; the eagle, beauty and supremacy; and man, intelligence and dominion on Earth. Each creature is the "king" of its respective domain: the lion over the wild animals of the earth; the ox over the domestic work animals; the eagle over the birds of the air; and man over the entire earth—together representing the Lord's dominion over His natural creation. The great mobility (each with six wings) and vision (each full of eyes) of the four creatures would seem to represent the omnipresence and omniscience of the Lord. Others have surmised from Biblical and extra-Biblical sources (e.g., the book of Enoch) that the four creatures or living beings are the four archangels, Michael, Gabriel, Raphael, and Uriel. Another possible correct interpretation is that whereas the 24 elders represent the Redeemed of the Lord who are seen by John in Heaven, the four creatures represent Yahuah's physical People the Jews who look forward in faith to the coming of the Messiah but have not yet accepted Yahushua as the Messiah. Jewish historians tell us that, during their 40-year sojourn in the wilderness on their way from Egypt to the Promised Land, the twelve tribes of Israel were separated into four groups which traveled and camped in those four groups behind the banners of Judah (on which was the figure of a lion), Reuben (on which was the figure of a man), Ephraim (on which was the figure of an ox), and Dan (on which was the figure of an eagle). When they camped, the Tabernacle, wherein was the presence of Yahuah, was in the midst of the four groups (cf. Numbers 2:3, 10, 18, 25), which would perfectly typify the scene that John saw in Heaven. Very similar creatures, in a vision combined with a vision of Yahuah on His throne, were also seen by Ezekiel when he was commissioned to prophesy concerning Israel (Ezekiel 1 and 10).

f.   The two roles of the four living creatures in Revelation are to worship Yahuah 24/7 (4:8; 5:9, 10, 12, 14; 7:12; 19:4) and to direct John's attention to what happens on Earth when the first four seals are broken (6:1; 3, 5, 7).

g.   Again, although the primary focus of Chapter 4 is on Yahuah the Father, there is no clear distinction between Him and Yahuah the Son, *"Who was, and is, and is to come!"*

4:9-11   (a) *Whenever the living creatures give glory and honour and thanks to Him who sits on the throne, who lives "forever" and ever, the twenty-four elders fall down before Him who sits on the throne and worship Him who lives "forever" and ever, and* (b) *cast their crowns before the throne, saying: "You are worthy, O [Yahuah], to receive glory and honor and power; for You created all things, and by Your will they exist and were created."*

a.   As the Israelites were the first to worship Yahuah on Earth, the living creatures appear to be the worship leaders in Heaven: The 24 elders follow their lead and worship the Lord.

b. As representatives of Yahuah's redeemed People, the 24 elders fall down casting their crowns before Him, Yahuah the Father and Yahuah the Son, acknowledging that He is the supreme Ruler, the King of Kings (19:16), because all things were created and are sustained by Him (cf. John 1:1-3; Colossians 1:16-17).

Chapter 5—The One Who is Worthy to Open the Scroll

5:1 And I saw in the right hand of Him who sat on the throne a scroll written inside and on the back, sealed with seven seals.

This apparently is the same scroll that, over six hundred years earlier, Daniel was told to seal *". . . until the time of the end"* (Daniel 12:4). Just before he was told to seal the book (scroll), it was revealed to him that at that time (the time of the end) a *"king"* would come who would *". . . do according to his own will: he shall exalt and magnify himself above every god, shall speak blasphemies against the God of gods, and shall prosper till the wrath has been accomplished"* (Daniel 11:36). Daniel was also told that his people (Israel) will be delivered (from the tribulation caused by the evil king) and that the resurrection of those whose names are written in the Book of Life will occur at that time (Daniel 12:1-2). As we proceed through Revelation, it will be clear that it is the revelation of the details of those events prophesied in Daniel and those contained in the scroll that was sealed by Daniel.

5:2-4 Then I saw a (a) strong angel proclaiming with a loud voice, "Who is worthy to open the scroll and to loose its seals?" And (b) no one in heaven or on the earth or under the earth was able to open the scroll, or to look at it. So I wept much, because no one was found worthy to open and read the scroll, or to look at it.

a. This *"strong angel"* appears to be in a special class of angels with Michael the archangel. Daniel 10:13, 21 states that "*Michael, the chief prince . . . upholds* (Hebrew: 'stands strong with') *me.*" Strong angels are also seen in connection with two other momentous events in Revelation—the proclamation that there would be no more delay (in the execution of Yahuah's judgments) (10:6) and the prophecy of the final destruction of modern prophetic Babylon (18:21).

b. The importance of the scroll is highlighted in that **no one** in all of Yahuah's creation was found worthy to open it, and John wept because of that. *"Under the earth"* (also in 5:13) may refer to under the surface of the earth (cf. Exodus 20:4) or to the realm of the dead or of demons (cf. Philippians 2:10).

5:5-7 But (a) *one of the elders said to me, "Do not weep. Behold* (b) *the Lion of the tribe of Judah, the Root of David, has prevailed to open the scroll and to loose its seven seals." And I looked, and behold, in the midst of the throne and of the four living creatures, and in the midst of the elders, stood a Lamb as though it had been slain, having seven horns and seven eyes, which are the seven Spirits of [Yahuah] sent out into all the earth.* (c) *Then He came and took the scroll out of the right hand of Him who sat on the throne.*

a. As the four creatures draw John's attention to the events of the six seals, the 24 elders also have another role besides worship: bearing witness to the Lord Yahushua and His redeemed ones (cf. 7:14).

b. Three of the *Bible's* identifiers of Yahuah the Son come together in one magnificent description: the Lion of Judah (cf. Hosea 5:14), the Root of David (cf. 22:16), and the Lamb of Yahuah (cf. Genesis 22:8; John 1:36). And although He was Yahuah the Father's helpless, sacrificial Lamb, He now lives with all the attributes of Yahuah, confirming that the Son and the Father are One. Also showing that the Son and the Father are One are the seven spirits of Yahuah, who belong to the Son as well as to the Father (cf. 1:4). In this verse, we see the spirits being sent out into all Earth in their roles as the active omnipotence (horns) and omniscience (eyes) of the Lamb during the Final Seven Years.

c. In Heaven and Earth, only the Lamb is worthy to take the scroll out of the right hand (the symbol of power and favor) of the Father.

5:8-10 Now when He had taken the scroll, (a) *the four living creatures and the twenty-four elders fell down before the Lamb, each having a harp, and golden bowls full of incense, which are the prayers of the saints. And they sang a* (b) *new song, saying: "You are worthy to take the scroll, and to open its seals, for You were slain, and have redeemed us to [Yahuah] by Your blood out of every tribe and tongue and people and nation, and have made us kings and priests to our God; and we shall reign on the earth."*

a. In 4:4, 11, the four living creatures and 24 elders worship Yahuah the Father; here, they worship Yahuah the Son who is worthy to open the scroll's seals because He has paid the ultimate price for the redemption of the Saints. (See the commentary on 4:4 as to whether the four living creatures and the 24 elders are literal or representative beings.) The Son is pleased by the singing and harp playing (the symbol of worship music in the *Bible*). (King Saul was pleased by David's harp playing—1 Samuel 16:23.) And the Son is pleased by the prayers of the Saints, which are probably prayers for deliverance and vengeance (cf. 6:10).

b. The beginning of the events of the Final Seven Years with the breaking of the seals is the occasion for the singing of the new song celebrating the redemption of the Saints and their soon-coming reign on the millennial earth (explained in the commentary on Chapter 20).

5:11-14 (a) *Then I looked, and I heard the voice of many angels around the throne, the living creatures, and the elders; and* (b) *the number of them was ten thousand times ten thousand, and thousands of thousands, saying with a loud voice: "Worthy is the Lamb who was slain to receive* (c) *power and riches and wisdom, and strength and honor and glory and blessing!" And* (d) *every creature which is in heaven and on earth and under the earth and such as are in the sea, and all that are in them, I heard saying: "Blessing and honor and glory and power be to Him who sits on the throne, and to the Lamb, "forever" and ever!" Then the four living creatures said, "Amen!" And the twenty-four elders fell down and worshiped Him who lives "forever" and ever.*

a. This is the climax of the throne room scene, setting the stage for what is about to happen on Earth.

b. Millions (an innumerable multitude) of heavenly beings surround the Lamb Who is in the *"midst of the throne"* (5:6).

c. The worthiness of the Lamb is perfectly summed up in seven attributes.

d. This is the *grande finale* of Chapters 2-5: *"Every creature"* in Heaven, on the earth, under the earth, and in the seas worships both Yahuah the Son and Yahuah the Father.

Chapter 6—The *"Beginnings of Sorrows"*—The Events of the Six Seals

6:1-2 (a) *Now I saw when the Lamb opened one of the seals, and I heard one of the four living creatures saying with* (b) *a voice like thunder, "Come and see." And I looked, and behold,* (c) *a white horse.* (d) *He who sat on it had* (e) *a bow; and* (f) *a crown was given to him, and he went out* (g) *conquering and to conquer.*

a. *"Now I saw"* or *"Then I saw"* (KJV) is a common phrase in Revelation that introduces a shift in what is seen, not necessarily a change in time period. Now that the stage has been set on Earth (Chapters 2 and 3) and in Heaven (Chapters 4 and 5), what will happen in the future (*"which will take place after this"*—1:19; 4:1) begins to be revealed to John with the breaking of the first seal.

b. *"Thunder"* indicates something radically different and ominous about to happen.

c. *"White horse"* is the symbol of a conqueror. When Yahushua returns as King of Kings to defeat His foes and establish His kingdom on Earth, He is depicted as riding on a white horse (19:11). This, however, is not the Messiah, because (1) the Lamb is the one opening the seal, not the one revealed in the opening of the seal; (2) it occurs at the beginning rather than at the end of the Final Seven Years; (3) his weapon is a bow—a worldly weapon; the Lord will destroy His enemies with a *"sword"* that comes from His mouth (His Word—cf. Ephesians 6:17); and (4) after the Messiah returns at the end of the seven years and defeats His enemies, He will establish peace on Earth, rather than His victory being followed by all the terrible events portrayed in the breaking of the succeeding six seals, especially the martyrdom of His People (6:9-10).

d. The rider of this white horse represents the evil *"prince who is to come"* (Daniel 9:26), the *"man of sin,"* the *"son of perdition"* (2 Thessalonians 2:3), the *"lawless one"* (2 Thessalonians 2:9), *"Antichrist"* (1 John 2:18), and the *"beast"* who rises out of the sea (13:1). Antimessiah's role as world conqueror during the Final Seven Years, until the plagues of the judgments of Yahuah destroy his global kingdom (cf. Daniel 11:36), will become clear as we proceed through Revelation.

e. The bow is the most common Biblical symbol of war. But notice that there is no mention of this conqueror having arrows. Both

Daniel and Revelation indicate that the evil prince who is to come will conquer not by brute force but primarily by sinister intrigue—by deceiving the world into following him (cf Daniel 8:23, 25; Revelation 13:3, 4).

f. His authority to rule is given to him by Satan (13:4). This is another indication that this conqueror is not Yahushua; the true Messiah has no need to be given the authority to rule the world, which He, as Yahuah the Son, created (John 1:1-3).

g. Antimessiah's obsession is to conquer the world and fully establish it as his kingdom in the place of the rightful King of Kings, as Satan wanted to supplant Yahuah in Heaven (cf. Isaiah 14:13-14). *"Antichrist"* (1 John 4:3) in the Greek does not just mean "against the Messiah," it also means "in the place of the Messiah." He is the false messiah. The white horse and golden crown also seem to indicate that this is not some dark, sinister-appearing figure, but is the counterfeit messiah whom the whole world will follow and worship (13:3, 4).

6:3-4 When He opened the second seal, I heard the second living creature saying, "Come and see." Another horse, fiery red, went out. And it was granted to (a) the one who sat on it to (b) take peace from the earth, and that people should kill one another; and there was given to him (c) a great sword.

a. The rider of the red horse may be a fallen archangel. There is a hierarchy of fallen angels, just as there is a hierarchy of heavenly angels. And just as Satan will give the anti-messiah authority to rule Earth, he gives fallen archangels authority over large realms and activity on Earth (cf. the *"Prince of Persia"*—Daniel 10:13).

b. Rather than resulting in "peace on Earth," as during the coming reign of the Messiah, the reign of the anti-messiah will result in widespread violence, bloodshed, and war.

c. The sword is a symbol of violence and bloodshed in general.

6:5-6 When He opened the third seal, I heard the third living creature say, "Come and see." So I looked, and behold, a black horse, and he who sat on it had (a) a pair of scales in his hand. And I heard (b) a voice in the midst of the four living creatures saying, (c) "A quart of wheat for a denarius; and do not harm the oil and the wine."

a. Balance scales were used by merchants in the ancient world to weigh out portions of grain.

b. The only One seen in the midst of the living creatures is the Lord (cf. 4:6, 9; 5:6). Although He does not directly cause the terrible events of the first four seals to occur, the Lord is ultimately in control of everything that happens on Earth and allows Satan, who has come to *"steal, and to kill, and to destroy"* (John 10:10), to bring them about, for several possible reasons, including: (1) setting Satan up to think that he is in total control of what happens on Earth, (2) sifting and refining His chosen People (cf. Psalm 66:10-12), and (3) partially executing His judgment—allowing those who refuse to repent to reap the consequences of their wickedness.

c. A denarius represented a day's wage. A quart of wheat or three quarts of barley provided barely enough food for a family to subsist on for a day or two. Oil and wine were luxury items, which, in times of famine (which inevitably follow wars), only the wealthy could afford. Therefore, what the Lord seems to be telling the rider of the black horse is, "Let the poor suffer, but do not harm the food of the wealthy," which could, ironically, be a curse on the wealthy because those who are poor and who suffer are much more likely to repent and accept the Lord's salvation than are those who prosper (cf. 1 Corinthians 1:26; James 2:5).

6:7-8 When He opened the fourth seal, I heard the voice of the fourth living creature saying, "Come and see." So I looked, and behold, a pale horse. And the name of him who sat on it was (a) *Death, and Hades followed with him. And power was given to them over* (b) *a fourth of the earth, to kill with sword, with hunger, with* (c) *death, and by* (d) *the beasts of the earth.*

a. Some think that Death and Hades are personified places or conditions, but they may also be fallen angels: Death the angel that separates the soul from the body and Hades the angel that carries the unsaved soul to its waiting place until the Final Judgment. Death is not cessation of existence; it is a separation. Physical death is the separation of the soul from the body, and spiritual death is the separation of the soul from Yahuah. As power is given to the riders of the first three horses, power is given to Death and Hades to kill (separate from life) and consign to Hades. Then, after the resurrection of the unsaved, Death and Hades are cast into the lake of fire (the final "Hell") (20:14).

93

b. The population of the earth at the present time (2013) is about seven billion people. That means that if the events of the fourth seal occurred today, about 1.75 billion people would die. At the present time, there are widespread wars, famines, diseases, natural catastrophes, and other causes of death on the earth, but, as is apparent, during the few years of the opening of the seals of Revelation, the suffering and carnage will increase exponentially and there will be no mistaking that we are at the *"End of the Age"* and the *"beginnings of sorrows."*

c. As was explained in the commentary on 2:23, *"kill with death"* is a Hebrew idiom that means to die a horrible, miserable death.

d. *"Beasts of the earth"* may refer not only to hungry animals seeking whom they may devour due to the famine, but to pestilence: disease-causing agents which result from unsanitary conditions and conditions of malnourishment, which are caused by wars and famine. So, the events of one seal lead to those of the next, indicating that they are in chronological order.

The events that occur as the first four seals are broken, terrible as they are, are not manifestations of the judgments and Wrath of Yahuah, which will be plagues sent forth from "heaven" (outside our solar system) ominously announced by natural cataclysms when the sixth seal is broken (cf. 6:16, 17) and beginning when the seventh seal is broken (cf. 8:1, 7). The events revealed by the breaking of the first four seals are pointed out to John by the living creatures which apparently represent Yahuah's natural creation and His power over it. They are natural manifestations and consequences of the wrath of Satan (cf. 12:12), released on the earth as his incarnation, the anti-messiah, goes forth conquering and to conquer. Notice also that the seals are on the **outside** of the scroll. So, they reveal events that are categorically different from the events that are revealed on the inside of the scroll. They must be opened first, therefore are precursors to the events of the judgments and Wrath of Yahuah—the plagues of the trumpet/bowl judgments (chapters 8, 9, 11, 15 and 16).

6:9-11 *When He opened the fifth seal, I saw* (a) *under the altar the souls of those who had been slain* (b) *for the word of [Yahuah] and for the testimony which they held. And they cried with a loud voice, saying, "How long, O [Yahuah], holy and true, until* (c) *You judge and avenge our blood on those who dwell on the earth?" Then* (d) *a white robe was given to each of them; and it was said to them that they should rest a little while longer,* (e) *until both the number of their fellow servants and their brethren, who would be killed as they were, was completed.*

John's attention is shifted back to Heaven where the souls of martyrs are seen *"beneath"* the altar. The Altar of Incense on Earth, also called the golden altar (8:3), was in the Temple in front of the curtain into the Holy of Holies. Burning coals from the Altar of Sacrifice were carried to the Altar of Incense to burn the incense there. In 11:1 John is told to measure the Temple and the altar, but to omit the court outside the Temple, apparently because, once the Lamb of Yahuah was offered as the "once for all" sacrifice for the sins of the world, it had served its purpose as a place of animal sacrifice and has no place in the New Jerusalem. So, it is apparently beneath the Altar of Incense (because incense represents the prayers of the Saints [5:8]) that incense, with the prayers of the Saints, is offered to the Lord (8:3; 8:4) that these souls are located. According to rabbinic tradition, the souls of all the Saints throughout history are stored under the altar. So, just because the souls of the martyrs are seen by John does not mean that the souls of all the Redeemed who have died, martyrs and non-martyrs, are not there. And there is even less reason to think that these are the souls of only those who are martyred during the Final Seven Years, as many propose.

a.   The martyrs were slain for the *"word of [Yahuah],"* that is, for speaking the Truth, and for the *"testimony which they held,"* that is, for testifying that Yahushua is the Lord (Yahuah). Not in the USA (yet) but in other parts of the world, there are more being martyred today for speaking the Truth and holding to the Testimony of the Messiah than at any other time in history, including the first and second centuries CE when the Revelation was written. For example, in Somalia, which is 98% Muslim, Followers of Yahushua are aggressively sought out and slain.

b.   This is another indication, even after the first four seals have been broken, that the judgments and Wrath of Yahuah have not yet begun to be poured out. That is what these souls are appealing to Yahuah to happen. As with the blood of Abel crying out to the Lord against his murderer, Cain (Genesis 4:10), the souls of the martyred Saints cry out to Yahuah for vengeance against their persecutors—*"those who dwell on the earth"* (in this commentary "earth dwellers"—those who do not believe in their hearts either in

95

the coming Messiah or that Yahushua is the Messiah, Yahuah incarnate, although they may say with their mouths that they do). Some may object, "Well, that is not very 'Christian' of them. Are we not supposed to forgive our persecutors?" But these souls are in Heaven—the purely spiritual realm—where the secrets of people's hearts and their ultimate destiny is known. Of course these martyrs are not crying out against those who will repent and be saved.

c. The martyrs are not yet resurrected. Although a white robe, a symbol of righteousness (19:8) worn by many of the Heavenly beings (overcomers—3:4-5, 18; the elders—4:4; the innumerable multitude—7:9; the armies of Heaven—19:14; the Lord Yahushua Himself—Luke 9:29; and angels—Mark 16:5, 20:12), is given to each of them, they are told to *"rest a little while longer." "Rest"* or *"sleep,"* also called Abraham's bosom (Luke 16:22) or Paradise (Luke 23:43), is a term in Scripture for the state of the Redeemed after they have died physically (cf. John 11:11-13). The souls of the unredeemed are in Hades, which is not a place of rest, but of torment (cf. Luke 16:23).

d. The Greek grammar is a little confusing here, but apparently, *"fellow servants"* and *"brethren"* are two different groups of the Redeemed. Otherwise, why would the Lord use the term, *"both"*? And apparently, the difference between the two groups is that *"fellow servants"* refers to those believers who are not martyred, and *"brethren who would killed as they were"* refers to those who will be martyred. In other words, what the Word seems to be saying here is that the number of both those who are saved but not martyred and those who are martyred is limited. And the time of the persecution of the believers, whether or not they are martyred, is limited. In fact, this period of *"great tribulation"* (7:14) is limited to a short period of time (*"a little while longer,"* or, in the KJV, *"a little season"*), which will be seen, as we continue through the Revelation, is, at the most, a few years of the Final Seven Years. No doubt, this was also included in Revelation to encourage those first century believers and believers who are persecuted throughout history to know that their time of suffering is limited to a very short period of time (compared to eternity in the presence of Yahuah).

6:12-14 *And I looked* (a) *when He opened the sixth seal, and behold,* (b) *there was a great earthquake; and the sun became black as*

sackcloth of hair, and the moon became like blood. And the stars of
(c) *heaven fell to the earth, as a fig tree drops its late figs when it is shaken by a mighty wind. Then the sky receded as a scroll when it is rolled up, and every mountain and island was moved out of its place.*

a.   And the next event on Yahuah's agenda for the Final Seven Years, after the Great Tribulation of the Saints, is that the martyrs begin to see their prayers answered with the sudden beginning of the often- and long-prophesied Day of the Lord (cf. especially Joel 2:1-2, 10; 3:15-16; Matthew 24:29).

b.   And what awful, cataclysmic events occur! There are hundreds of "stars" that fall from the sky, impacting the earth and causing an earthquake so powerful that every mountain and island is moved out of its place, the sun is darkened to almost total darkness and the moon is darkened by a dark red haze by the smoke and debris from the explosions, and the sky seems to disappear like a scroll being rolled up as the heat from the impact explosions evaporate the water in the atmosphere. Note that every one of the above phenomena occur when a nuclear bomb explodes: a large nuclear explosion can cause earthquakes, darkening of the sun and moon by the cloud of smoke and ash it produces, and the blue sky to dis- appear, revealing the blackness beyond. But scientific studies have shown that a comet or comet fragments impacting the earth will produce exactly the same results.[5]

---

[5]There is much disagreement and confusion among *Bible* expositors con- cerning the disasters and plagues of the Day and the Wrath of the Lord Yahuah. The causes of these terrible, soon-coming events have been attribut- ed variously to nuclear explosions, extraordinary natural catastrophes, attacks by demonic creatures, human warfare and direct action of the Lord.

However, ancient civilizations, including those of the Sumerians, Akkadi- ans, Babylonians, Assyrians, Hebrews and Greeks, in recognition that a su- pernatural power ultimately controls celestial objects, attributed catastrophes like those prophesied in the Revelation to the gods who they believed used the "stars" (comets and meteors) as "messengers" of their wrath against Earth's inhabitants with whom they were displeased. Although such beliefs have been largely dismissed by modern "rational" and scientific "authorities," there are many indications in Scripture that the Lord Yahuah has used comets or comet fragments as His "weapons of indignation" to execute His judg- ments (e.g., Job 38:22-23; Isaiah 13:3-5). The descriptions of many of the

c. "Heaven" in Scripture may refer to the visible, blue sky (the atmosphere surrounding the earth), space beyond Earth's atmosphere, far outer space beyond Earth's solar system, or Heaven where the Lord Yahuah dwells, depending on the context. In this context, it would appear to refer to outer space beyond Earth's solar system where there is a cloud of billions of comets, called the Oort Cloud, surrounding our solar system. It is apparently this cloud of comets to which Job 38:22-23 refers where it speaks of the treasuries or storehouses of snow and ice (comets are giant balls of snow, ice, dirt and other substances).

6:15-17 (a) *And* (b) *the kings of the earth, the great men, the rich men, the commanders, the mighty men, every slave and every free man,* (c) *hid themselves in the caves and in the rocks of the mountains, and said to the mountains and rocks, "Fall on us and hide us from the face of* (d) *Him who sits on the throne and from the wrath of the Lamb! For* (e) *the great day of His wrath has come, and who is able to stand?"*

a. These three verses are key verses in Revelation and give us some

---

disasters brought on those opposed to the Lord and the enemies of His People (the destructions of Babylon and of Sodom and Gomorrah, some of the "plagues" brought on Egypt, and so forth) exactly match what scientists have learned during just the past half century about the effects of comets and comet fragments exploding in Earth's atmosphere or impacting the ground. And scientist Jeffrey Goodman's recently published, thoroughly researched and documented book *The Comets of God* (Tucson, AZ: Archaeological Research Books, LLC, 2011) convincingly explains that **every one** of the Revelation's descriptions of the preliminary catastrophes of this chapter (verses 12-17), the trumpet (chapters 8 and 9) and bowl (chapter 16) catastrophes of the judgments of Yahuah, as well as the annihilation of Babylon the Great (chapters 17 and 18), clearly indicates the results of the impact of one or more comets, comet fragments, meteorites or asteroids with the earth or exploding in the atmosphere above the earth.

Therefore, in this commentary, the descriptions and explanations of those terrible events brought on by the judgments of the Lord during the Final Seven Years are based on Dr. Goodman's research as presented in the *Comets of God*. For fascinating details about how any of the catastrophes of the Wrath of the Lord, as presented in the Revelation, may very well be caused by cometary impact, read about them in *The Comets of God* or visit www.thecometsofgod.com.

very important insights into the correct interpretation of the whole book.

b.   After the breaking of the sixth seal, **every person on the earth**—great or common, slave or free—reacts in terror to the events that occur, knowing that they are caused by the Lord.

c.   And the people on the earth (the "earth dwellers") would rather be crushed by rocks or in the flattened caves of mountains than to face the Wrath of Yahuah. It is interesting to note that, although the catastrophes that occur at the breaking of the sixth seal are natural occurrences, the earth dwellers know that it is ultimately the Lord who is causing these events. Every person, even the most hardened "atheist," knows somewhere deep in his soul that there is a God and that if he is not saved, he is going to have to face the Wrath of Yahuah someday.

d.   Here is another key to fully understanding Revelation: the Wrath of Yahuah is not just the Wrath of Yahuah the Father, but of Yahuah the Son (the Lamb). As we will see, the Son is fully involved, in Heaven and on Earth, in the orchestration and execution of the judgments and Wrath of Yahuah. In other words, He does not sit on His throne in Heaven while the plagues of Yahuah's judgments are poured out on Earth, but He is in Heaven *and* on Earth (as we will see) and traveling back and forth between Heaven and Earth participating in all the events that affect His creation during the Final Seven Years, and afterwards.

e.   As has already been explained, the events of the sixth seal are not the manifestations of the judgments and Wrath of Yahuah, which are the events on the inside of the scroll and begin with the opening of the seventh seal (cf. 8:1, 7). This recognition by the earth dwellers of the coming Wrath of Yahuah is anticipatory. The events of the sixth seal occur just before and announce the beginning of the Day of Yahuah (cf. Joel 3:14, 15; Matthew 24:29; Acts 2:20) which includes the trumpet judgments and *"last plagues"*—the plagues of the *"Wrath of [Yahuah]"* (15:1); the resurrection of the righteous; the return of the Lord Yahushua for His Bride; the catching away of the His Bride (the "Rapture"); the return of the Lord Yahushua with the armies of Heaven; the Battle of "Armageddon"; the establishment of the Lord's millennial kingdom on Earth; the Final Judgment; and the destruction of the heavens and the earth (cf. 2 Peter 3:10). Some may object that the *"Day of [Yahuah]"* is one day, but the term *"day"* in scripture frequently refers to longer periods of time which include a series of related events (cf. Genesis 2:4; Psalm 50:15, 95:8; et al.). Others may object that the "second coming" of the Lord is a single event, but when we speak of His "first coming," are we not talking about His entire thirty or so years on Earth? Why could His "second coming" not likewise include all the events from His return to catch away the Redeemed until His return with the armies of Heaven to destroy His enemies and to establish His kingdom on Earth? As we have noted, the Messiah is no longer bound by an earthly body and by space and time; He is free to come and go as He pleases. But too often our puny minds try to limit Him to our concepts of the natural world. Let us expand our thinking to more fully comprehend the breathtaking glimpse of ultimate reality given to us in the Revelation.

At this point, by comparing Scripture with Scripture, we can fill in more details included in the events that are revealed when the six seals are broken. Some of those details are given to us through the prophet Daniel who told us of the coming of the anti-messiah who signs a peace treaty with Israel for seven years (the Final Seven Years) but treacherously breaks that treaty at the midpoint of the seven years (Daniel 9:27). He then persecutes Yahuah's People (the Great Tribulation), martyring most of them (except those specially protected by Yahuah) during the last half of the seven years (Daniel 7:24, 25). Yahushua also previewed the events of the six seals for his Disciples by outlining them exactly as described in the Revelation, including the same details that Daniel foretold, with special emphasis on the Great Tribulation (which begins with the *"abomination of desolation"*) and the cataclysmic sixth seal events that announce the trumpet judgments and the bowls of the Wrath of Yahuah (cf. Matthew 24:5-29).

Chapter 7— Yahuah's Provision for the 144,000 of Israel and for the Believers in Yahushua During the Great Tribulation

7:1-3 (a) *After these things I saw* (b) *four angels standing at the four corners of the earth, holding the four winds of the earth, that the wind should not blow on the earth, on the sea, or on any tree. Then I saw another angel ascending from the east, having* (c) *the seal of the living God. And he cried with a loud voice to the four angels* (b continued) *to whom it was granted to harm the earth and the sea, saying, "Do not harm the earth, the sea, or the trees* (c continued) *till we have sealed the servants of our God on their foreheads."*

a. *"After these things I saw"* indicates another major shift in subject matter (cf. 4:1), from the breaking of the first six seals in Heaven and the events on the earth associated with those six seals to what happens to the 144,000 sealed of Israel during the intermission between the events of the sixth seal and the breaking of the seventh seal, then a preview of the ultimate destiny of Yahuah's People the Disciples of Yahushua at the end of the Final Seven Years.

b. This is apparently a brief time period during which the cataclysmic events following the breaking of the sixth seal have ceased wreaking their havoc on Earth. Imagine a time of eerie quiet and stillness that suddenly falls during a great thunderstorm, just before a tornado comes roaring through. The winds that blew during the ferocious events of the sixth seal have stopped blowing because the four angels who have the power to release the winds and cause great damage to the earth, its vegetation, and the sea (which is exactly what will happen when the first plagues of the judgments of Yahuah (the trumpet judgments) are released on the earth—8:7-10) have been told to hold them back. As we shall see in the next chapter (8:1), there is also a half-hour period of total silence in Heaven just before the plagues of the judgments of Yahuah start to be released on the earth. Perhaps this time period on Earth when the winds are being held back is the same as the half-hour of silence in Heaven.

c. Before the plagues of the judgments of Yahuah begin to be released, the *"servants"* of Yahuah must be sealed on their foreheads. As we shall see, this is a seal of protection applied to Yahuah's People on the earth, Israel, in the same way that He placed a mark on Cain to protect him as he wandered the earth an alien to those he met (cf. Genesis 4:14-15). In the same way, the

Remnant of Israel who are chosen by Yahuah to be sealed will be considered aliens by the followers of the anti-messiah.

7:4-8 *And I heard the number of those who were sealed.* (a) *One hundred and forty-four thousand of all the tribes of the children of Israel were sealed: of* (b) *the tribe of Judah twelve thousand were sealed; of the tribe of Reuben twelve thousand were sealed; of the tribe of Asher twelve thousand were sealed; of the tribe of Naphtali twelve thousand were sealed; of the tribe of* (c) *Manasseh twelve thousand were sealed; of the tribe of Simeon twelve thousand were sealed; of the tribe of Levi twelve thousand were sealed; of the tribe of Issachar twelve thousand were sealed; of the tribe of Zebulon twelve thousand were sealed; of the tribe of* (d) *Joseph twelve thousand were sealed; of the tribe of Benjamin twelve thousand were sealed.*

a. Some may object, "Do you mean to tell me that after being scattered among the nations of the world and unidentified for over 2,700 years, there will be exactly 144,000 of Israel—12,000 from each tribe—who are given the protective seal of Yahuah during the Final Seven Years?" Yes, if we are going to hold to a literal interpretation of Scripture, that is what the *Bible* says. Unless the context indicates differently, specific numbers and names in Scripture must be interpreted literally. And there is no reason to deduce, from the context, that the names and numbers of the tribes of Israel in these verses are figurative. In fact, the phrase, "*children of Israel*," occurs 656 times in the *Bible* and not once does it refer to anyone other than the physical descendants of Abraham, Isaac, and Jacob (Israel). The Northern Kingdom of Israel, the *"House of Ephraim"* or the *"House of Israel"* (ten tribes), was destroyed by the Assyrians in about 720 BCE and many of the people of those tribes—some entire tribes—were carried away into captivity beyond the Euphrates into Assyria (later, Medo-Persia) and subsequently scattered among the nations of the world. And the Southern Kingdom, the *"House of Judah"*—who was composed not only of the tribe of Judah but also the tribe of Benjamin, much of the tribe of Levi, plus many from other tribes who lived among them—was also dispersed worldwide beginning with the Babylonian captivity in 586 BCE, then especially by the Roman dispersions in 70 CE and 135 CE. There are many groups all over the world today who claim to be descendants of the various tribes of Israel. And although, according to Yahuah's birthright promise to

102

Abraham, Isaac, Jacob, and Joseph (cf. Genesis 48:16), their descendants are an innumerable multitude among the peoples of the world, the majority will be destroyed during the *"day of the Wrath of the Lord"* (Ezekiel 6:11-12, 19). Only a very small remnant will be saved (Isaiah 1:9, Ezekiel 6:8). And Yahuah knows exactly who and where Israel's descendants—all twelve tribes—are, and He is preparing 144,000 of them, who are totally devoted to Him and who are still looking for the coming of the Messiah (cf. 14:3-4), to come out of (modern, prophetic) Babylon (cf. 18:4) back into the land of Israel (cf. Isaiah 10:20-22) where they will be sealed on their foreheads for their protection during the Final Seven Years. More details about the role of the 144,000 during and after the Final Seven Years are given in Chapter 14.

b. Judah, although not the firstborn of Israel (who was Reuben), was chosen by Yahuah, as was prophesied by Jacob on his deathbed, to father the tribe from which the kings David and Solomon, who would rule over all the tribes of Israel, would come. Judah was also the tribe to which all the other tribes of Israel will eventually gather, to be ruled by the ultimate, eternal King of Israel, the Messiah, who is also a descendant of Judah, David, and Solomon (cf. Genesis 49:10). This designation of Judah by Yahuah to be the royal tribe of Israel is apparently why he is listed first in Revelation 7.

c. Manasseh, the son of Joseph and adopted son of Israel, replaces Israel's son, Dan, on this list. The reason for Dan being replaced by Manasseh is not clear, but it may be because, as seems to be prophesied by Israel (Genesis 49:17), that Dan was a treacherous, violent *"serpent"*—a satanically-influenced character. Rather than establishing cities in the territory allotted him, the tribe of Dan ruthlessly attacked and took over other cities (e.g., Judges 18:27-29), and the tribe of Dan was heavily involved in idolatry (Judges 18:30; 1 Kings 12:29; Amos 8:14). So, although the tribe of Dan will have a place in the millennial Messianic Kingdom (cf. Ezekiel 48:1, 2), he will be not be represented among the righteous 144,000.

d. Another puzzling part of this prophecy is that Joseph is listed among the tribes of the 144,000 rather than Ephraim. Joseph's inheritance was divided between his sons (Israel's adopted sons), Ephraim and Manasseh. And Israel told Joseph that Ephraim would become a *"multitude of nations"* (Genesis 48:19). Then, when Israel died, his first-born's birthright inheritance went to

103

Ephraim rather than to Reuben (1 Chronicles 5:1). So, why is the tribe of Ephraim not among the twelve tribes listed in Revelation 7? A possible answer might be that the tribes are listed in the *Tanakh* (1 Chronicles 5-8) according to their natural, physical birth order, but they are listed in the Revelation according to their place in the plan of Yahuah and their relationship to Him. That is why Judah, the ancestor of King David and of the King of Kings who will reign from David's throne over all Israel in the ultimate Kingdom of Yahuah (cf. Isaiah 9:6-7), is listed first, and why Manasseh is listed in the place of Dan, the evil, idolatrous tribe. Likewise, although Ephraim, as was prophesied, received the double-portion birthright inheritance, Jeroboam, an Ephraimite, rebelled against Solomon, King of Israel (cf. 1 Kings 11:26). Then later, after Solomon's death, when his son, Rehoboam, took over as King of Judea, Jeroboam led the northern ten tribes in rebellion against Rehoboam and Judea, establishing the Northern Kingdom, which continued to be called *"Israel,"* with Shechem, in the mountains of Ephraim, as its capital. (cf. 1 Kings 12:19, 25). After that, Israel (then also called *"Ephraim"*), moved farther and farther away from the religious practices of the Southern Kingdom (which, after the division of the kingdom, was stripped of the name *"Israel"* and was just called *"Judah"*) and into idolatrous practices that were instituted by Jeroboam. And although Ephraim had received the birthright inheritance in the Promised Land, he actually received it as the proxy for his father, Joseph, who remained in Egypt until he died and to whom, as the natural son of Israel, the inheritance technically belonged (cf. 1 Chronicles 5:2). In fact, in some *Tanakh* passages, the names Israel, Joseph, and Ephraim are used interchangeably (e.g., Ezekiel 37:16). And that is probably why Joseph, who is the clearest type of the Messiah of any of the sons of Israel, is listed rather than his son Ephraim among the tribes of the 144,000. [6]

---

[6] After the captivity and dispersion of much of the Northern Kingdom of Israel into the nations of the world, and the flight of thousands into the Southern Kingdom to escape the Assyrians, the House of Judah, the Southern Kingdom, began to again refer to themselves as "Israel" (cf. Daniel 9:7, 11, 20). And, because at that time Judah was the primary intact, clearly identifiable tribe remaining, all Israelites began to be referred to as "Jews" (cf. Romans 9:24, 27). Although today most of the dispersed of Israel have lost track of

7:9-10 (a) *After these things I looked, and behold, a* (b) *great multi-tude which no one could number, of all nations, tribes, peoples, and tongues, standing before the throne and before the Lamb, clothed with white robes, with* (c) *palm branches in their hands, and crying out with a loud voice, saying, "Salvation belongs to our God who sits on the throne, and to the Lamb!"*

a. *"After these things I looked"* indicates another major shift in fo-cus—back to Heaven and to Yahuah's People the Believers in Yahushua (the Redeemed Believers, the Bride of the Messiah).
b. This innumerable multitude from all nations (Gr. *ethnos*—ethnic groups), tribes, peoples (Gr. *phule*—a better word to translate as "nations"), and languages is also seen shouting similar words of praise following the final destruction of Babylon, the kingdom of Satan, at the end of the seven years (19:1-2). So, this scene is ap-parently a preview of what will occur at the end of the Final Seven Years, after the blowing of the Last Trump (cf. the commentary on 11:14-19). (Remember, scenes in Heaven transcend time, so their time and sequence must be determined by contextual clues rather than by a strict time-line chart of events on earth.) These are the redeemed, resurrected, and glorified Saints of all ages, because no other group of human beings, wearing white robes of righteousness and salvation, is seen in Heaven before, during, or after the Final Seven Years. At this point in time, following the resurrection and ascension of the Redeemed at the end of the Final Seven Years, they must have been joined by those whose souls who had been under the altar and had been given their white robes but had been told to *"rest a little while longer, until both the number of their fel-low servants and their brethren, who would be killed as they were, was completed"* (6:11).
c. Waving palm branches was a traditional greeting for a conquering hero or king, as when those who believed that Yahushua was the Messiah greeted Him as he rode into Jerusalem while they sang,

---

their genealogies, some have strong oral traditions and a very small number of the   descendants of David seem to have clear genealogical links all the way back to David. Genealogical and genetic research are also claiming to have identified links back to the original tribes. In other words, the Lord knows who among the Gentiles are Hebrews, although we may not.   So, in this commentary, the term "Jews" refers to all Israelites, whether or not they are of the House of Judah, who do not yet recognize that Yahushua is the Messiah.

"Hosanna [Hebrew: *hoshia-na*—"O save!"] *to the Son of David!* '*Blessed is He who comes in the name of the LORD!' Hosanna in the highest!"* (Matthew 21:9)

7:11-12 (a) *All the angels stood around the throne and the elders and the four living creatures, and fell on their faces before the throne and worshiped [Yahuah], saying:* (b) *"Amen!* (c) *Blessing and glory and wisdom, thanksgiving and honor and power and might, be to our God "forever" and ever. Amen."*

a. All the other inhabitants of Heaven in John's vision—the angels, elders, and living creatures—join the innumerable multitude in absolute, submissive adoration of the Lord.
b. *"Amen"* means "So be it" or "That settles it."
c. This is another seven-fold ascription of praise similar to the one at 5:12.

7:13-14 *Then one of the elders answered, saying to me,* (a) *"Who are these arrayed in white robes, and where did they come from?" And I said to him, "Sir, you know." So he said to me, "These are the ones who* (b) *come out of the* (c) *great tribulation, and* (d) *washed their robes and made them white in the blood of the lamb."*

a. The elder asks John two rhetorical questions: *"Who are these?"* and, *"Where did they come from?"* the answers to which must be important, because the elder answers them himself.
b. The innumerable multitude comes *"out of"* the Great Tribulation. The Greek word (*ek* or *ex*) for *"out of,"* from which the English word "exit" is derived, means exactly as it is translated: *"out of,"* "from," or "away from," as when someone exits an event. And this confirms what Yahushua said:

> *For then there will be a great tribulation, such as has not been since the beginning of the world until this time, no, nor ever shall be. And unless those days were shortened, no flesh would be saved; but for the elect's sake those days will be shortened.* (Matthew 24:21-22)

In other words, the Redeemed will come out of the Great Tribulation when it is cut short (Matthew 24:22) by the events of the Last (seventh) Trump, including the return of the Messiah for His Elect (Mark 13:27) and the *"last plagues"* of the judgments of Yahuah

106

(15:1). Yahushua goes on to explain that, at that time, He will return to gather His Elect (the "Rapture") *"from the four winds, from the farthest part of the earth to the farthest part of heaven"* (Matthew 24:27-31; Mark 13:27). Some argue that *"His elect"* in Matthew 24:31 refers only to the Remnant of Israel who will be hidden, protected, and nourished on Earth during the Final Seven Years, but both common sense and Yahuah's Word negate that interpretation: (1) *"Elect"* is used to refer to ancient Israel in only three *Tanakh* passages, and all three of those are in Isaiah (Isaiah 45:4; 65:9, 22), in prophecies regarding the Millennium. But in the *B'rit Hadashah, "elect"* refers to both ancient Israel (e.g., Romans 11:7) and the Followers of Yahushua (e.g., Colossians 3:12), but mostly the Followers of Yahushua. (2) Yahushua's prophecy as recorded in Matthew 24 (also Mark 13 and Luke 17), involves both the Jews and the Followers of Yahushua. He appears to be alluding to what will happen to the Jews in the near future when Jerusalem was destroyed by the Romans in 70 CE and the Jews were dispersed, Yahushua appears to be alluding to what will happen to the Jews in the near future when Jerusalem was destroyed by the Romans in 70 CE and the Jews were dispersed; but the language of the text indicates that when He speaks of gathering His elect, He is speaking of gathering His Disciples *"to the farthest part of Heaven"* (the Rapture) when He returns at *"the end of the age"* (Matthew 24:3). Another clue that the Lord is speaking both of the Jews and His Disciples is that He uses terms that refer to both; for example, He states, *"For false [**messiahs**] and false **prophets** will rise and show great signs and wonders to deceive, if possible, even the elect"* (Matthew 24:24). (3) The direction of the action (from Earth to Heaven) when He returns and gathers His Elect appears to be vertical, toward Heaven, not horizontal on the earth (cf. Matthew 24:30-31). Later, the apostle Paul gave us exactly the same scenario in greater detail:

> *For the Lord Himself will descend from heaven with a shout, with the voice of an archangel, and with the trumpet of [Yahuah]. And the dead in [the Messiah] will rise first. Then we who are alive and remain shall be caught up together with them in the clouds to meet the Lord in the air. And thus we shall always be with the Lord.* (1 Thessalonians 4:16-17)

This is a clear reference to what is commonly called "The Rapture" (which is from the Latin word, *rapio*, translated "caught up" in 1 Thessalonians 4:17 in the Latin Vulgate translation of the *Bible)*. (cf. Matthew 24:7-30). For exactly when, in the sequence of End-Times events, the Rapture will occur, please read "Appendix 6—When is the Rapture?"

So again, a major key to understanding the End Times prophecies of Yahushua, as recorded in both the gospels and the Revelation, is knowing that they are given to **both** the Jews and the Disciples of Yahushua, and knowing which parts refer to the Jews who have not yet accepted Yahushua as their Messiah, which parts refer to the Disciples of Yahushua, and which parts refer to both. And that can be determined only by comparing Scripture with Scripture.

c. Most *Bible* teachers refer to the entire Final Seven Years as "the tribulation." But that is a contrived label with no textual support. What is the *"Great Tribulation"*? Again, Yahushua makes that clear. He states that it will be that terrible time *"such as has not been since the beginning of the world until this time, no, nor ever shall be"* after the *"'abomination of desolation,'* spoken of by Daniel the prophet, standing in the holy place" (Matthew 24:15, 21). When we turn to the book of Daniel, we find that what Yahushua told His Disciples exactly parallels—almost quotes—what is written there:

> *Then he* [the anti-messiah] *shall confirm a covenant with many for one week* [of years—seven years]; *but in the middle of the week he shall bring an end to sacrifice and offering. And on the wing of abominations shall be one who makes desolate, even until the consummation, which is determined, is poured out on the desolate . . . . And there shall be a time of trouble, such as never was since there was a nation, even to that time.* (Daniel 9:27; 12:1)

In other words, the Great Tribulation will be the 42 months (cf. 13:5) following the anti-messiah's desecration of the Temple in Jerusalem and declaring himself to be "God" (cf. 2 Thessalonians 2:4) at the mid-point of the seven years when, through him, Satan's wrath (cf. 12:12) will be poured out on the Elect. These events will be further clarified when we get to Chapter 13.

d. This is a description not just of martyrs but of all the Redeemed of the Lord (cf. 1:5).

7:16-17 *"Therefore they are before the throne of [Yahuah], and serve Him day and night* (a) *in His temple. And He who sits on the throne*

108

(b) *will dwell among them.* (c) *They shall neither hunger anymore nor thirst anymore; the sun shall not strike them, nor any heat; for the Lamb who is in the midst of the throne will shepherd them and lead them to living fountains of waters. And [Yahuah] will wipe away every tear from their eyes."*

a. Typified by the Temple on the earth where the priests of Israel served, there is a Temple in Heaven where the Redeemed, who are all priests in the Kingdom of Heaven (cf. 1:6), will serve.
b. As Jewish grooms prepared a home, which was attached to their parents' home, for their brides before they were married, Yahushua told His Disciples, before His ascension into Heaven, that He was going to prepare a place for them in His Father's house so that where He was they could be also, and He would dwell with them (cf. John 14:2, 3; 21:3).
c. This is a preview of the eternal state of the Redeemed (cf. 21:3-4). So, once the Bride of Christ is with Him in Heaven, she will be, as promised (1 Thessalonians 5:9), safe from the Wrath of the Lord.

Already, by reading and interpreting the *Bible* in a literal, common-sense way and by comparing Scripture with Scripture, a large part of Yahuah's Revelation mural has been painted for us, has it not? We see that there will be a seven-year period of time, which we are calling the Final Seven Years and which Yahushua's Disciples called *"the end of the age"* (Matthew 24:3), when world history will be brought to a tremendously tumultuous and cataclysmic close. The seven years will begin with a totally evil man—called, in the Bible, the *"prince who is to come,"* the *"man of sin,"* the *"son of perdition,"* the *"lawless one,"* *"[Antimessiah],"* and the *"beast"*—signing a peace treaty with Israel then going forth to conquer the world. But he will not conquer primarily by force; he will conquer by deceit and intrigue. Nevertheless, his insidious maneuvers to conquer Earth will result in wars, bloodshed, famine, pestilence, and death (including the martyrdom of Followers of Yahushua) on a global, unprecedented scale. Then, at the midpoint of the seven years, the anti-messiah will set up what both Daniel and Yahushua refer to as *"the abomination that causes desolation"* in the rebuilt Jewish Temple in Jerusalem. Then, a time of *"great tribulation"* for the people of the world, especially the Jews and the Followers of the Messiah, will begin in which, for 42 months, the anti-messiah will ruthlessly destroy anyone who does not worship and submit to him. But, at the end of those three and one-half years, the Great Tribu-

109

lation will be cut short by the events announced by the Last Trump: the return of the Messiah Yahushua in the clouds, the Rapture of the Assembly of Believers in the Messiah, and the outpouring of the final plagues of the Wrath of Yahuah following the sounding of the seventh trumpet (cf. 11:14-15; 15:1).

Chapter 8—The Events of the First Four Trumpet Judgments

The calamities of the first five seals are caused by the anti-messiah going forth to conquer the world (6:2-11). Then, the events of the sixth seal (6:12-17) are the overture to the Day and the Wrath of the Lord Yahuah. But now, following the sealing of the 144,000 of Israel (7:4-8) and John's vision of the Redeemed of the Lord in Heaven who *"come out of the Great Tribulation"* (7:14), the terrible events of the trumpet/bowl judgments commence.[7]

Some try to naturalize these plagues by saying the blood is the blood of humans and animals killed, merely naturally occurring cycles of events, and so forth. Others attribute them to nuclear holocaust. Others allegorize them, asserting that they are symbols of spiritual or social disintegration, or something other than literal events. But, as scientific discoveries within just the past half century about comets and their effects when impacting Earth or other celestial objects have clearly shown, **every one** of the trumpet/bowl catastrophes may be attributed to cometary impact.

Of course, *Bible* translators and expositors down through the centuries have not had access to the extensive information from the sciences of archaeology, geology, anthropology and astronomy now

---

[7]There are two primary different interpretations of the sequence of events of the Day and the Wrath of the Lord—the plagues of the the trumpet judgments (chapters 8, 9 and 11) and the bowls of wrath (chapters 15 and 16). One view is that the trumpet and bowl judgments occur sequentially—the bowl judgments following the trumpet judgments as listed in the text—and the other view is that they parallel each other in sequence (the first trumpet judgment occurs at the same time the first bowl of wrath is poured out, the second trumpet judgment occurs at the same time the second bowl of wrath is poured out, and so forth). There is textual support for both interpretations and problems with both. The Lord has not given this commentator (Watchman Bob) revelation as to which, if either, is correct, and he will not be dogmatic about it. But, in his opinion, the view that the trumpet and bowl judgments parallel each other and occur simultaneously has more textual support. (See a detailed exposition in the commentary on 15:1-8a.) So this commentary is based on that interpretation. However, whichever interpretation is correct, the terrible plagues of the trumpet and bowl judgments **will literally occur**, and the Lord has graciously given His People this Revelation of what they will be like so, when we see them coming to pass, we will understand what is happening and, like the tribe of Issachar, will know what to do (cf. 1 Chronicles 12:32).

available, so it is understandable that they would interpret the prophecies of Scripture in whatever way made the most sense to them. But sadly, the vast majority of current commentators are no more aware of the relevance of current discoveries to *Bible* prophecy than were the ancients and continue to perpetuate the old, misguided interpretations and myths.

However, this commentator (Watchman Bob), after much study and prayer, is totally convinced that, in these Last Days, the Creator is making His Revelation of exactly what will transpire during the Final Seven Years very clear to those who have eyes that see and ears that hear. And it is his prayer that the reader will be as astonished as he is at how clear it all is, as explained in the following commentary.

8:1 *When He opened the seventh seal, there was silence in heaven for about half an hour.*

> When the seventh seal is opened revealing the contents of the scroll, there is an ominous, awesome calm in Heaven (the only such silence mentioned in Scripture) before the greatest, most destructive "storm" in history—the plagues of the judgments and the Wrath of Yahuah. After the 144,000 are sealed, the four angels (7:1) will now release the winds of destruction on Earth.

8:2-6 *And I saw* (a) *the seven angels who stand before [Yahuah], and to them were given* (b) *seven trumpets. Then another angel, having a golden censer, came and stood at the altar. He was given much incense, that he should offer it with* (c) *the prayers of all the saints upon the golden altar which was before the throne. And the smoke of the incense, with the prayers of the saints, ascended before [Yahuah] from the angel's hand. Then the angel took the censer, filled it with fire from the altar, and threw it to the earth. And there were* (d) *noises, thundering, lightnings, and an earthquake. So the seven angels who had the seven trumpets prepared themselves to sound.*

a. Perhaps one way the seven Spirits before Yahuah's throne (1:4) manifest themselves will be through the actions of these angels.
b. Trumpets were used in Israel to warn of danger and to announce significant events, including, in prophesy, the Day of the Lord (Joel 2:1).
c. One precursor to the judgments of the Lord being executed is

the prayers of the Saints—another indication that the events of the six seals, which include the prayers of the martyrs (cf. 6:10), are precursors to, rather than manifestations of, the plagues of the judgments of Yahuah.

d. More ominous sounds and sights announcing the terrible, destructive events to follow

8:7-12 The first angel sounded: And (a) *hail and fire followed, mingled with blood, and they were thrown to the earth. And* (b) *a third of the trees were burned up, and all green grass was burned up. Then the second angel sounded: And something like* (c) *a great mountain burning with fire was thrown into the sea, and a third of the sea became blood. And a third of the creatures in the sea died, and a third of the ships were destroyed. Then the third angel sounded: And* (d) *a great star fell from heaven, burning like a torch, and it fell on a third of the rivers and on the springs of water. The name of the star is Wormwood. A third of the waters became wormwood, and many men died from the water, because it was made bitter. Then the fourth angel sounded: And* (e) *a third of the sun was struck, a third of the moon, and a third of the stars, so that a third of them were darkened. A third of the day did not shine, and likewise the night.* (f)

a. Scientific studies of comets have revealed that they are giant balls of ice or compacted snow *("hail")*, covered with a crust of rocky dirt and venting toxic gases and other substances, which burn as they pass through Earth's atmosphere. If they explode before striking the ground, they incinerate all living organisms within range in the air and on the ground below. If they impact the ground (with the force of one or many nuclear bomb explosions), they leave deep craters, some of which may even penetrate the earth's crust into the soft, superheated mantle below. They also produce seismic shock waves in the earth's crust, send out superheated waves of wind, and shoot clouds of toxic smoke, dust and debris high into the atmosphere, exactly like the effects of a nuclear bomb explosion.

b. On June 30, 1908, a relatively small comet fragment with a cross section about the size of a football field exploded over the Tunguska River Basin in Siberia with what scientists estimate to be the force of a large, 30-megaton nuclear bomb. This mid-air explosion devastated and burned over 1,000 square miles of forested area and incinerated several herds of reindeer. Eye witnesses 40

113

miles away reported that they were burned by the blast of what they described as a blindingly bright "star" exploding in the sky. Geological studies have shown that a similar explosion caused the annihilation of all life in Sodom and Gomorrah. For more details, read *The Comets of God*, pages 54-57 and 143-152. This much larger first trumpet comet, exploding with the force of probably thousands of nuclear bombs, destroys a third of Earth's forests, all green grass, and probably a third of all land-dwelling living organisms (in prophetic Scripture *"blood"* is a symbol of death).

c.   This is a clear description of a burning comet plunging into the sea. Recently (2005) an eighteen mile wide cometary impact crater was discovered in the floor of the Indian Ocean. Scientific studies have shown that the impact that caused this crater, which has been named the Burckle Crater, produced a huge tsunami wave over a mile high and several miles wide that rushed out at over 400 miles per hour in all directions, including up the plain of the Tigris and Euphrates Rivers until it crashed into and ran up and over the Ararat mountains over 3,000 miles from the comet's point of impact. This impact, which occured about 2800 BCE, is apparently what caused the Great Flood of Noah's day. For evidence of this read *The Comets of God*, pages 104-105. Also, a much larger crater 112 miles in diameter, named the Chicxulub Crater, which was produced by a cometary fragment about six miles in diameter, has been discovered in the floor of the Gulf of Mexico. Computerized virtual re-construction of the cometary impact that caused this massive crater and geological studies of land topography surrounding the crater show that it penetrated the earth's crust, threw trillions of gallons of ocean water superheated to thousands of degrees Farenheit high into the air, triggered a massive earthquake that shook the whole planet and produced a series of tsunamis higher than the Rocky Mountains, plus created a giant fireball of steam and molten ejecta that leveled everything in its path within a distance of over a thousand miles. It also would have produced a dense cloud of toxic smoke, steam and debris that covered the whole planet for months or years, killing much of Earth's vegetation and, many scientists believe, brought about the end of the dinosaurs and other prehistoric forms of life. See *The Comets of God*, pages 125, 213, 216, 270 and 422 for more details about the Chicxulub Crater.

Scientific studies of the Burckle Crater, the Chicxulub Crater and other even larger craters have clearly shown that *"something like a great mountain thrown into the sea,"* causing a third of the sea to become *"blood"* (filled with death), a third of the sea to die and a third of the ships on that sea to be destroyed is very feasible indeed. The second trumpet prophecy could be easily, simply and quickly fulfilled, for example, if a large comet 50 or 100 miles in diameter plunged, at over 25,000 miles per hour, into either the Atlantic Ocean or the Pacific Ocean.

d. A *"great star"* (comet) named Wormwood (a bitter herb in the Holy Land) falling on and contaminating the *"springs"* (sources) and rivers of fresh water is also very possible in light of what we now know about comets. Studies have shown that comets contain numerous toxic radicals like hydrogen cyanide, carbon monoxide and sulfur which, when combined with water and other substances in extreme heat, form deadly, poisonous chemicals. There are several large freshwater lakes (e.g., North America's Great Lakes and Russia's Lake Baikal), each of which, with the rivers that flow from them, contain close to 20% of Earth's fresh water. Coincidentally, the Great Lakes and Lake Baikal are at approximately the same latitude (45° N), so, if a comet breaks up over the earth at that latitude, fragments might very well land in all those lakes and contaminate over one-third of Earth's fresh water.

e. Comets exploding when they impact the earth produce mushroom shaped plumes of fire, smoke and debris exactly like that of a nuclear bomb exploding. Just a small comet fragment 100 meters in diameter will result in an explosion on impact equal to that of a large, thirty megaton bomb. A somewhat larger comet or comet fragment six miles in diameter will produce the explosive force of thousands of nuclear bombs on impact. It is easy to see that a comet that size or larger (some are over 100 miles in diameter) will produce enough smoke and ash to darken the light from the sun, moon and stars that shines on one-third or more of Earth.

f. The net result of the first four trumpet judgments, which destroy a third of the earth's life-support resources, is that perhaps a third or more of the earth's human population dies. If that is a third of the remaining population after the events of the six seals have killed 25% (cf. 6:8), then over three billion or almost half of the earth's population will have died during the Final Seven Years, up to this point in time, with the worst yet to come.

115

8:13 *And I looked, and I heard an angel flying through the midst of heaven, saying with a loud voice, "Woe, woe, woe to the inhabitants of the earth, because of the three angels who are about to sound!"*

The destruction of the earth and the decimation of its inhabitants is already terrible, but now, with the last three trumpet judgments combined with the last three bowl judgments, the Wrath of the Lord is going to intensify, becoming indeed *woe*-ful. The final results, following the seventh and final trumpet/bowl judgment, will be the total destruction of the surface features of the earth and the death of virtually all of Earth's inhabitants (except those supernaturally protected by the Lord). Following that, the earth and its *"heaven"* (sky or atmosphere) will be renewed and the millennial reign of the Messiah Yahushua will begin. But, we are getting ahead of ourselves. Next come the fifth and sixth judgments of the Day and the Wrath of the Lord Yahuah—the first and second *"woes."*

Chapter 9—The Events of the Fifth and Sixth Trumpet Judgments

9:1-12 Then the fifth angel sounded: And I saw (a) *a star fallen from heaven to earth. To* (b) *him was given the key to the bottomless pit. And he opened the bottomless pit, and smoke arose out of the pit like the smoke of a great furnace. So the sun and the air were darkened because of the smoke of the pit. Then out of the smoke* (c) *locusts came upon the earth. And to them was given power, as the scorpions of the earth have power. They were commanded not to harm the grass of the earth, or any green thing, or any tree, but* (d) *only those men who do not have the seal of [Yahuah] on their foreheads. And they were not given authority to kill them, but to torment them for* (e) *five months. Their torment was like the torment of a scorpion when it strikes a man. In those days men will seek death and will not find it; they will desire to die, and death will flee from them.* (f) *The shape of the locusts was like horses prepared for battle. On their heads were crowns of something like gold, and their faces were like the faces of men. They had hair like women's hair, and their teeth were like lions' teeth. And they had breastplates like breastplates of iron, and the sound of their wings was like the sound of chariots with many horses running into battle. They had tails like scorpions, and there were stings in their tails. Their power was to hurt men five months. And* (g) *they had as king over them the angel of the bottomless pit, whose name in Hebrew is Abaddon, but in Greek he has the name Apollyon. One woe is past. Behold still two more woes are coming* (h) *after these things.*

a. Of course, if a star (our sun is a relatively small star) literally fell to Earth, Earth would instantly be annihilated. The description given in these verses seems to fit that of a cometary impact. Scientific studies have shown that a large comet impacting the earth at over 25,000 miles per hour would (as some have in the past) penetrate Earth's crust into the molten mantle, producing a "bottomless" crater, the explosive force of thousands of atomic bombs, a mushroom-shaped cloud exactly like that of the explosion of a nuclear bomb and fill the atmosphere with toxic smoke and debris for hundreds or thousands of miles around, exactly as did the volcanic eruption in Iceland in 2010. It would also send seismic shock waves through and around the earth that would shake the whole planet.

117

b. The ancient Hebrews and Greeks (and, before them, the Sumerians, Akkadians, Babylonians and Assyrians) called any luminous celestial object (star, meteor or comet) a "star." And they personified falling stars as "messengers of the gods." So, the *"star"* in this verse could, ironically, be a comet sent as a "messenger" from the one true God Yahuah to wreak destruction on the ungodly earth dwellers. The Lord uses symbolic language here to communicate to the mindset of the first century Believers.

c. These are not literal locusts because they do not harm vegetation. These *"locusts"* are apparently microorganisms that cause painful diseases. Like locusts, bacteria and other microbes amass in great numbers and are carried, in smoke and dust, wherever the wind takes them.

d. Of Earth's inhabitants, only the Jews who have not yet recognized that Yahushua is the Messiah but who still cling to their faith in the coming Messiah, refusing to take the mark of the anti-messiah, plus those Gentiles who do not take the mark, are protected from the plagues of the judgments of Yahuah.

e. What horrible suffering!—tormented with excruciating pain (like the sting of a scorpion), wanting but not being able to die, for five months. This is a foretaste of "eternity" in the Lake of Fire (cf. Mark 9:47, 48). This description makes it clear that these terrifying creatures are like an innumerable swarm of locusts in number, and the torment that they inflict on the inhabitants of the world, from which there is no escape, makes it more woeful than the previous plagues or calamities.

f. There are several types of deadly bacteria (including streptococcal and viral bacteria) that, when viewed through a microscope, closely resemble this description of *"locusts."* Although not yet confirmed, scientists have discovered evidence of viruses and bacteria in comets.

g. The language here also seems to be highly personified and symbolic. Remember, the Greek word translated "angel" (*aggelos*) can also be translated "messenger." And the Greek word translated "king" (*basilleus*) can be translated "controller." Also, the Greek term translated "over" (*epi*) can mean "to give direction." Plus, Psalm 147:4 states, *"He* [the Lord] *tells the number of the stars* [the luminous celestial objects]; *He calls them by their names."* The names *Abaddon* (Hebrew) and *Apollyon* (Greek) mean "destroyer." So, if we can suspend the usual interpretation that these verses are speaking of supernatural beings and events,

118

we will see that an equally valid, literal translation of 9:11 might be, "And the direction from which the harmful organisms came was controlled by a comet (named *Abaddon* in Hebrew or *Apollyon* in Greek) that created the 'bottomless' pit from which the creatures ascended."

h. Unlike *"after these things I looked"* (4:1, et al.), which denotes primarily a change in visions, *"after these things"* (without the *"I looked")* indicates a new time-sequence event.

9:13-19 *Then the sixth angel sounded: And I heard* (a) *a voice from the four horns of the golden altar which is before [Yahuah], saying to the sixth angel who had the trumpet, "Release* (b) *the four angels who are bound at the great river Euphrates." So the four angels, who had been prepared for* (c) *the hour and day and month and year, were released to kill a third of mankind. Now the number of* (d) *the army of the horsemen was two hundred million; I heard the number of them. And thus I saw* (e) *the horses in the vision: those who sat on them had breastplates of fiery red, hyacinth blue, and sulfur yellow; and the heads of the horses were like the heads of lions; and out of their mouths came fire, smoke, and brimstone. (f) By these three plagues a third of mankind was killed—by the fire and the smoke and the brimstone which came out of their mouths. For their power is in their mouth and in their tails; for their tails are like serpents, having heads; and with them they do harm.*

a. This voice is not the voice of the Lord or, apparently, the voice of any of the other heavenly beings. The only voice mentioned as coming from an altar in Heaven is the cry of the martyrs crying out to Yahuah for vengeance (6:1).

b. An incorrect translation. Again, the Greek word (*aggelos*) translated *"angels"* can also be translated "messengers"; also, the Greek word (*epi*) translated *"in"* can be translated "toward" or "for." So, this sentence could and apparently should read, *"Loose the four messengers* [comets or comet fragments] *which are bound for the river Euphrates."* This latter translation of the description of what occurs to start the execution of the sixth trumpet judgment perfectly parallels the description of what happens when the sixth bowl judgment is executed—the water of the Euphrates River is dried up (16:12). Comets or comet fragments striking the river will instantly vaporize its water.

119

c. These *"angels"* (comets) have been prepared for their role in executing Yahuah's judgments at this specific point in time. Some claim that the events of Revelation occurred during the first century or two of the "Church Age," or have been occurring throughout the past 2,000 years, but this verse argues strongly against those hypotheses: At no specific hour, day, month, or year in history has one-third of the earth's population been killed, much less by the objects described here or in the ways described here.

d. Some have claimed that these two hundred million comprise a vast human army from the East (the direction of the Euphrates River from Israel). But that hypothesis cannot be true either, without allegorizing the details beyond reasonable recognition. Why not just accept the literal interpretation that, as with the events of the fifth trumpet, these are terrifying natural objects (comet fragments) that had been prepared by the Lord Yahuah for this point in time to release more of the plagues of His judgments on Earth? The *Bible* speaks of the *"treasures* [storehouses] *of the hail"* (the Oort Cloud of billions of comets that surrounds our solar system?) which the Lord has *"reserved against the time of trouble"* (a phrase in Scripture that refers to the Great Tribulation and the Day of the Lord) (Job 38:22-23). Prophetic Scripture also speaks of *"the weapons of* [the Lord's] *indignation"* which *"come . . . from the end of heaven* [the edge of our solar system?] *. . . to destroy the whole land"* (Isaiah 13:5).

e. According to scientist Jeffrey Goodman (*The Comets of God*, page 283), this is a perfect, symbolic description of comet fragments plummeting through Earth's atmosphere. Comets (and comet fragments) eject gases and dust through vents in their surfaces that rise up in a plume away from the "head" of the comet, like the mane of a horse or lion, and trail behind like a long, serpentine tail. And when plunging through Earth's atmosphere at thousands of miles per hour, comets burn with an intense heat of thousands of degrees Farenheit, reflecting the exact colors (*fiery red, hyacinth blue and sulfur yellow*) mentioned in this verse. Plus, a comet or comets entering Earth's atmosphere could disintegrate into millions of fragments.

f. So, by the three agents of death released by the two hundred million comet fragments—the fire, the smoke, and the brimstone (brimstone is burning sulfur which is common in comets)—another third of humanity is killed. That is over five and one-half billion or two-thirds of Earth's population who have been killed so far during the Final Seven Years, with the last and most terrible trumpet/bowl judgment of Yahuah's Wrath plus "Armageddon" yet to come.

Dr. John S. Lewis, a professor of planetary science and Co-Director of the NASA Space Engineering Research Center at the University of Arizona, in his book *Rain of Iron and Ice: The Very Real Threat of Comet and Asteroid Bombardment* (Reading Massachusetts: Addison-Wesley Publishing, 1996, pages 11-13), made an interesting observation:

> . . . the description of future events in *Revelation* leans heavily upon the phenomenology of violent cosmic events. . . . The central theme is clear and unambiguous: the events described in *Revelation* are of astronomical origin and describe real physical events, not mere portents or symbols. Did John (the author of the *Book of Revelation*) somehow know more about impact phenomena than any scientist before the present decade?

9:20-21 *But* (a) *the rest of mankind, who were not killed by these plagues, did not repent* (b) *of the works of their hands, that they should not worship demons, and idols of gold, silver, brass, stone, and wood, which can neither see nor hear nor walk. And they did not repent of their murders or their sorceries or their sexual immorality or their thefts.* (c)

a. Indicating that virtually all of mankind, other than the Jews and Gentiles who have not taken the mark of the beast and are protected by Yahuah from physical harm, have either been killed or are unrepentant.

b. The one-third or so of mankind remaining on the earth are so hardened in the confidence that they can save themselves (by "*the works of their hands*") and in their confidence in the power of riches or inanimate objects (which is actually the worship of demons [cf. 2 Chronicles 11:15]), that they refuse to repent of the sins that result from such idolatry, including murders (destroying people in thoughts, words, or actions), sorceries (confidence in spiritual powers, forces, or beings other than Yahuah), sexual immorality (including lust), and thefts (including dishonest business practices, defrauding people, and extortion).

c. Notice that by this point in time, mankind is beyond hope; the Gospel has no effect. There is no appeal for anyone to repent; it is just noted that no one does repent. The only inhabitants left on the earth (other than the Israelites and the Gentiles who have not taken the mark of the beast) are earth dwellers— *"vessels of wrath prepared for destruction"* (Romans 9:22).

Chapter 10 provides an intermission after the description of the events of sixth trumpet (the second woe) to give us more details about what is happening during the execution of the Lord's judgments on Earth and what it all means.

Chapter 10—The Seven Thunders and the Little Book

10:1 *I saw still* (a) *another mighty angel* (b) *coming down from heaven, (c) clothed with a cloud. And a rainbow was on his head, his face was like the sun, and his feet like pillars of fire.*

a. This is the second of three *"mighty"* angels who appear in Revelation. The first was at 5:2 and the third will be at 18:21. Each has a significant role to play in the events of the Final Seven Years: the first, drawing attention to the One who was worthy to open the sealed book (scroll); the second (this angel), setting the stage for the sounding of the seventh trumpet and the final plagues of the judgments of Yahuah; and the third, executing the final destruction of modern, prophetic Babylon.

b. The appearance of this angel is similar to the that of the awesome angel who appeared to Daniel (Daniel 10:5-8) and who told Daniel to seal the book of prophecy until *"the time of the end"* (Daniel 12:4). His appearance, including coming clothed in a cloud (in this vision, John is on the earth), is also very similar to that of the One like the Son of Man (the Messiah) here in Revelation (1:13-15). So, it would seem that this angel is a direct representative of the Lord Yahushua in giving to John some important details of the Revelation.

10:2-7 *He had* (a) *a little book open in his hand. And he set* (b) *his right foot on the sea and his left foot on the land, and cried with (c) a loud voice, as when a lion roars. When he cried out, (d) seven thunders uttered their voices. Now when the seven thunders uttered their voices, I was about to write; but I heard* (e) *a voice from heaven saying to me, "Seal up the things which the seven thunders uttered, and do not write them." The angel whom I saw standing on the sea and on the land* (f) *raised up his hand to heaven and swore by Him who lives "forever" and ever, who created heaven and the things that are in it, the earth and the things that are in it, and the sea and the things that are in it, (g) that there should be delay no longer, but* (h) *in the days of the sounding of the seventh angel, when he is about to sound, the mystery of [Yahuah] would be finished, as He declared to His servants the prophets.*

a. This is a book or scroll smaller than the one which reveals the events of the six seals and the judgments of Yahuah (5:1). It is already open.

b. The planting of one foot on the sea and the other on the land may indicate that the implications of what the angel is about to reveal will affect all the people of the world. The sea may represent the tumultuous, pagan people of the world, as in 13:1 and 17:15, and the earth may represent organized religion (which seems to be the implication of *"earth"* in 13:11). Also, the Greek for *"earth"* (*ge*) is translated *"land,"* as in the *"land of Israel"* (Matthew 2:20). Organized religion would include Christianity and Judaism.

c. If the angel represents Yahushua, the Lion of Judah (5:5), then what he utters is the roar of the Lord.

d. As also is mentioned in 4:5, 8:5, 11:19, 16:18, and 19:6, thunder appears to be associated with the power of the Lord. Here, the seven thunders seem to represent the awesome power of the Lord in executing His perfect, complete judgment of the world.

e. As though the angel is overridden, John is commanded from Heaven not to write—to seal up—the utterances of the seven thunders, perhaps indicating that they portend the terrible *"last plagues"* of the judgments of Yahuah (15:1), or the ultimate, Great White Throne Judgment (cf. 20:11-15), the details of which are not yet ready to be revealed. But that is conjecture; the contents of the seven thunders are nowhere revealed in the *Bible* as far as this commentator knows.

f. The angel, apparently in response to the voice from Heaven, with the little book in one hand, raises the other hand toward Heaven and utters a binding oath . . .

g. That there will be no more delay in the execution and completion of the (final) Wrath of the Lord. This may be a response to the cry of the martyrs under the altar: *"How long, O Lord, holy and true, until You judge and avenge our blood on those who dwell on the earth"* (6:10).

h. The KJV and NKJV translations of this sentence are not clear and complete. The Greek word (*euallegizo*) translated *"declared"* means "to bring good news or glad tidings." A better translation of the statement might be: *"The hidden plan* [revealed only to those who have "eyes that see and ears that hear"] *of [Yahuah], the Good*

News that was communicated to the prophets, is about to be brought to completion as soon as the seventh angel sounds his trumpet and during the days of the sounding of that trumpet." This statement makes it clear that there is something special about the seventh trumpet judgment. And indeed there is! It, combined with the seventh bowl judgment (which apparently is just another aspect of the same judgment) is the judgment in which the *"hidden plan"* of Yahuah (to restore His Creation to its original state under the reign of the true Messiah—*"the restoration of all things"*—Acts 3:21) is *"brought to completion."* The seventh bowl, which contains the final plagues of the judgments of Yahuah, completing His Wrath (cf. 16:17-21), is poured out following the sounding of the seventh trumpet, which also prompts worship in Heaven *"of our Lord and of His [Messiah]"* for bringing His plan to completion (cf. 11:15-19). The Day of the Lord, including His Wrath, is explicitly foretold many times in the *Tanakh* (Isaiah 2:12; Jeremiah 46:10; Joel 2:1; Amos 5:18; Obadiah 1:15; Zephaniah 1:14; Zechariah 14:1; Malachi 4:5 [one example from each of these prophets; there are many others]) and mentioned several times in the *B'rit Hadashah* (Acts 2:20; 1 Corinthians 5:5; 2 Corinthians 1:14; 1 Thessalonians 5:2; 2 Peter 3:10).

10:8-11 *Then (a) the voice which I heard from heaven spoke to me again and said, "Go, take the little book which is open in the hand of the angel who stands on the sea and on the earth." So I went to the angel and said to him, "Give me the little book." And he said to me, (b) "Take and eat it; and it will make your stomach bitter, but it will be as sweet as honey in your mouth." Then I took the little book out of the angel's hand and ate it, and it was as sweet as honey in my mouth. But when I had eaten it, my stomach became bitter. And he said to me, (c) "You must prophesy again about many peoples, nations, tongues, and kings."*

a. Some have suggested that, because of his appearance, the *"angel"* is Yahushua, but this passage clearly indicates otherwise: John obeys the voice from Heaven and tells the angel to give him the book. The angel is subservient to both the One who speaks from Heaven and to John. He is just a representative and a messenger of the Lord. (The literal meaning of the Greek word for angel, *aggelos*, is "messenger.")

b. John was told to eat the book—to consume its contents, which were apparently the revelation of the seven thunders, and was told that those contents would initially taste sweet but would then become bitter, which, when he ate the book, he discovered was true. Note that Ezekiel, over 600 years earlier, had been told by the Lord to do exactly the same as John was told to do here—eat a book (scroll) that would taste sweet—before he prophesied the judgments of the Lord (Ezekiel 2:8–3:3).

c. In the context, the contents of the book appear to be a revelation of the final plagues of the Day and the Wrath of Yahuah still to come after the parenthetical details of Chapters 11-14 are revealed, the seventh trumpet has sounded, and *"the mystery of [Yahuah] is finished"* (10:7). The Day of the Lord is sweet news to the Redeemed but bitter to those who are perishing. And John is told that he must prophesy again about the people of this world. So, the contents of the seven thunders and of the little book may reveal the plagues of the Wrath of Yahuah that are poured out after the seventh trumpet has sounded, the carnage of "Armageddon," the terror of Great White Throne Judgment, or all three. They may also, in the same way that the sweetness and bitterness of the contents of the scroll that Ezekiel ate foretold the destruction of Jerusalem (cf. Ezekiel 2:9-3:3; 4:1-3), refer to the destruction of Jerusalem which, at the end of the Final Seven Years, will become, spiritually, like Sodom and Egypt (cf. 11:8, 13; 16:19).

126

Chapter 11—Measuring the Temple, the Two Witnesses, and the Blowing of the Seventh Trumpet

11:1-2 *Then* (a) *I was given a reed like a measuring rod. And* (b) *the angel stood, saying, "Rise and measure the temple of [Yahuah], the altar, and those who worship there. But* (c) *leave out the court which is outside the temple, and do not measure it, for it has been given to the Gentiles. And they will tread the holy city underfoot for forty-two months."*

a. After eating the little book, John is given a measuring stick (a reed—a variety of cane that grows in the area of the Jordan River, which was used for measuring, among its other functions).

b. The angel stands to give John another assignment: to measure the Temple, the altar, and those who worship there. Because the bulk of the evidence indicates that the Revelation was written about 95 AD, this is apparently not the Temple which was destroyed in 70 AD, approximately 25 years before John received the Revelation, but is a vision (not a literal temple) illustrating how Yahuah is going to deal with the Gentiles vis-à-vis Yahuah's People Israel during the last half of the Final Seven Years. In Jewish symbolism, to measure something is to preserve it. In his vision, John is told to measure the part of the Temple where (true) Israel worships, because that numbered (measured) Remnant of Israel will be saved (not trodden down by the Gentiles). (The literal, rebuilt Temple will be totally taken over by the Gentiles and by Antimessiah when he desecrates it and sits in it proclaiming himself to be "God" at the midpoint of the Final Seven Years [cf. Daniel 9:27; Matthew 24:15; 2 Thessalonians 2:3, 4; Revelation 13:4-6]).

c. John is told not to measure the court outside (not part of) the Temple, where the Gentiles had been permitted to worship in the past and where Yahushua taught, because during the last half of the seven years (42 months), the *"holy city"* (Jerusalem) will be given totally over to and trodden down by the Gentiles, who, in the end will be destroyed—not saved.

11:3-13 *And* (a) *I will give power to my two witnesses, and they will prophesy one thousand two hundred and sixty days, clothed in sackcloth."* (b) *These are the two olive trees and the two lampstands standing before the God of the earth. And if anyone wants to harm them,* (c) *fire proceeds from their mouth and devours their enemies. And if any-*

one wants to harm them, he must be killed in this manner. These have power to shut heaven, so that no rain falls in the days of their prophecy; and they have power over waters to turn them to blood, and to strike the earth with all plagues, as often as they desire. When they finish their testimony, (d) the beast that ascends out of the bottomless pit will make war against them, overcome them, and kill them. And their dead bodies will lie in the street of the (e) great city which spiritually is called Sodom and Egypt, where also our Lord was crucified. Then (f) those from the peoples, tribes, tongues, and nations will see their dead bodies three-and-a-half days, and not allow their dead bodies to be put into graves. And those who dwell on the earth will rejoice over them, make merry, and send gifts to one another, because these two prophets tormented those who dwell on the earth. Now (g) after the three-and-a-half days the breath of life from [Yahuah] entered them, and they stood on their feet, and great fear fell on those who saw them. And they heard (h) a loud voice from heaven saying to them, "Come up here." And they ascended to heaven in a cloud, and their enemies saw them. (i) In the same hour there was a great earthquake, and a tenth of the city fell. In the earthquake seven thousand people were killed, and (j) the rest were afraid and gave glory to the God of heaven.

a. The angel, still speaking for the Lord, who had just told John that Jerusalem will be trodden down by the Gentiles during the last half of the seven years, tells him that during that time, 1260 days (42 Hebrew months, which are 30 days each), there will be two *"witnesses"* in the city who will be empowered by the Lord to prophesy.

b. The witnesses are identified as olive trees and lampstands. The olive tree is a symbol of Israel (cf. Jeremiah 11:16; Romans 11:17) and the lampstand is a symbol of the presence and light of the Lord (cf. Matthew 5:15; Revelation 2:5) in Scripture. So, a logical interpretation is that the two witnesses are Israelites prophesying the truth (light) of the Lord. Some have speculated that they are Israel and the Church, but common sense and literal interpretation argues to the contrary because they are **both** represented by olive trees and lampstands, and they wear sackcloth. Besides, there is no difference between "true Israel" and "the Church."

c. There are many ideas as to the identity of the two witnesses, but common sense would also seem to indicate that they are Moses and Elijah. Or, they may be *types* of Moses and Elijah, working in the Spirit and power of Moses and Elijah, just as did John the Baptist—another type of Elijah who testified that Yahushua was the Messiah at His first coming (Matthew 17:12, 13; Mark 9:12; Luke 1:13-17). However, the glorified Christ appeared with Moses and Elijah as His witnesses at the Transfiguration (Matthew 17:3), so they will probably be the same two individuals. These plagues may be clues to their identity: Moses and Elijah brought the same types of plagues on the earth (cf. Exodus 7-11; 1 Kings 17:1, 7; Luke 9:54). And Yahushua had told his Disciples that Moses (through whom the law, which testifies of Yahushua, was given) and the prophets (of whom Elijah was the primary representative) testified of Him (Luke 24:44; John 1:45). He also hinted that Elijah would be coming again after the Transfiguration (cf. Mark 9:12). So, the fact that the central focus of Revelation is the second coming of the Messiah would seem to lend support to the interpretation that the two witnesses (undoubtedly testifying in the streets of Jerusalem that Yahushua, not Antimessiah, is the true Messiah) are Moses and Elijah, His primary two witnesses throughout the *Bible*. Children in Israel today sing a song about the return of Moses and Elijah.

d. Antimessiah (cf. 17:8), who undoubtedly had been extremely annoyed, even tormented, by the testimony and power of the two witnesses, is finally enabled to kill them at the end of the seven years.

e. This is Jerusalem (*"where our Lord was crucified"*), but, during the reign of Antimessiah, it has sunk to such depths of depravity that it is called spiritual Sodom and Gomorrah.

f. The unredeemed people of the world allow the bodies of the two witnesses to lie in the streets of Jerusalem for three and one-half days, where they can view them and celebrate their death and the murderous power of Antimessiah over them.

g. But, their revelry is short lived; after the three and one-half days, the two witnesses are resurrected, filling those who had been celebrating their death with fear.

h. Then, with the same words that John had been summoned to Heaven (4:1), the Two Witnesses are told, *"Come up here,"* and ascend into Heaven, as if to proclaim prophetically to their enemies on Earth, "In the same way that we were dead and you gloated over us for three and one-half days, your three and one-half years of treading down Jerusalem and gloating in your power over Yahuah's People is at an end!"

129

i.   This appears to be the final event of the sixth trumpet judgment (the second woe) (cf. verse 14). A tenth of Jerusalem, which has become as Sodom and Egypt, is destroyed and 7,000, presumably of the ungodly Gentiles who have been trampling the city underfoot for the past 42 months, are killed.

j.   These who fear the Lord and give Him glory are apparently Jews who have not been allowed to take the mark of the beast (the anti-messiah) so they can engage in commerce (cf. 13:16-17), but have been subjected to horribly harsh conditions and servitude by the anti-messiah and his followers, just as the Israelites were oppressed by Pharaoh before they were saved from his dominion. Notice an important difference here in the response of the inhabitants of Jerusalem who are not killed (the Jews) from the response of the earth dwellers to the plagues of the Lord. The Jews who have not taken the mark of the beast fear Yahuah and give Him glory, preparing them to be saved in the end (cf. Romans 11:26), but the ungodly Gentiles refuse to repent and blaspheme the Lord (cf. 9:20-21; 16:11, 21), dooming themselves to destruction.

11:14-19 (a) *The second woe is past. Behold, the third woe is coming quickly.* Then (b) *the seventh angel sounded: And there were loud voices in heaven, saying, "The kingdoms of this world have become the kingdoms of our Lord and of His [Messiah], and He shall reign 'forever and ever'!" And the twenty-four elders who sat before [Yahuah] on their thrones fell on their faces and worshiped God, saying: "We give You thanks, O Lord [Yahuah] Almighty, The One who is and who was and who is to come, Because You have taken Your great power and reigned. The nations were angry, and Your wrath has come, And* (c) *the time of the dead, that they should be judged, And that You should reward Your servants the prophets and the saints, And those who fear Your name, small and great, And should destroy those who destroy the earth."* Then (d) *the temple of [Yahuah] was opened in heaven, and the ark of His covenant was seen in His temple. And* (e) *there were lightnings, noises, thunderings, an earthquake, and great hail.*

a.   Some have postulated that the two witnesses appear during the first half of the Final Seven Years. But, because it states here that they ascend just before the catastrophe that ends the second woe (sixth trumpet judgment), it is clear that their time on Earth spans the second half of the seven years.

b. It is also clear that, because the two witnesses ascend on the last day of the seven years, the seventh trumpet sounds immediately following the 1260 days of the last half of the Final Seven Years. And the scene in Heaven is one in which the 24 elders are rejoicing and praising Yahuah because, at the time that the seventh angel sounds his trumpet, the battle is virtually over; Antimessiah has been dethroned. So, the voices in Heaven begin to celebrate the victory and dominion of the Lord, even before the *"last plagues"* of the Wrath of Yahuah are poured out on Earth (cf. 15:1) during the ten "Days of Awe" between Yom Teruah (the Feast of Trumpets) and Yom Kippur (the Feast of Atonement).

c. Throughout Israel's history, the awesome day known as Yom Teruah (the Feast of Trumpets), Yom haDin (the Day of Judgment), or Rosh haShanah (the Head of the New Year) has been celebrated as a rehearsal for (1) the sounding of the Last Trump, (2) the judgment of the dead, (3) the resurrection of the Righteous (*teruah* means "an awakening blast"), and (4) the gathering of the Righteous for the coronation of the Messiah. So, this day—the day of the sounding of the Last Trump—will be the day of the coming of the Messiah in the clouds to gather His Elect (His Bride) and take them to Heaven for the marriage of the Lamb and His coronation as the King of Kings (cf. Matthew 24:31; 1 Corinthians 15:51, 52; 1 Thessalonians 4:16, 17; Revelation 19:7, 16).

d. The Temple on the earth, including the Ark of His Covenant, which was the location of the Lord's presence with His People Israel (cf. Leviticus 16:2), was apparently a model of the Temple in Heaven. His presence with His resurrected and ascended People after the seventh trumpet has sounded will be in Heaven.

e. These are ominous precursors to the final execution of the judgments of Yahuah which follow the blowing of the seventh trumpet blast.

Chapters 12-14 are parenthetical chapters inserted between the sounding of the seventh trumpet (11:15) and the description of the bowls of wrath events (Chapters 15-16) to give us some background information about Satan's antagonism toward the Lord Yahuah's People and His coming Messiah throughout history and to fill in more details of what happens during the Great Tribulation (the wrath of Satan) of the second half of the Final Seven Years.

Chapter 12—Satan versus Yahuah's People Israel and Her Children throughout History

By combining images from the past, present, and future, Chapter 12 provides more details about what is happening behind the scenes with Satan vis-à-vis the Messiah and Yahuah's People Israel. The imagery in this chapter does not appear to be strictly sequential or time-specific: The events manifest a pattern of conflict between the devil and Israel, including her spiritual children the Disciples of the Messiah, throughout history, culminating during the Final Seven Years.

12:1-2 *Now (a) a great sign appeared in heaven:* (b) *a woman clothed with the sun, with the moon under her feet, and on her head a garland of twelve stars. Then being* (c) *with child, she cried out in labor and in pain to give birth.*

a. *"Sign"* means symbolic—not an actual person, object, or event. Its appearance in Heaven rather than on the earth indicates that it transcends time and space; it is not specific to a single person, object, or event at a certain point in time on the earth.
b. Thankfully, we are not left to the mercy of the fickleness and frailty of men's imaginations in interpreting the *Bible*. **Scripture is its own best interpreter.** Other Scriptures tell us very clearly what or who the sun, moon, and stars represent. In Joseph's dream (Genesis 37:9), which was very similar to the vision of 12:1, he dreamed that the sun (Jacob), the moon (Rachel) and eleven stars (Joseph's brothers) were bowing down to him, the twelfth star. So, the sun, moon, and stars represent the family of Israel in Joseph's vision. Why could not they represent the same in John's vision? Most of the early Assembly of Believers in Yahushua, including the apostles, was comprised of Jewish believers. They would have immediately understood the symbolism: The woman is Israel. So, the Remnant of Israel, including the grafted in Gentiles, who have

truly believed in the coming Messiah throughout history (even though many of them did not recognize Him the first time He came), the ones to whom Paul refers as "true Israel" (cf. Romans 9:6), is symbolized in John's vision as the woman. And in 12:1, this woman—clothed with the sun, moon, and stars—appears in Heaven, indicating that the imagery in this chapter is not bound by time and is not in strict chronological sequence, but represents the timeless plan of Yahuah, which originates in Heaven.

c. *For unto us **a Child is born**, unto us a Son is given; and the government will be upon His shoulder. And His name will be called Wonderful, Counselor, Mighty God, Everlasting Father, Prince of Peace* (Isaiah 9:6). Who else could this Child of Israel be other than Yahuah the Son, the Messiah, the focus of Revelation? In an extended sense, His birth might refer to His second coming as Head of the Kingdom of Yahuah on Earth, because the Final Seven Years are prophesied to be a time of great travail and pain, referred to as *"the time that she* [Israel] *who is in labor has given birth; then the remnant of His* [the Messiah's] *brethren shall return to the children of Israel."* During the Final Seven Years, a remnant of the tribes of Israel scattered throughout the world will return to the Land of Israel and be reunited with the Jews who are already there. Then, the Messiah will return to rule them from David's throne in New Jerusalem during His millennial kingdom on Earth. (cf. Micah 5:2-3; Isaiah 9:7)

12:3-4 *And another sign appeared in heaven: behold,* (a) *a great, fiery red dragon having seven heads and ten horns, and seven diadems on his heads. His tail drew* (b) *a third of the stars of heaven and threw them to the earth. And* (c) *the dragon stood before the woman who was ready to give birth, to devour her Child as soon as it was born.*

a. This is Satan, the devil, the *"serpent of old"* (cf. verse 9; 17:3; 20:2). As will be clarified in Chapters 13 and 17, *"heads"* is synonymous with *"mountains"*—worldly kingdoms or empires; *"horns"* refers to worldly authority or power; and *"diadems"* (crowns) refers to the kings or rulers who wield that authority over the kingdoms of the world. Satan is, at the present time, the source and sustainer of the authority and power of the kings of the world—the one who controls those kings and, in effect, rules the world from behind the scenes (cf. John 12:31; 14:30; 16:11).

b. These are Satan's angels (cf. verse 9).

134

c. Satan, through Herod, attempted to kill Yahushua soon after He
    was born (cf. Matthew 2:8; 16-18). He also attempted to kill him
    at various times during his ministry on Earth and at His crucifix-
    ion. He will attempt to kill him again at "Armageddon," and final-
    ly at the end of the Millennium. Some attempt to mistranslate and
    over-allegorize *"Child"* into "Children" ("the Church"), but a
    good principle to follow in interpreting Scripture is that symbolism
    does not violate common sense or correct grammar.

12:5-6 (a) *She bore a male Child who was to rule all nations with a
rod of iron. And her Child was caught up to* [Yahuah] *and His throne.*
(b) *Then the woman fled into the wilderness, where she has a place
prepared by* [Yahuah], *that (c) they should feed her there one thousand
two hundred and sixty days.*

a. But Israel, through Mary, a descendant of David (cf. Matthew 1:1-
    16), bore the Child who was to rule all nations with a rod of iron
    (cf. Genesis 3:15; Psalm 2:9; Revelation 19:15).[8]   And He es-
    caped being destroyed by Satan when He ascended into Heaven
    (cf. Acts 1:11).
b. Then, when he failed to destroy the Son of Yahuah, the devil went
    after His mother Israel who fled into the *"wilderness"* (rural,
    sparsely inhabited areas). Actually, in anticipation of the coming
    Messiah, Satan has been trying to destroy Israel throughout her
    history: when she came out of Egypt, by Antiochus Epiphanes, by
    the Roman persecutions and dispersion, by the Russian pogroms,
    by the German Holocaust, and by worldwide anti-Semitism and
    anti-Zionism today. If he can destroy Israel, then he will prevent
    the Messiah from "giving birth" through her to the redeemed na-
    tion of Israel when He returns to rule over her from David's throne
    in Jerusalem. Satan will attempt to destroy Yahuah's physical

---

[8]Matthew 1:16, in stating that Joseph was Mary's **husband**, is an error in
translation. Recently-discovered Hebrew manuscripts of the Gospel of Matthew state that Joseph (a Joseph other than Mary's husband) was her **father**.
The genealogy of Mary's husband Joseph is listed in Luke 3. So, as was
prophesied, Yahushua was a descendant of the kingly line of David and Solomon through only one human parent, His mother (cf. Genesis 3:15; Isaiah
7:14). For a complete explanation of the genealogy of Yahushua, get the
DVD *Raiders of the Lost Book* at www.michaelrood.tv or view the YouTube
videos by the same name.

135

people Israel when his incarnation, Antimessiah, pursues her into the wilderness at the midpoint of the Final Seven Years.

c. But she will escape and *"they"* will feed her the last half of the seven years (1260 days). Who *"they"* are is not clear—perhaps the angels who ministered to Yahushua after His 40 days in the wilderness (cf. Matthew 4:11), or Jordanian Arabs who the *Bible* indicates will aid Israel after she flees into the wilderness (e.g., Isaiah 16:3-4). Although this imagery may have multiple references, including Yahuah's taking care of Israel in the Sinai wilderness after her exodus from Egypt and His taking care of her in the "wilderness" of the world today before the Remnant returns to Israel, it will have a literal fulfillment during the Final Seven Years when the Jews in Jerusalem and that area who recognize that Antimessiah is the false messiah flee into hiding places in the mountains of *"Judea"* (Central Israel) at the midpoint of the Final Seven Years when he stands in the Temple proclaiming himself to be "God" (cf. Matthew 24:15-20; 2 Thessalonians 2:3-4).

12:7-17 And war broke out in heaven: (a) *Michael and his angels fought with the dragon; and the dragon and his angels fought, but they did not prevail, nor was a place found for them in heaven any longer. So the great dragon was cast out, that serpent of old, called the devil and Satan, who deceives the whole world; he was cast to the earth, and his angels were cast out with him. Then I heard* (b) *a loud voice saying in heaven, "Now salvation, and strength, and the kingdom of our God, and the power of His [Messiah] have come, for the accuser of our brethren, who accused them before our God day and night, has been cast down. And they overcame him by the blood of the Lamb and by the word of their testimony, and they did not love their lives to the death. Therefore rejoice, O heavens, and you who dwell in them!* (c) *Woe to the inhabitants of the earth and the sea! For the devil has come down to you, having great wrath, because he knows that he has a short time." Now when the dragon saw that he had been cast to the earth,* (d) *he persecuted the woman who gave birth to the male Child. But the woman was given two wings of a great eagle, that she might fly into the wilderness to her place, where she is nourished for a time and times and half a time, from the presence of the serpent. So* (e) *the serpent spewed water out of his mouth like a flood after the woman, that he might cause her to be carried away by the flood. But the earth helped the woman, and* (f) *the earth opened its mouth and swallowed up the flood which the dragon had spewed out of his mouth. And* (g)

136

the dragon was enraged with the woman, and he went to make war with the rest of her offspring, who keep the commandments of [Yahuah] and have the testimony of [Yahushua the Messiah]. (h)

Verses 7-17 appear to repeat the content of verses 1-6, adding more details about what has happened in cosmic history, what will happen to Israel's physical children during the last half of the Final Seven Years, and culminating with what will happen to Israel's spiritual children the Believers in the Messiah Yahushua during the Great Tribulation.

a. Although Satan, when he was Lucifer, was expelled from Heaven before he appeared as the serpent in the Garden of Eden (cf. Isaiah 14:12; Genesis 3:1), he still seems to be able to come, with his angels, into the presence of Yahuah. But apparently, during the Final Seven Years, at the midpoint of the Final Seven Years (cf. verses 12 and 13), he and his angels are permanently cast out of Heaven after a war with the archangel Michael and his angels.

b. The devil's ejection from Heaven prompts rejoicing by the Redeemed in Heaven (notice that it is just a voice that John hears; there is no indication that the Redeemed are in their final, glorified bodies, which would make the prophecy time-specific), because he can no longer accuse their brethren, especially the martyrs, before Yahuah. It is by virtue of the sacrifice of the Lamb of Yahuah and their faithful testimony to the Truth that Yahushua is the true Messiah and salvation is only through Him, even to the point of sacrificing their own lives, that the Redeemed Brethren are able to overcome the constant accusations of Satan, resulting in his being cast out of Heaven.

c. But woe to the inhabitants of both Israel and the Gentile world (cf. 10:2) because the devil, full of desperate wrath because he knows that his time is short, will be a total tyrant in attempting to establish his dominion on the earth.

d. This verse appears to reiterate verse six in which Satan, through His incarnation the anti-messiah, trys to destroy the Jews, who, specially enabled by Yahuah, flee into the mountains of central Israel at the midpoint of the Final Seven Years and are protected and nourished there for *"a time and times and half a time,"* three and one-half years. The majority of the Jews in Jerusalem will probably not escape, however, and will be subjected to harsh servitude by Satan's incarnation, Antimessiah, just as the Israelites were oppressed in Egypt by Pharaoh.

137

e. Then, Satan's last attempt to destroy Yahuah's physical people Israel before their Messiah takes back His throne on Earth will be when the anti-messiah pursues those remaining in Jerusalem into the wilderness at the end of the Final Seven Years, when the Messiah returns with the armies of Heaven to destroy the forces of Antimessiah and the kings of the earth. His feet will land on the Mount of Olives which will split, half of it moving to the south and half moving to the north, creating a valley that runs from Jerusalem to the north end of the Dead Sea (Azal). And that valley will provide a way of escape for the Jews through the mountains east of Jerusalem, just as the "valley" through the sea provided a way of escape for the Israelites fleeing from Egypt (cf. Zechariah 14:3-5).

f. And, just as the valley through the sea became a death trap for Pharaoh's army pursuing the children of Israel (Exodus 15:2), a crevasse (caused by an earthquake) will open in the valley created for the Israelites' escape from Jerusalem and *"swallow up"* Antimessiah's army *("flood")* pursuing them.

g. Now, the scope of John's vision broadens to include the whole earth. Satan's failure to destroy the Jews in Jerusalem enrages him that much more, so he goes off to destroy *"the rest of her offspring, who keep the commandments of [Yahuah] and have the testimony of [Yahushua the Messiah]."* These spiritual offspring of Israel are the redeemed Believers in Yahushua (cf. John 14:21). They are the seed of Abraham by grace through faith (cf. Romans 4:16; 1 John 2:3; Revelation 1:9; 19:10), who are not exempt from the Great Tribulation, but whom the Lord "catches up" to Heaven before the final plagues of His Wrath (the plagues of the seventh trumpet/bowl judgment) fall on the earth dwellers.

h. And, in time sequence, that brings us to Chapter 13.

Chapter 13—Satan versus the Community of Believers in Yahushua through Antimessiah and the False Prophet

This chapter details how the devil goes about destroying the Followers of Yahushua and others who refuse to take his incarnation's mark and establishing his tyrannical dominion over Earth.

13:1-2 Then I stood on the sand of (a) the sea. And I saw (b) a beast rising up out of the sea, having seven heads and ten horns, and on his horns ten crowns, and on his heads (c) a blasphemous name. Now (d) the beast which I saw was like a leopard, his feet were like the feet of a bear, and his mouth like the mouth of a lion. (e) The dragon gave him his power, his throne, and great authority.

a. This is the mass of humanity (cf. 10:2).
b. This is Antimessiah, the incarnation of Satan. Notice that he is very similar to Satan (12:3) but has crowns on his horns rather than on his heads. The significance of this difference will be clarified when we get to Chapter 17. During the last half of the Final Seven Years, Antimessiah embodies the spirit of Satan and, as we will see, rules over the fourth kingdom described by Daniel (Daniel 7:7), the "Revived Roman Empire."
c. It is not clear what the blasphemous name is, but it must vainly use and violate the name of the Lord (cf. Exodus 20:7).
d. Antimessiah also embodies the spirit of the first three kingdoms described by Daniel (Daniel 7:1-6). Daniel had previously interpreted an image that had been seen in a dream by Nebuchadnezzar, King of Babylon, as representing four ancient empires: Babylon, Medo-Persia, Greece, and Rome (Daniel 2:26-43). The spirit of the beasts of Daniel 7:1-7, although they represent four modern empires, is the same as that of ancient Babylon, Medo-Persia, Greece, and Rome. And all of these empires have one thing in common: They have sought or will seek to oppress and destroy Yahuah's People Israel and Israel's Messiah to prevent His reign on Earth.
e. This confirms that the beast of this chapter is not Satan—He receives his power, throne and authority to rule from the dragon (Satan).

13:3-5 And I saw (a) one of his heads (b) as if it had been mortally wounded, and his deadly wound was healed. And (c) all the world marveled and followed the beast. So they worshiped the dragon who gave authority to the beast; and they worshiped the beast, saying, "Who is like the beast? Who is able to make war with him?" And he was given a mouth speaking great things and blasphemies, and (d) *he was given authority to continue for forty-two months.*

a. As we will see, when we get to 17:9, *"heads"* is synonymous with *"mountains"*—worldly kingdoms or domains.

b. *"As if it had been mortally wounded"* is a misleading translation. The Greek (*hos esphagmenen*) should be translated, "as having been slain." In other words, the kingdom represented by *"one of his heads"* was actually destroyed. Likewise, the literal translation of the next clause, *"and his deadly wound was healed"* (Greek: *kai plege thanatos autos therapeuo*) is "and the wound of his death was healed." So, the kingdom or empire represented by the beast's head that was slain will be revived.[9]

c. Naturally, the whole world, including the Jews and the Followers of Yahushua, who were deceived, no doubt thinking he was the true Messiah, was amazed by the anti-messiah's power in reviving his kingdom that was destroyed by war, followed Him and worshiped both him and his spiritual father Satan/the devil; hence, Antimessiah's name, which means "false messiah."

d. And he was given authority to rule as "Lord of the World" for 42 months (the last half of the seven years) which, as we have seen, will be cut short by the seventh trumpet/bowl judgment (cf. Matthew 24:22). And Scripture does make it clear that Satan, the prince of this world, has the authority to turn the world over to whomever he pleases, as he offered to Yahushua if He would worship him (cf. Matthew 4:9). Antimessiah accepts the offer, becoming the ultimate Satanist.

---

[9]The vast majority of *Bible* prophecy expositors state that the anti-messiah himself will be slain then miraculously revived, causing the whole world to follow after him in awe. However, that is clearly **not** what the text states. Only one of his seven *"heads,"* which 17:9 states is synonymous with *"mountains"* (kingdoms or empires), is, consistent with the personification, *"slain"* (destroyed). In Chapter 17 we will see it is the seventh empire— modern Babylon the Great—that is destroyed then revived as the global empire ruled over by ten *"kings"* (represented in this chapter by ten *"crowns"*) who yield their authority over their individual domains in the empire to Antimessiah.

13:6-10 (a) *Then he opened his mouth in blasphemy against* [Yahuah], *to blaspheme His name, His tabernacle, and those who dwell in heaven.* (b) *It was granted to him to make war with the saints and to overcome them. And* (c) *authority was given him over every tribe, tongue, and nation. All who dwell on the earth will worship him, (d) whose names have not been written in the Book of Life of the Lamb slain from the foundation of the world. (e) If anyone has an ear, let him hear. He who leads into captivity shall go into captivity; he who kills with the sword must be killed with the sword. (f) Here is the patience and the faith of the saints.*

So begins Antimessiah's campaign against Yahuah and His People the Followers of Yahushua.

a. He starts by blaspheming ("cursing in an irreverent manner") Yahuah, His Tabernacle (a temporary dwelling place for Yahuah among His People on Earth—*"Do you not know that your body is the temple of the Holy Spirit?"*—1 Corinthians 6:19), the living creatures, the 24 elders, the angels, and others who dwell in Heaven.

b. Next, he makes war with the Saints (Gr. *hagios*—"holy ones") and overcomes them. Although *"saints"* can refer to either the Jews or the Believers in Yahushua in the *Bible*, here the term seems to refer to the Disciples of Yahushua, because, as Chapter 12 indicates, the Remnant of Israel who have not yet recognized that Yahushua is the Messiah have already fled into and are being protected in the wilderness at this time. After pursuing Israel into the wilderness but failing to destroy her, Satan, through Antimessiah, goes after Yahushua's Followers. More than 50 times the term *"saints"* refers to the Disciples of Yahushua in the *B'rit Hadashah*, including in the Revelation (5:8; 8:3, 4; 14:12; 19:8). There are numerous places in Revelation, as it is written to both the Community of Believers in Yahushua and to the Jews, where *"saints"* refers to both the Jews and the Believers in Yahushua (11:18; 15:3; 16:6; 17:6; 18:24; 20:9). But in the context of Chapter 13, the term seems to refer to the Community of Believers. So, whereas Chapter 12 was primarily about Satan versus the Jews, in Chapter 13 the emphasis is apparently on Antimessiah's campaign to annihilate Yahuah's People the Followers of Yahushua during the Great Tribulation. Notice that this same exact scenario was also prophesied by Daniel: *Then the saints shall be given into his hand for a time and*

times and half a time [three and one-half years—42 months]*"*
(Dan 7:25).

c. Antimessiah is not only given the authority and power to overcome the Saints, he is given the authority to rule the whole, unsaved, perishing world (*"those who dwell on earth"*—a term frequently used in Revelation for the unsaved people of the world—3:10, 6:10, 11:10, here, 13:14, 14:6, 17:8), all of whom will worship him.

d. The earth dwellers—the unsaved, those who worship Antimessiah, the ones who are alien to the Kingdom of Heaven—are those whose names have not been written in the Lamb's Book of Life. And no matter how bad it gets, they will not repent and be saved from the Wrath of Yahuah (cf. 9:20; 16:9; 16:11). They are the *"vessels of wrath fitted to destruction"* spoken of by the Apostle Paul (Romans 9:22).

e. *"If anyone has an ear, let him hear"* is a statement in Scripture that refers to an enigma. In this case it seems to refer to the destiny of Antimessiah (and, by association, his followers): They who take Yahuah's People captive and kill them will "reap what they have sown"—be destroyed in the same way.

f. One purpose of the Revelation is to encourage Yahuah's People to "hang in there" until the end. One way to do that is to let them know exactly what to expect so that they can be prepared for it, patiently and faithfully enduring Antimessiah's persecution, knowing that it will end; and, in the same way that Antimessiah persecutes and kills them, he will be destroyed.

13:11-18 *Then I saw* (a) *another beast coming up out of the earth, and he had two horns like a lamb and spoke like a dragon. And* (b) *he exercises all the authority of the first beast in his presence, and causes the earth and those who dwell in it to worship the first beast, whose deadly wound was healed. He performs great signs, so that he even makes fire come down from heaven on the earth in the sight of men. And* (c) *he deceives those who dwell on the earth by those signs which he was granted to do in the sight of the beast, telling those who dwell on the earth to make an image to the beast who was wounded by the sword and lived. (d) He was granted power to give breath to the image of the beast, that the image of the beast should both speak and cause as many as would not worship the image of the beast to be killed. (e) He causes all, both small and great, rich and poor, free and slave, to receive a mark on their right hand or on their foreheads, and that no one may buy or sell except one who has the mark or the name*

142

*of the beast, or the number of his name. Here is wisdom. Let him who
has understanding* (f) *calculate the number of the beast, for it is the
number of a man:* (g) *His number is 666.* (h)

a. As was suggested in the commentary on 10:2, *"the earth"* seems
    to refer to organized religion. This second beast, having two horns
    like a lamb (a symbol of authority and power combined with reli-
    gious meekness—like Yahushua) is deceitful in that his speech is
    satanic (probably full of lies and blasphemy like that of the first
    beast).
b. This second beast, who is later identified as the False Prophet
    (19:20), is the head of Satan's false, global religion and his chief
    executive for world control. He stands in the presence of
    Antimessiah and falsely prophesies (to "prophesy" is to speak for
    Yahuah) that Antimessiah is "God" (Paul called this *"the lie"*—2
    Thessalonians 2:11), and causes the *"earth"* (members of orga-
    nized religion) and all the earth dwellers to worship the one whose
    fatal wound was healed.
c. Exactly as Paul foretold (cf. 2 Thessalonians 2:3-10), the primary
    method that the False Prophet uses to get the earth dwellers to
    worship Antimessiah is deception (in the same power and authority
    given to Antimessiah to perform incredible, supernatural signs and
    wonders that rival those of the ancient prophets of Yahuah).
d. The most powerfully deceptive and compelling sign is an image of
    Antimessiah made by the earth dwellers, which the False Prophet
    causes to come to life, speak, and cause those who refuse to wor-
    ship it to be killed. It is not difficult to imagine, with today's hol-
    ographic technology, how a life-like image that speaks could be
    made, but this image actually comes to life and causes people to be
    killed. And, just as a holographic image can be projected any-
    where in the world (as Al Gore's was when he opened the Live
    Earth concert series from Sydney, Australia, and his holographic
    image was projected onto a stage in Tokyo, Japan, on July 7,
    2007), it is not that difficult to imagine how an image of
    Antimessiah could be projected anywhere and simultaneously eve-
    rywhere in the world to facilitate total world control.
e. Another way the False Prophet facilitates control of the earth
    dwellers is to permanently identify each with a *"mark,"* and to al-
    low only those with the mark to buy or sell, effectively isolating
    and/or starving to death all those who refuse to take the mark. The
    mark is specifically identified as the name of the beast (the *"blas-*

143

phemous name," whatever that is—13:1) or the number of that name. It is also easy to imagine how, with today's technology, a person could be implanted with a micro-computer chip that could be read or with some kind of bar code that could be scanned, accessing all of that person's information. And computers exist (e.g., the NSA computer in Fort Meade, Maryland, and the EU computer in Brussels, Belgium) that could be used to hold information about and track every individual on the earth.

f. This statement confirms that Antimessiah is not a spiritual or allegorical being or entity, a group or category of people, or a kingdom or nation; he is a man, a person, a human being—the false messiah.

g. And he is identified by the number *666*. Theories as to what *666* represents are endless, and Yahuah has not given this commentator insight into what it means. He will venture only a common-sense opinion: The number *7* represents perfection or completeness—it is the number of Yahuah. So, *777* could represent the Trinity—Yahuah the Father, Yahuah the Son, and Yahuah the Holy Spirit. The number *6* represents imperfect man —"*a little lower than the angels* [Hebrew: *elohim* – gods]" (Psalm 8:3). So, *666* could represent the unholy trinity—Satan the father, Antimessiah the son, and the False Prophet, executor of the will of Satan on Earth—or man putting himself in the place of Yahuah. *666* may well represent a specific name, but until Antimessiah is specifically identified, and he will be (cf. 2 Thessalonians 2:3), perhaps this is a step in the direction of understanding who he is. The "*number of the name*" may simply refer to the fact that the name of the beast is converted to a number which can be read by a scanner, of which, of course, no one had any concept at the time Revelation was written.

h. So, this second half of the seven years includes the Great Tribulation (Antimessiah pursuing the Jews into the wilderness then persecuting and killing Yahuah's People the Followers of Yahushua); then the Day of the Lord begins with the events of the sixth seal, the sealing of the 144,000, and a preview of the raptured Saints in Heaven, followed by the Wrath of Yahuah falling on the earth dwellers. This whole period of time is called The Birthpains of the Messiah (Hebrew: *Chevlai shel Mashiach*) and The Time of Jacob's Trouble (Jeremiah 30:7), because it will be a time of such persecution, suffering, and devastation of Yahuah's People before the Messiah returns to give birth to His Kingdom that it is compared to the pains of a woman in the labor of childbirth (cf. Micah 4:9, 10; 1 Thessalonians 5:3).

Chapter 14—The Gospel According to the Revelation

In the commentaries that I have read, there is a lot of confusion about this chapter—what the images and events mean and where they fit in the sequence of events of the Final Seven Years. However, as with every other part of the Revelation, when we step back and consider this chapter in a literal, common-sense manner, in the light of other relevant Scriptures, it comes clearly into focus. So, to facilitate that clarification before we get into the verse-by-verse commentary, the following overview of Chapter 14 is offered:

The events of this chapter are not in strict chronological sequence or scope, but in giving us more details of what happens during the second half of the Final Seven Years and after that, they focus on a very important theme that is appropriately in focus at this point in the Revelation: the Gospel. The term *"gospel"* is the translation of a Greek word (*euaggelion*) which literally means "good tidings" or "good news." We also get our term "evangelize" from *euaggelion*. The Gospel is a key theme throughout the *B'rit Hadashah*, the term appearing 100 times there. Yahushua's final words to his Disciples before He ascended into Heaven comprise what we call the "Great Commission"—His directive to take the Gospel to all the world, proclaiming it to *"every creature"* (Mark 16:15). Why? Because it is through the proclamation of the Gospel that people, both Jews and Gentiles, are saved—brought out of this sinful, doomed world into the glorious Kingdom of Yahuah (Romans 1:16)!

And that gives us a clue as to why this chapter is inserted at this particular point in Revelation—immediately following the description of the wrath of Satan against Israel and her children in Chapter 12 and the description of Antimessiah's persecution of the Community of Believers in Yahushua in Chapter 13. It is inserted here to encourage Yahuah's People to, in the face of "great tribulation," "endure to the end" (cf. verses 12 and 13 vis-à-vis Matthew 24:13).

The Gospel is three-fold in the *B'rit Hadashah*: the Gospel of the establishment of the Kingdom of Yahuah on Earth, including the destruction of the enemies of Yahuah and His People, which is promised especially to the Jews; the Gospel of the salvation of the Followers of Yahushua; and the *"everlasting gospel"* (verse 6), which is the promise of the eternal Kingdom of Heaven to all of Yahuah's People. All aspects of the Gospel are reflected in this chapter: the Kingdom of Yahuah on Earth and in Heaven in verses 1-6, the destruction of the enemies of Yahuah and His People in verses 8-11 and 17-20, and the salvation of the Disciples of Yahushua in verses 12-16.

14:1-5 (a) *Then I looked, and behold,* (b) *a Lamb standing on Mount Zion, and with Him* (c) *one hundred and forty-four thousand, having His Father's name written on their foreheads.* (d) *And I heard a voice from heaven, like the voice of many waters, and like the voice of loud thunder. And I heard* (e) *the sound of harpists playing their harps.* (f) *They sang as it were a new song before the throne, before the four living creatures, and the elders; and* (g) *no one could learn that song except the hundred and forty-four thousand who were* (h) *redeemed from the earth. These are* (i) *the ones who were not defiled with women, for they are virgins. These are the ones who follow the Lamb wherever He goes. These were redeemed from among men, being* (j) *firstfruits to* [v] *and to the Lamb. And in their mouth was found no deceit, for* (k) *they are without fault before the throne of [Yahuah].* (l)

a. In the sequence of events, this episode apparently occurs following the events of the sixth seal, which announce the Day of Yahuah, because the 144,000 are not sealed until after the cataclysmic events of the sixth seal while the four angels are holding back the winds of Yahuah's wrath (7:4). So it is appropriately inserted here, immediately following the description of the tyrannical reign of Antimessiah (alluded to in 6:2, 9), to highlight the ultimate victory of the Messiah and His chosen People over Antimessiah—which is part of the Gospel.

b. John sees the Lord Yahushua (He is called the "*Lamb*" throughout Revelation—27 times) standing on Mount Zion, the highest mountain in Jerusalem. (Jerusalem is also referred to as "*Zion, the city of David,*" in Scripture—i.e., 2 Samuel 5:7.) There is no indication anywhere in Scripture (except figuratively—e.g., Hebrews 12:22) that there is a Mount Zion in Heaven.

c. There is no reason to think that these are other than the 144,000 of Israel who were sealed on their foreheads to protect them from the wrath of Satan and the Wrath of Yahuah (7:3).

d. Perhaps this is the voice of the Lord (cf. 1:5) combined with the voice of others in Heaven (cf. 6:1; 10:3).

e. Apparently, this refers to the Redeemed in Heaven who are standing before the throne on the sea of glass mingled with fire, having the harps of Yahuah (15:2). Time is transcended in Heaven, so here John sees the Redeemed of the past, present, and future who are in Heaven.

f. Previously, the four living creatures and 24 elders had sung a new song (5:8, 9), but here it is sung *"**before** the four living creatures and 24 elders."* There are numerous passages in the *Tanakh*, especially in the Psalms, that speak of the new song. See especially Psalm 144:9 which speaks of singing a new song and playing a harp.

g. This apparently means that none **on Earth**, other than the 144,000 of Israel, could learn the new song that was being sung by the Redeemed in Heaven.

h. The 144,000 are among the Redeemed, but this apparently does not refer to the Redeemed who are in Heaven, because Israel was also called redeemed when the Lord brought them out of Egypt (Deuteronomy 13:5). These may be those who were "redeemed" when Yahuah enabled them to escape from Satan into the wilderness then sealed them on their foreheads.

i. If this is to be taken literally, this is a very special group, who, like the apostle Paul (cf. 1 Corinthians 7:7), remain unmarried so that they can devote themselves totally to the Lord, following Him wherever He goes. But, it may simply refer to the fact that they are a portion of the Remnant of true Israel who have not been absorbed by the world into which they were dispersed and have remained faithful to the Lord. Ancient Israel was also called, in several passages, *"the virgin daughter of Zion"* (e.g., 2 Kings 19:21) or *"the virgin of Israel"* (e.g., Jeremiah 18:13).

j. The children of Israel were called *"firstfruits"* when the Lord brought them out of Egypt (Jeremiah 2:3). In other words, the ones Yahuah saved from Egypt were the firstfruits of the people chosen by Yahuah to become the nation Israel. Then, regarding modern-day Israel, Paul wrote, *"If the **firstfruit** is holy, the lump* [mass] *is also holy"* (Romans 11:16). According to Jewish interpreters, this is a saying that means the firstfruits of Israel (the 144,000 in Revelation) must be sanctified (saved) before the whole nation can be saved, which Romans 11:26 says will happen.

k. This is problematic because, from its first impression, it sounds like the 144,000 are standing before the throne in Heaven. The problem is solved, however, when we remember that it is *"the accuser of the brethren,"* who can find no fault in the 144,000, who is in Heaven before the throne accusing them day and night (cf. 12:10).

l. In summary, the 144,000 seem to be those of the twelve tribes of Israel who, because of their unwavering devotion to the Lord and faith in the coming Messiah, are chosen for a special task during the Final Seven Years. Apparently, as the firstfruits of those who are saved out of Israel, after they flee Modern Babylon, they will lead many of their Israelite brethren out of the nations of the world back to the land of Israel (cf. Jeremiah 50:4-8, 16), witnessing to them that Yahushua is the true Messiah. Indicative that they are protected in a miraculous way during the latter half of the seven years—the time of the Great Tribulation of the terrible, despotic reign of Antimessiah—is that here, *"following the Lamb wherever He goes,"* they appear with Him on Mount Zion.

14:6-13 *Then I saw (a) another angel flying in the midst of heaven, (b) having the everlasting gospel to preach to those who dwell on the earth—to every nation, tribe, tongue, and people—saying with a loud voice, "Fear [Yahuah] and give glory to Him, for the hour of His judgment has come; and worship Him who made heaven and earth, the sea and springs of water." And (c) another angel followed, saying, "Babylon is fallen, is fallen, that great city, because she has made all nations drink of the wine of the wrath of her fornication." Then (d) a third angel followed them, saying with a loud voice, "If anyone worships the beast and his image, and receives his mark on his forehead or on his hand, he himself shall also drink of the wine of the wrath of [Yahuah], which is poured out full strength into the cup of His indignation. He shall be tormented with fire and brimstone in the presence of the holy angels and in the presence of the Lamb. And the smoke of their torment ascends "forever" and ever; and they have no rest day or night, who worship the beast and his image, and whoever receives the mark of his name." Here is the patience of the saints; here are those who keep the commandments of [Yahuah] and the faith of [Yahushua]. Then I heard a voice from heaven saying to me, "Write: 'Blessed are the dead who die in the Lord from now on.'" "Yes," says the Spirit, "that they may rest from their labors, and their works follow them."*

a. Prior to the appearance of the three angels of this chapter, the first angel seen flying *"in the midst of Heaven"* was the angel who announced the three woes (8:13).

b. The first angel seen here announces the judgment of Yahuah. Notice that this angel preaches the *"everlasting gospel* [good news]."

But, for whom could these announcements of gloom and doom, the judgment of the Lord, possibly be good news? There is no mention of hope or salvation for the earth dwellers here, not even a call to repentance. There is only the proclamation of their judgment and "eternal" punishment, and the command to worship the Creator, as all earth dwellers, even though they have rejected the saving grace of Yahuah, will in the end be compelled to do (Philippians 2:10, 11). Although there is a warning not to take the mark of the beast, it appears to be directed to the Saints who are still on the earth enduring the persecution of Antimessiah and his followers during the Great Tribulation. As we continue to read, we see that the good news (Gospel) of the judgment and destruction of their enemies is for the encouragement of the Redeemed—for those who are being killed and who, like the 6:11 martyrs, cry out, "*How long, O Lord, holy and true, until You judge and avenge our blood on those who dwell on the earth?*" So John writes (verse 12), "*Here is the patience of the saints.*" The Lord is saying to His beloved Bride, "Look, good news: the judgment of Yahuah has already started to come on your persecutors; Babylon has been destroyed. So don't take Antimessiah's mark, continue to worship Yahuah, be patient, and in the end you will be saved."

c. This announcement of the destruction of Babylon seems out of sequence. But, as will be seen when we get to Chapters 17 and 18, there are **two** destructions of Babylon (indicated here by the repetition, "*is fallen, is fallen*"): one before the midpoint of the seven years, and one at the end of the seven years.

d. This is a warning and word of encouragement to the Community of Believers in Yahushua and to those Jews and Yahuah-fearing Gentiles who, although they do not yet recognize that Yahushua is the Messiah, will not take the mark of the anti-messiah following the Rapture: "Do not take the mark like have the earth dwellers whose end is 'eternal' torment in the lake of fire and brimstone. Remain faithful until the end. And if you should die in your faith in the coming Messiah, rejoice, for you are blessed. You will rest from your labors and you will be rewarded in Heaven for your good works done on Earth in the name of the Lord Yahuah."

14:14-20 (a) *Then I looked, and behold, a white cloud, and on the cloud sat* (b) *One like the Son of Man, having on His head a golden crown, and in His hand a sharp sickle. And another angel came out of the temple, crying with a loud voice to Him who sat on the cloud,*

151

"Thrust in Your sickle and reap, for the time has come for You to reap, for the harvest of the earth is ripe." So (c) He who sat on the cloud thrust in His sickle on the earth, and the earth was reaped. Then another angel came out of the temple which is in heaven, he also having a sharp sickle. And (d) another angel came out from the altar, who had power over fire, and he cried with a loud cry to him who had the sharp sickle, saying, "Thrust in your sharp sickle and gather the clusters of the vine of the earth, for her grapes are fully ripe." So (e) the angel thrust his sickle into the earth and gathered the vine of the earth, and threw it into the great winepress of the wrath of [Yahuah]. And the winepress was trampled outside the city, and blood came out of the winepress, up to the horses' bridles, for one thousand six hundred furlongs.

a. These events apparently foretell the fulfillment of Yahushua's prophetic parable of the tares of the field (Matthew 13:24-43). In that parable, a farmer plants his wheat seeds, but an enemy comes along and sows the seeds of tares (weeds) in the field. Then, the tares and the wheat sprout together. The farmer's workers ask him if they should remove the tares, to which he replies, *"No, let them grow together until the harvest, lest you uproot the wheat along with the tares."* Later, his Disciples asked Yahushua the meaning of the parable. He replied that the planter of the good seeds is the *"Son of Man"* (Yahushua), the field is the world, the good seeds are the *"sons of the kingdom"* (the children of Yahuah), the tares are the *"sons of the wicked one,"* and the enemy who sows them is the devil. The saints and the earth dwellers will continue together until the *"harvest"* at the *"end of this age,"* at which time,

> *The Son of Man will send out His Angels, and they will gather out of His kingdom all things that offend, and those who practice lawlessness, and will cast them into the furnace of fire. There will be wailing and gnashing of teeth. Then the righteous will shine forth as the sun in the kingdom of their Father.*

b. Notice that those who do the reaping of the harvest, both of the saved and the lost, are angels sent out by the Lord. So, *"One"* in verse 14 should not be capitalized, as it is in the NKJV. Also, see the comment on 1:13 regarding *"the Son of Man."* He, like the angel of 10:1, is an angel who clearly represents the Messiah, but he is not the Messiah. Another clue that he is an angel rather than the Messiah is that another angel, who comes out of the Temple, the dwelling place of Yahuah, commands him to reap. It is doubtful that any angel will tell the Lord Yahushua what to do, especially when angels will do the reaping.

c. So the angel who represents the Messiah reaps the harvest of the wheat—the Redeemed of Yahuah.

d. But, there is another harvest. And the reaping of this harvest is commanded by another angel—one who comes out from the altar and who has *"power over fire."* If this angel comes out from the altar of incense, from which the prayers of the Saints are offered up with the incense being burned (cf. 8:3-4), then the second harvest may be in answer to the prayers of the martyrs, pleading, *"How long, O Lord, holy and true, until You judge and avenge our blood on those who dwell on the earth?"* (6:10)

e. And the angel who represents the Messiah harvests *"the clusters of the vine of the earth"* (the "grapes of wrath") and throws them into *"the winepress of the Wrath of [Yahuah],"* where their blood flows out to such an extent that it fills up wherever they are to a depth of five to six feet, approximately 7.25 miles in length (indicating a massive slaughter). Some have linked this second harvest to the final battle between the Messiah and His adversaries (cf. 16:14-16; 19:11-21), but it is apparently more comprehensive than that, including not only the annihilation of the Messiah's enemies, the *"kings of the earth and of **the whole world** [universe]"* (16:14), but of *"mighty men, captains* [military leaders]; *horses and of those who sit on them* [military equipment and soldiers]; [and] ***all people, both small and great"*** (19:18, 19). It also includes capturing Antimessiah and the False Prophet and casting them alive into the lake of fire (19:20), and finally, casting all enemies of Yahuah, including the devil (20:10), Death, and Hades (20:14), and *"anyone not found written in the Book of Life"* (20:15), into the lake of fire (the *"furnace of fire"* in the parable).

So, Chapter 14 is included at this point in the Revelation to encourage and assure all of Yahuah's People—the Jews, the Yahuah - fearing Gentiles, and the Community of Believers in Yahushua—who are in the midst of great tribulation, to remain faithful to The End, because **all** of their enemies are being judged and will continue to be judged . . . all the way until the Final Judgment at the end of the Millennium.

153

Chapter 15—Precursors to the Bowls of Wrath

Now that we have completed the parenthetical details of Chapters 10-14, the seventh trumpet has sounded prompting those in Heaven to praise the Lord for bringing the Final Seven Years to culmination in restoring the kingdom of this world to Himself and to His Messiah (11:15), and ominous warnings of the final plagues of Yahuah's judgments have occurred (11:19), we are back to the description of the events that initiate those *"last plagues"* of the *"Wrath of Yahuah"* being poured out.

15:1-8 *Then I saw another sign in heaven, great and marvelous: seven angels having* (a) *the seven last plagues, for in them the wrath of [Yahuah] is complete. And I saw something like* (b) *a sea of glass mingled with fire, and* (c) *those who have the victory over the beast, over his image and over his mark and over the number of his name, standing on the sea of glass, having harps of [Yahuah].* (d) *They sing the song of Moses, the servant of [Yahuah], and the song of the Lamb, saying: "Great and marvelous are Your works, Lord [Yahuah] Almighty! Just and true are Your ways, O King of the saints! Who shall not fear You, O Lord, and glorify Your name? For You alone are holy. For* (e) *all nations shall come and worship before You, for Your judgments have been manifested." After these things I looked, and behold, the temple of the tabernacle of the testimony in heaven was opened. And out of the temple came* (f) *the seven angels having the seven plagues, clothed in* (g) *pure bright linen, and having their chests girded with golden bands. Then one of the four living creatures gave to the seven angels seven golden bowls full of the wrath of [Yahuah] who lives "forever" and ever.* (h) *The temple was filled with smoke from the glory of [Yahuah] and from His power, and no one was able to enter the temple till the seven plagues of the seven angels were completed.*

a. But now we have a problem with sequence (cf. Footnote 7, Chapter 8). Do the trumpet judgments and bowl judgments occur simultaneously or do the trumpet judgments precede the bowl judgments? This section (15:1-8), following the description of the trumpet judgments in chapters 8, 9 and 11, makes it seem like the bowl judgments follow the trumpet judgments and are the *"seven last plagues."* Also, the descriptions of the first, second, third, fourth and sixth trumpet judgments state that **a third** of the natural creation and humans are affected by the trumpet plagues, but the descriptions of the corresponding bowl plagues state that **the entire** natural creation and **all** inhabitants of Earth (except those protected by the Lord) are affected.

However, there are some strong indications that the trumpet and bowl plagues occur simultaneously and are different aspects or different phases of the same judgments. There are remarkable similarities between the plagues of the trumpet and bowl judgments, and they occur in the same sequence: The first trumpet and bowl judgments impact the earth (8:7; 16:2); the second judgments impact the sea (8:8; 16:3); the third impact the sources of fresh water (8:10; 16:4); the fourth impact the sun (8:12; 16:8); the fifth cause humans to be physically tormented (9:1; 16:10); the sixth impact the Euphrates River (9:14; 16:12). Finally, before the seventh trumpet sounds, an angel declares that the *"mystery of [Yahuah] would be finished"* (10:7). Then, also before the trumpet sounds, the two witnesses are killed, resurrected and ascend to Heaven (which occurs on the last day of the Final Seven Years), and there is an earthquake that collapses a tenth of Jerusalem killing seven thousand people (11:7-14). Then, when the seventh trumpet sounds, loud voices are heard from Heaven proclaiming the transformation of the *"kingdoms of this world"* into the Messianic Kingdom (11:15) (the same exultation as that of the multitude in Heaven following the destruction of Babylon after the final plague described in the Revelation is poured out on that kingdom [cf. 18:21; 19:1-6]). Finally (following the sounding of the seventh trumpet), there are "lightnings, noises, thundering, an earthquake and great hail" (11:19). Now, notice this: **Exactly the same events occur** when the seventh angel pours out his bowl of Yahuah's wrath: "noises and thunderings and lightnings . . . a great earthquake," the partial destruction of Jerusalem, the total destruction of Babylon . . . and "great hail" (16:17-21).

So, it is hard to deny, isn't it, with all these "coincidences" between the trumpet and bowl judgments, that they are just different aspects or phases of the same judgments? (The bowl judgments, rather than being separate from and following the trumpet judgments, may be basically the same but more intense phases of those judgments.) And understanding that the plagues of each of the seven trumpet/bowl judgments can be caused by the same types of cometary impact makes it all the more certain that the catastrophes of the trumpet and bowl judgments are basically the same events.

So why does this verse, which follows the descriptions of the trumpet judgments way back in chapters 8, 9 and 11, seem to indicate that the bowl judgments, the descriptions of which follow in Chapter 16, are the *"seven last plagues"* in which *"the wrath of Yahuah is complete"*? A clue to the answer might be that Chapter 15 is the perspective from Heaven, which, as has been previously noted in this commentary, transcends time and views events on Earth as a mural rather than as a strict time-line sequence of events. So, from Heaven's point of view, the *"seven last plagues"* might include the plagues of both the trumpet and bowl judgments. In fact, Chapter 15 seems to be an overview of all the events of the Day and the Wrath of the Lord, from Heaven's point of view, during the last half of the Final Seven Years.

Nevertheless, it is possible that the bowl plagues, compacted into a short period of time following the seventh and final trumpet blast, will follow the trumpet plagues and be the *"seven last plagues"* of *"the Wrath of Yahuah."* But it is clear that the final plagues, whether they are the plagues of the seventh trumpet/bowl judgment or the plagues of all seven bowls of wrath, by which the surface features of the earth and all those remaining on Earth who have rejected the Gospel message and have taken the mark of the beast are destroyed, **will literally occur.** And, they will occur at the end of the Final Seven Years following the blast of the seventh trumpet, the resurrection and ascension of the two witnesses and the resurrection, transformation and catching up of the Redeemed of the Lord (see "Appendix 6—When is 'The Rapture'"?).

b. Cf. 4:6

c. Cf. 14:2-3

d. The praises of the Redeemed in Heaven (cf. 7:14), singing the song of Moses and of the Lamb, continue.

e. This must refer to the nations formed from the descendants of the tribes of Israel, including the descendants of Ephraim (a *"multitude of nations"*) (Genesis 48:19), plus the Gentile nations who will inhabit the millennial Messianic Kingdom (cf. Zechariah 14:16-17), because all present-age unbelievers will have been killed (cf. 19:18, 21).

f. These are executioners of the final Wrath of Yahuah. Notice the references to purity and value—pure linen, golden bands, golden bowls.

g. The purpose of the final manifestations of Yahuah's Wrath is to cleanse Earth of all corruption, restoring its value and consecrating it as the pure, unpolluted creation of Yahuah.

h. No one can approach Yahuah when His glory is manifested in His sovereign works of consecration (e.g., 2 Chronicles 7:1, 2).

Chapter 16—The Events of the Seven Bowls of Wrath

16:1-11 *Then I heard* (a) *a loud voice from the temple saying to* (b) *the seven angels, "Go and pour out the bowls of the wrath of [Yahuah] on the earth." So the first went and poured out his bowl upon the earth, and* (c) *a foul and loathsome sore came upon the men who had the mark of the beast and those who worshiped his image. Then the second angel poured out his bowl on the sea, and* (d) *it became blood as of a dead man; and every living creature in the sea died. Then the third angel poured out his bowl on the rivers and springs of water, and* (e) *they became blood. And I heard* (f) *the angel of the waters saying: "You are righteous, O Lord, the One who is and who was and who is to be, because You have judged these things.* (g) *For they have shed the blood of saints and prophets, and You have given them blood to drink. For it is their just due." And I heard another from the altar saying, "Even so, Lord [Yahuah] Almighty, true and righteous are your judgments." Then the fourth angel poured out his bowl on the sun, and power was given to him to scorch men with fire. And (h) men were scorched with great heat, and* (i) *they blasphemed the name of [Yahuah] who has power over these plagues; and they did not repent and give Him glory. Then the fifth angel poured out his bowl on* (j) *the throne of the beast, and his kingdom became* (k) *full of darkness; and they gnawed their tongues because of the pain.* (l) *They blasphemed the God of heaven because of their pains and their sores, and did not repent of their deeds.*

a. This must be the voice of Yahuah telling the angels what to do, because we have just been told that no one can enter the Temple until the seven final plagues are completed because it is filled with smoke from the glory of Yahuah and His power (15:8).
b. Perhaps, since the plagues of the trumpet judgments and the plagues of the bowl judgments are apparently different aspects or phases of the same judgments, the same seven angels both blow the trumpets and pour out the bowls of wrath.
c. The Greek term for *"sore"* (*helkos*) indicates a particularly painful and disgusting sore, like a boil oozing pus that is potentially fatal if not healed. As was noted in the commentary on the first trumpet judgment (8:7), comet fragments impacting the earth or exploding in the atmosphere produce very similar effects to those of nuclear bomb explosions, including toxic fallout. Scientific studies have shown that when comets or comet fragments impact another celes-

159

tial object (planet, moon, asteroid and so forth), all kinds of hazardous substances (ammonia, sulfur, nitrous oxide, cyanide and so forth) are released into the atmosphere, and some of them react with the elements in the atmosphere producing substances (like nitric acid) that will indeed produce *"foul and loathsome"* sores on human beings.

d. This is saltwater turning to "blood," as with the second trumpet plague; except with this plague, because it is *"blood as of a dead man"* (not oxygenated—no life in it), **all** salt-water creatures, which take their oxygen from the water in which they swim, die. Again, blood separated from a living body is symbolic of death in Scripture. So, this reference to the sea turning to blood is apparently a figurative reference to death in the sea. Also, some of the substances in comets react with water turning it red, so this might also be a reference to that phenomenon.

e. Coincidental with the third trumpet plague, the fresh water also turns to "blood" (lifeless).

f. Apparently, angels are assigned to various parts of Yahuah's creation.

g. Yahuah's judgments are just and appropriate for the offense, in this case "drinking blood" ("tasting death") for shedding the blood of (murdering) the saints and prophets.

h. Searing, unbearable heat. This may be caused by cometary impact explosions destroying the protective ozone layer surrounding the earth. Also, this verse and others (e.g. Isaiah 30:26; Malachi 4:1) seem to indicate that massive corona ejections (sun flares) may be involved in the plagues of the Wrath of the Lord.

i. The earth dwellers will not repent but, realizing that it is Yahuah who is causing these plagues, blaspheme Him and refuse all the more to worship Him.

j. This plague targets the *"throne* [seat of authority] *of the beast"* (Antimessiah). Rather than the throne of the beast referring to a specific location, it probably is the whole earth, over which the anti-messiah has temporarily been given dominion (cf. 13:5, 7), because his entire *"kingdom"* (Earth) is filled with darkness by this plague.

k. Scientific studies have shown that a comet fragment just six miles in diameter impacting the earth at 25,000 miles per hour will produce the equivalent explosive force of **billions** of nuclear bombs and smoke, ash and debri that will darken the light from the sun

160

and reduce temperatures drastically all over the earth for months or even years.

l. But, in spite of all these torturous plagues, the earth dwellers who have received the mark of the beast and worship him **still** refuse to repent and they continue to blaspheme the Most High God.

16:12-16 *Then* (a) *the sixth angel poured out his bowl on the great river Euphrates, and its water was dried up, so that the way of* (b) *the kings from the east might be prepared. And I saw* (c) *three unclean spirits like frogs coming out of the mouth of the dragon, out of the mouth of the beast, and out of the mouth of the false prophet. For they are spirits of demons, performing signs, which go out to the kings of the earth and of the whole world, to gather them to the battle of that great day of [Yahuah] Almighty.* (d) *"Behold, I am coming as a thief. Blessed is he who watches, and keeps his garments, lest he walk naked and they see his shame." And they gathered them together to the place called in Hebrew,* (e) *Armageddon.*

a. The sixth angel prepares the way for the kings of the east to bring their armies to Israel.
b. Some, in connecting this plague to 9:16, think it refers to an army of two hundred million from China, which is capable of mobilizing such an army. But, as was explained in the commentary on 9:16-19, although the two hundred million *"horsemen,"* breathing fire, smoke and brimstone, by no stretch of the imagination fit the description of a human army, they match the description of small, boulder-size comet fragments perfectly. So, although the drying up of the Euphrates does apparently clear the way for the kings of the east who, along with the kings of the other nations of the world and their armies, advance on Jerusalem, the two hundred million of Chapter 9 are **not** those armies.
c. The unclean spirits from Satan, Antimessiah and the False Prophet go out, as demons, to the rulers of *"the earth and of the whole world"* (both human and spiritual—cf. the commentary on 14:19), and, through miraculous signs, entice them to gather their armies for the battle that will climax the Day of the Lord.
d. This battle is linked with the surprise coming of the Lord (cf. 1 Thessalonians 5:2) with the armies of Heaven (19:14) to destroy His enemies and restore His kingdom on Earth (19:15-21; 20:4).
e. The Hebrew is *Har-Megiddon* (the "mountain of Megiddo"). This is, according to most commentators, a reference to the 15-

161

mile-wide battle plain of the Valley of Jezreel in the northern part of Israel where numerous famous battles in Israel's history took place. The city of Megiddo was located there. However, Charles Cooper of Prewrath Resource Institute (www.prewrathrapture.com) builds a strong case that there is no such place as "Armageddon" (there was no mountain named Megiddo), which he suggests is both a mistranslation and mistransliteration of the term "Har Moed," which is another Biblical name for Mount Zion. If Cooper is correct, the final battle between the *"kings of the earth"* and the King of Kings will be centered on Jerusalem, which seems to concur with other passages of Scripture (cf. Zechariah 12:2; 14:2; Micah 4:11-12; Revelation 14:19-20; et al.).

16:17-21 *Then the seventh angel poured out his bowl into the air, and* (a) *a loud voice came out of the temple of heaven, from the throne, saying, "It is done!" And* (b) *there were noises and thunderings and lightnings; and there was a great earthquake, such a mighty and great earthquake as had not occurred since men were on the earth.* (c) *Now the great city was divided into three parts, and the cities of the nations fell. And* (d) *great Babylon was remembered before [Yahuah], to give her the cup of the wine of the fierceness of His wrath.* (e) *Then every island fled away, and the mountains were not found.* (f) *And great hail from heaven fell upon men, each hailstone about the weight of a talent.* (g) *Men blasphemed [Yahuah] because of the plague of the hail, since that plague was exceedingly great.*

Just as Pharaoh and the citizens of Egypt were given ten plagues as warnings to repent and let Yahuah's People go before the Hebrews were led out of Egypt and Paraoh and his entire army perished in the Red Sea (Exodus 7:10-12:30; 14:27-29), Antimessiah and his followers are given a series of plagues, but they repeatedly and continuously refuse to repent. Now, their time is up; after the completion of the plagues of the previous six judgments and the sounding of the seventh and final trumpet (10:7; 11:15), they are all destroyed.

All the prophecies (Isaiah 13:6, 9; Jeremiah 46:10; Joel 1:15; 2:12; Amos 5:18, 20; Obadiah 1:15; Zephaniah 1:14-18; 3:8; et al.) regarding the climax of the Day of the Lord, one of the most frequently prophesied events in the *Bible*, converge in these few verses. As was mentioned in the commentary on 6:17, the term, *"Day of the Lord,"* involves much more than this battle or this single day. It includes the return of the Messiah to gather His Bride and take her to Heaven, all the events of the Wrath of Yahuah, the establishment of the millennial kingdom of the Lord, and the Final Judgment. But **this one day, when all the remaining enemies of the Lord, spiritual and human, and the earth corrupted by them are destroyed, is the climax that Israel has been anticipating throughout her history**. Apparently, the Battle of "Armageddon" has already occurred and the armies of the *"kings of the earth"* have been destroyed when the following events occur:

a. The voice of the Lord speaks again from the Temple in Heaven.

b. The (climax of) the Day of the Lord begins with the usual ominous noises, thunderings, and lightnings, but they are immediately followed by the greatest earthquake in history by far. This earthquake could be caused by the cumulative effect of all the previous cometary impacts with the earth.

c. The earthquake causes the *"great city"* to divide into three parts. There are two cities in Revelation called *"the great city"*— Jerusalem (11:8) and modern, prophetic Babylon (17:18; 18:10)— which are the antitheses of one another. The instance in this verse appears to refer to Jerusalem, because she is distinguished from the cities of the nations, of which Babylon is the prototype. And the purpose of this verse seems to be to contrast the fate of each on the Day of the Lord:

d. Babylon in her second destruction (the first occurred prior to the midpoint of the seven years) is not just split into sections, as is the *"great city"* of this verse, but is totally annihilated—physically made to disappear from the earth (18:21). Details of Babylon's two destructions are given in the next two Chapters, 17 and 18.

e. This indicates radical changes in the topography of the earth. Both the islands and the mountains disappear, leaving only the level continents. There is a theory that, in the beginning, when the world was first created, the dry land of the earth was one, huge continent. Apparently, this cataclysm is in preparation for the restoration of Earth to its original, Edenic state.

f. This is the final plague to be directly poured out on human beings.

g. And they blasphemed Yahuah even as they were dying. Who could possibly survive 100-pound "hailstones" (boulder-size comet fragments), especially after all the other plagues?—only those specially protected by Yahuah—the chosen Remnant of physical Isra-

el and the Yahuah-fearing Gentiles who have not taken the mark of
Antimessiah and who had helped the Jews during the Final Seven
Years.

Chapters 17 and 18 are parenthetical chapters inserted to give more details about the destruction of modern, prophetic Babylon—the kingdom of Satan on Earth (cf. Isaiah 14:4)—immediately before and during the Final Seven Years of world history. Chapter 17 focuses on spiritual, religious Babylon and Chapter 18 focuses on material, secular Babylon. But, as we will clearly see, the two are inextricably intertwined in one, great, modern city-state (nation). In the original Greek, there were not two separate chapters describing Babylon; the description was of two different aspects of the same city-state/nation/empire. And understanding the identity and destiny of *"Babylon the Great"* is a major key to understanding the sequence of events of the Revelation. But Chapters 17 and 18 are highly symbolic—in the form of a riddle. Let us see if we, by the enlightenment of the Holy Spirit, can solve the riddle.

Chapter 17—Spiritual, Religious Babylon

17:1-5 *Then (a) one of the seven angels who had the seven bowls came and talked with me, saying to me, "Come, I will show you the judgment of (b) the great harlot (c) who sits on many waters, (d) with whom the kings of the earth committed fornication, and the inhabitants of the earth were made drunk with the wine of her fornication." So he carried me away in the Spirit into (e) the wilderness. And I saw a woman (f) sitting on a scarlet beast which was full of names of blasphemy, having seven heads and ten horns. The woman was (g) arrayed in purple and scarlet, and adorned with gold and precious stones and pearls, having in her hand a golden cup full of abominations and the filthiness of her fornication. And on her forehead a name was written: (h) MYSTERY, BABYLON THE GREAT, THE MOTHER OF HARLOTS AND OF THE ABOMINATIONS OF THE EARTH.*

a.   This angel is probably the seventh, as it was during the pouring out of his bowl that *"Babylon was remembered before [Yahuah], to give her the cup of the wine of the fierceness of His wrath"* (16:19). In this chapter and in Chapter 18, he is giving John more details about the identity, characteristics, and destiny of modern, prophetic Babylon.

b.   In both Chapters 17 and 18 (18:3), Babylon is described as a harlot—one who gives herself to others, not because she loves them or is interested in their welfare, but to gain their favors, which ultimately results in their destruction as well as hers. In this chapter the emphasis is on her spiritual/religious harlotry; in Chapter 18 the emphasis is on her political/commercial harlotry.

c. She sits on (dominates and controls) the earth dwellers (cf. verse 15).

d. Her seductive enticements entangle all classes of earth dwellers, nobility as well as the masses.

e. The *"wilderness"* in this verse is a symbol of the unsaved world.

f. The harlot is supported by and empowered by Satan. She is his spiritual kingdom on earth (cf. Isaiah 14:4, 12; Revelation 12:3).

g. Her attractions—riches, beauty, and intoxicating drink—appeal to the flesh, not to the spirit.

h. And, she *is* Babylon. The fact that, in this chapter, her identification is a mystery—not obvious—and her real power over the earth dwellers is spiritual—not physical—indicates that this is Babylonian spirituality or religion. The religion of ancient Babylon was centered on sex rites involving thousands of temple prostitutes. It was the religious duty of every Babylonian woman to serve as a temple prostitute at least once in her life. Ishtar was called "the mother of [temple] prostitutes." When Israel was worshiping pagan gods, she was referred to as a harlot (e.g., Hosea 4:15). Some say that the whore of Revelation 17 is the apostate Christian Church or the Roman Catholic Church, but she is much more than that. Babylonian religion was very eclectic, consolidating the worship of many gods, not only Babylonian but of the surrounding nations. The eclectic religion of modern, prophetic Babylon will be centered in Babylon, the city-state/nation/empire, but it will ultimately consolidate all the religions of the world into a global religion led by the False Prophet. It may resemble Christianity because it will consist of the worship of the false messiah and his "father," Satan (13:4), but it will also resemble Islam and other religions of the world which anticipate a coming god-man or messiah.

17:6-11 *I saw (a) the woman, drunk with the blood of the saints and with the blood of the martyrs of [Yahushua]. And when I saw her, (b) I marveled with great amazement. But (c) the angel said to me, "Why did you marvel? I will tell you the mystery of the woman and of the beast that carries her, which has the seven heads and the ten horns. The beast that you saw was, and is not, and will ascend out of the bottomless pit and go to perdition. And (d) those who dwell on the earth will marvel, whose names are not written in the Book of Life from the foundation of the world, when they see the beast that was, and is not, and yet is. Here is the mind which has wisdom:* (e) *The seven heads are seven mountains on which the woman sits. There are also* (f) *seven kings. Five have fallen, one is, and the other has not yet come.* (g) *And when he comes, he must continue a short time.* (h) *And the beast that was, and is not, is himself also the eighth, and is of the seven, and is going to perdition.*

a. The religion of Babylon, which is energized and controlled by the spirit of the devil, is responsible for the death of the Saints and martyrs of Yahushua.

b. John is amazed by the incongruity of the religion of Babylon being responsible for the death of members of the true Community of Believers in Yahushua.

c. The angel explains that the religious spirit of Babylon gets her power from Satan and his incarnation, Antimessiah. Notice that both Satan and Antimessiah have seven heads and ten horns, but here they are not distinguished by the crowns being on their heads or their horns as they are in 12:3 and 13:1. So, the scarlet beast, Satan, and the beast that *"was, and is not, and will ascend out of the bottomless pit and go to perdition,"* Antimessiah, are spiritually one, just as Yahuah the Father and Yahuah the Son are One.

d. The earth dwellers marvel at Antimessiah because of his *"head"* (kingdom) that was destroyed but then revived and the signs and wonders performed in his name (cf. 13:3, 13).

e. Some have reasoned, because of her garments of purple and red (the colors of the Roman Catholic Church) and the seven *"mountains"* (Rome is the "city of seven hills"), that the woman, Babylon, is the Roman Catholic Church or Rome. However, the Greek word (*oros*) translated *"mountains"* here really means, just as it is translated, *"mountains"* or large land masses, not "hills." The Greek word (*buonos*) for "hills" (actually a Latin word, borrowed by the Greeks, which commonly referred to Rome) is not used here. (See Luke 3:5 where both terms are used.) In Scripture, mountains also symbolize large areas of political power and dominion. So, the harlot Babylon holds religious/spiritual sway over large realms of the earth—perhaps continents or large administrative areas. It would seem that Rome and its dominating religion, the Roman Catholic Church, is a prototype of modern Babylon, but Rome does not come close in her religious influence (or, as in Chapter 18, in political or economic influence) to the total global

167

dominance of the eclectic, pseudo-messianic, Babylonian religion described in this chapter.

f.   The seven kings that manifest the spirit of Satan and Antimessiah on Earth apparently represent rulers of the seven empires that ruled over and persecuted Yahuah's People Israel and the rulers that will will persecute Yahuah's People during the Great Tribulation period of the Final Seven Years. Those seven kingdoms or empires were: Egypt, Assyria, Babylonia, Medo-Persia, and Greece (the five that *"have fallen"*), Rome (the one that *"is"* at the time Revelation was written), and modern, prophetic Babylon (the one that *"has not yet come"*). Modern religious and secular Babylon will be annihilated by fire, as we will see in 17:16 and 18:8, but will then be replaced by the global kingdom of Antimessiah (17:17), the Revived Roman/Ottoman Empire (cf. Daniel 7:7, 23).[10]

---

[10]Current events are rapidly confirming the fulfillment of the prophecies concerning the rise of the revived Roman/Ottoman Empire and its ruler, the anti-messiah.

The capital of the ancient Roman Empire under Constantine (a type of the anti-messiah) was Constantinople (now Istanbul, Turkey). The Roman Empire was then divided into the Western Empire with Rome as its capital and the Eastern Empire with its capital still Constantinople. After the destruction of the Western Empire, the Eastern Roman Empire became the Byzantine Empire, which later became the Islamic Ottoman Empire in 1299 CE. The Ottoman Empire had a long history, finally falling in 1923 CE.

However, Islam, with its goal of establishing a new Caliphate (empire ruled by *Sharia*—Islamic—law) is, by far, the world's fastest-growing religion and Muslims are, by far, the fastest-growing religious population group world-wide, literally invading the nations of the world, particularly the Western nations. And Turkey, a Muslim-dominated nation, is considered a "Eurasian" nation because of its location as a land-bridge between Europe and Asia and its strong economic and political ties with both Eastern and Western nations. So, it is not too difficult to see that Turkey, which is also the primary location of the peoples who will come against Israel in the Last Days (cf. Ezekiel 38), may very well be the location of the capital of the Revived Roman Empire just as it was the location of the capital of the ancient Roman Empire. Is it not interesting that Turkey recently cut off diplomatic ties with Israel and has sided with other Arabic nations in their determination to destroy Israel?

Also, it is clear from Obadiah's prophecies (e.g., Obadiah 4) vis-à-vis other Bible prophecies (e.g., Isaiah 14:13; Daniel 8:10; 11:37) that the

g. The seventh "king"—the ruler or president of modern Babylon—will rule a short time.

h. Antimessiah, the ultimate counterfeit of the true Messiah, *"is of the seven"* previous kings (embodies the spirit of all seven) and is the eighth and final worldly king. An intriguing possible interpretation of this description, when it is combined with the prophecy of 13:3 and the rather curious prophecy that the seventh king will rule a short time, is that, before it is destroyed by fire, the kingdom

---

anti-messiah will be an Arabic Muslim—specifically a descendant of Jacob's twin brother Esau.

The descendants of Abraham's son and Isaac's outcast half-brother Ishmael (the Arabs) mirror Israel in many ways, including being descendants of twelve patriarchs (the sons of Ishmael), their belief in one god (Allah), and looking forward to a messiah (the Mahdi). And they have always been the rivals of Israel, coveting Israel's inheritance from Yahuah through Abraham (the Promised Land, its capital Jerusalem, and dominion over the world).

When Edom, the nation formed by the descendants of Esau (Ishmael's nephew)—Judea's treacherous kinsman-neighbor to the south—was conquered by Nebuchadnezzar, although she remained an identifiable province of Babylon, many of her inhabitants migrated into the surrounding areas, including what is now Saudi Arabia and into Israel. In the absence of the Judeans, who had been carried away into captivity into Babylon, the Edomites were permitted to occupy Jerusalem. But then, the Jews were permitted to return to their homeland by Cyrus, King of Persia, in 536 BCE. And, in 130 BCE, when Jerusalem and Judea were again occupied and controlled by the Jews, the ruler of Judea at that time, John Hyrcanus, forced the Edomites to convert to Judaism. Nominally, they complied, but maintained a treacherous presence in Jerusalem and Judea. The Jews remained suspicious of them, calling them "half-Jews." Then, when the Romans subjugated Judea, they made Herod I ("the Great"), an Edomite (Latin: *Idumean*) "Jew," King of the Jews. And it was Herod the Great who, in his maniacal determination to get rid of the newborn Messiah Yahushua, had all baby boys under the age of two in and around Bethlehem killed.

Get the picture: the "King of the Jews," a descendant of Israel's displaced twin brother Esau, in a diabolical frenzy trying to kill the true King of the Jews. What clearer type of the false messiah could there be?

Then, exactly as prophesied (Jeremiah 49:10 and numerous other passages), the Edomites seem to have disappeared after the destruction of the Temple by the Romans in 70 CE. Apparently, they were absorbed into the surrounding, now Arabic/Muslim nations, especially into what is now Turkey.

But, at the End of the Age, one of their descendants will again ascend to the throne of David, claiming to be not only King of the Jews, but Lord of the World.

over which he rules (modern religious and secular Babylon) will be destroyed by war, but will then be "miraculously" revived, and he will become the eighth king after whom the whole world will follow in wonder and awe. (Cf. Footnote 9 Chapter 13)

17:12-15 (a) *The ten horns which you saw are ten kings who have received no kingdom as yet, but they receive authority for one hour as kings with the beast. These are of one mind, and they will give their power and authority to the beast.* (b) *These will make war with the Lamb, and the Lamb will overcome them, for He is Lord of lords and King of kings; and those who are with Him are called, chosen, and faithful."* Then he said to me, (c) *"The waters which you saw, where the harlot sits, are peoples, multitudes, nations, and tongues."*

a. After Antimessiah takes over at the midpoint of the Final Seven Years, for the short time (signified by *"one hour"*) that he is in control, the world will be ruled by ten *"kings"* under him, who yield their authority and power to rule to him. Verses 3, 7 and 9 indicate that Earth will be divided up into seven "kingdoms" or administrative areas *("heads"* or *"mountains")* that will be ruled by ten *"kings"* under the *"beast"* or Antimessiah. This is exactly the same scenario prophesied by Daniel, except that he provides the additional detail that three of the ten kings will be "subdued" (brought down) by the anti-messiah (Daniel 7:24).
b. This is a reference to 16:14-16 and 19:11-21, when the King of Kings and Lord of Lords returns with the armies of Heaven at "Armageddon" to defeat and destroy *"the kings of the earth and of the whole world . . . who are gathered . . . to the battle of that great day of [Yahuah] Almighty."*
c. The waters where Babylon sits (17:1) are explained as *"peoples* (Greek: *laos*—tribes or nations), *multitudes, nations* (Greek: *ethnos*—ethnic groups), *and tongues"* (people who speak various languages)—in other words, all the earth dwellers of the world.

17:16-18 (a) *"And the ten horns which you saw on the beast, these will hate the harlot, make her desolate and naked, eat her flesh and burn her with fire.* (b) *For [Yahuah] has put it into their hearts to fulfill His purpose, to be of one mind, and to give their kingdom to the beast, until the words of [Yahuah] are fulfilled.* (c) *And the woman whom you saw is that great city which reigns over the kings of the earth."* (d)

170

a. Verse 16 may be one of the most poorly translated and misleading verses in the *Bible*. Virtually every translation, following the lead of the KJV, states that the ten kings are the ones who burn Babylon. But the structure of the Greek is somewhat ambiguous. When correctly translated, it indicates that *"fire"* is the subject of the sentence rather than the ten kings, who may be passive. In other words, it is the fire that does the burning of Babylon, not the ten kings, who may be just passive onlookers.[11] That they "hate" the harlot does not necessarily mean that they are involved in her destruction. To this commentator, that makes more sense than the way this verse is commonly translated, because it is difficult to conceptualize how the ten kings, who will not even receive their kingdoms until *after* Babylon is destroyed, could destroy in *"one hour"* (cf. 18:10, 17, 19) the most powerful, world-dominating kingdom (nation or empire) in the history of the world. Also, BCE prophecy indicates that Babylon will be destroyed in the same way that Sodom and Gomorrah were destroyed—by fire from Heaven—after which no human will dwell there, only demons and unclean spirits, which seems to fit the scenario of Chapters 17 and 18 (cf. Jeremiah 50:32, 39, 40; 51:25, 30, 58; Revelation 18:2, 8).

Most *Bible* expositors, because of the confusion caused by the mistranslation of this verse, state that the harlot of Chapter 17 (religious Babylon) is destroyed at a different point in time than is secular Babylon of Chapter 18. But that is a false distinction and a forced interpretation that over-allegorizes and mutilates the meaning of the text. It is impossible to conceive how spiritual, religious Babylon could be separated from the secular state and destroyed without destroying the government with whom she is inextricably intertwined and supports (cf. 13:11-18).

b. And here is another indication that the annihilation of all natural life in Babylon will be caused by the Lord rather than by her human enemies: The reason for the burning of Babylon is because Yahuah has put it in the hearts of the ten kings to give their kingdom (singular), which they have not yet received (verse 12), to Antimessiah. The ten kings may indeed hate Babylon because she, under her present ruler (the seventh king) and system of government, is dominating the world, making it impossible for them to

---

[11]For an excellent technical analysis of 17:16 (which is beyond the competency of this commentator), please see the book *America the Babylon: America's Destiny Foretold in Biblical Prophecy*, available through Amazon.

receive and consolidate their domains into the global kingdom of Antimessiah. But they are powerless to do anything about it until the Lord intervenes and destroys her by fire.

c. So, the woman who rides the beast is *"that great city"* which reigns over the kings of the earth. This *"great city"* is Babylon, because the *"great city"* Jerusalem (11:8) has never reigned over the kings of the earth. Notice that here she is not just the harlot—religious, spiritual Babylon—but a physical place—a *"city"*—the same Babylon as in Chapter 18.

d. Again, notice that the ten kings and Antimessiah will not receive their kingdom until **after** all natural life in Babylon is destroyed by fire. That means that, although Babylon is the spiritual "headquarters" of Satan, she is not the ultimate global kingdom ruled by Antimessiah—the "Revived Roman Empire." It also means that Babylon must be burned **before** the midpoint of the Final Seven Years because that is when Antimessiah takes over as world ruler. But that presents a problem because the details of Babylon's destruction are placed here, in Chapter 17, and in 18, just before the celebration of her destruction in Chapter 19, which appears to be at the end of the seven years, just before the Lord returns with the armies of Heaven to defeat and destroy His enemies at "Armageddon." However, as will be seen as we continue through Chapter 18, that apparent dilemma is easily and clearly resolved. Remember that the details of Chapters 17 and 18 are parenthetical—not in strict chronological sequence.

Chapter 18—Material, Secular Babylon

18:1-3 (a) *After these things I saw another angel coming down from heaven, having great authority, and the earth was illuminated with his glory. And he cried mightily with a loud voice, saying,* (b) *"Babylon the great is fallen, is fallen, and has become* (c) *a dwelling place of demons, a prison for every foul spirit, and a cage for every unclean and hated bird! For* (d) *all the nations have drunk of the wine of the wrath of her fornication, the kings of the earth have committed fornication with her, and the merchants of the earth have become rich through the abundance of her luxury."*

a. *"After these things I saw"* indicates a change in perspective, but not in time (cf. the commentary on 4:1). As we will clearly see the Babylon of Chapter 18 is exactly the same as the Babylon of Chapter 17. The only difference is that Chapter 18 focuses on the material, secular aspect of Babylon whereas Chapter 17 focuses on the spiritual, religious aspect of Babylon. But, in actuality, although Babylonian spirituality is universal, religious and secular Babylon cannot be separated; they are indissolubly married, just as was religion and state in ancient Babylon. In fact, modern physical Babylon (the city-state/nation/empire) is the main purveyor of Babylonian spirituality/religion throughout the world.

b. Exactly the same name, *"Babylon the Great,"* is used here as in 17:5. Chapter 18 just takes up where Chapter 17 left off, with the fall (burning) of *"that great city,"* Babylon the Great.

c. This is total annihilation of all natural life![12] After Babylon is

---

[12]As scientist and scholar Jeffrey Goodman has pointed out in his well researched and thoroughly documented book *The Comets of God*, it would be impossible for even thousands of simultaneously detonated nuclear bombs to annihilate all natural life in an area the size of modern Babylon (for a complete, irrefutable, Scriptural exposition of the identity of modern, prophetic Babylon, read "Appendix 1—Who is Modern Babylon?"). But a comet less than a mile in diameter exploding in the atmosphere above a 10,000 square mile area would very quickly incincerate all living plants, animals and humans in that area, rendering it uninhabitable. Scientific studies of the sites of Sodom and Gomorrah have proven that those cities were destroyed by a comet fragment exploding in the atmosphere above them. Likewise, on June 30, 1908, at 7:15 a.m., a relatively small comet fragment approximately 100 meters (the length of a football field) in diameter exploded in the atmosphere

destroyed by fire (her first destruction), resulting in desolate desert conditions, no human can dwell there, only demons and evil spirits (cf. the commentary on 17:16; also Isaiah 13:19-21). After she is burned, Babylon is uninhabited by natural living things, but is still the kingdom and base of operations, so to speak, of Satan and his evil spiritual horde.

d. As in Chapter 17, Babylon is the whore of Earth, but Chapter 18 focuses on her political whoredom with the rulers of the earth and her material whoredom with the merchants of the earth.

18:4-8 And I heard (a) another voice from heaven saying, (b) "Come out of her, my people, lest you share in her sins, and lest you receive of her plagues. For her sins have reached to heaven, and (c) [Yahuah] has remembered her iniquities. (d) Render to her just as she rendered to you, and repay her double according to her works; in the cup which she has mixed, mix double for her. In the measure that (e) she glorified herself and lived luxuriously, in the same measure give her torment and sorrow; for she says in her heart, (f) `I sit as queen, and am no widow, and will not see sorrow.' Therefore her plagues (g) will come in one day—death and mourning and famine. And she will be utterly burned with fire, for (h) strong is the Lord [Yahuah] who judges her."

a. The voice of the Lord
b. As the Revelation is written to both the Jews and to the Followers of Yahushua, *"come out of her"* would seem to apply in a literal sense to Yahuah's physical People the Jews who have not yet accepted Yahushua as their Redeemer and who remain on the earth throughout the Final Seven Years and into the Millennium, and in a spiritual sense to His People the Community of Believers in Yahushua who are taken to Heaven at the sounding of the *"Last Trump"* (1 Corinthians 15:52) on Yom Teruah at the end of the

---

above the Tunguska River Basin in Siberia, incinerating a 1,000 square mile forested area and several herds of reindeer below, and scorched the skin of eye witnesses 40 miles away (*The Comets of God*, pages 54-57 and 143-152). Also, computer simulations have shown that a comet just two miles in diameter exploding in Earth's atmosphere will engulf the entire planet in flames. So, it is easy to see, is it not, how a comet exploding above modern Babylon the Great will very quickly annihilate all living plants and animals in that city-state/nation?

seven years, because the Believers in Yahushua are promised that,as long as they remain faithful, they will not have to endure the *"last plagues"*—the plagues of the Wrath of Yahuah (cf. 1 Thessalonians 5:9; Revelation 15:1) or be subjected to His judgment (cf. John 5:24). But those *"last plagues,"* as well as the preceding *"Great Tribulation"* (Matthew 24:21; Revelation 7:14)— the wrath of Satan (12:12)—will the time of *"Jacob's trouble"* (Jeremiah 30:7) for those of Yahuah's People who have not yet recognized that Yahushua is their Messiah, separating the *"sheep"* from the *"goats"*—"true Israel" (cf. Romans 9:6) from those who do not really believe in Yahuah or in the coming Messiah Yahushua. For proof that this command is directed to both Yahuah's BCE People the Jews and His CE People the Disciples of Yahushua, see the parallel commands in Jeremiah 50:8; 51:6, 45 and 2 Corinthians 6:17.[13]

c. Cf. 16:19
d. Babylon will reap what she has sowed—double: two separate judgments—the judgment by fire (destroying all natural life) and total physical annihilation (destroying Satan's spiritual base of operations—verse 21).
e. She sees herself as a queen of those nations to whom she is
f. She is a proud, wealthy, luxurious nation.
    illicitly married. A title of Ishtar, chief goddess of Babylon, was "Queen of Heaven."
g. She will be utterly destroyed by fire in a very short period of time, indicated by *"one day"* in this verse and by *"one hour"* in verses 10, 17 and 19.
h. Confirming that it is because of the judgment of the Lord and by His power, not by the power of the ten kings, that Babylon is destroyed.

18:9-17a [The prophecy of the voice from Heaven continues:] (a) *"The kings of the earth who committed fornication and lived luxuriously with her will weep and lament for her, when they see the smoke of her burning, standing at a distance for fear of her torment, saying, 'Alas, alas, that great city Babylon, that mighty city! For in one hour your judgment has come.' And* (b) *the merchants of the earth will weep and*

---

[13]For a detailed explanation of who the People of Yahuah are, read "Appendix 3—Who are the People of Yahuah?"

mourn over her, for no one buys their merchandise anymore: merchandise of gold and silver, precious stones and pearls, fine linen and purple, silk and scarlet, every kind of citron wood, every kind of object of ivory, every kind of object of most precious wood, bronze, iron, and marble; and cinnamon and incense, fragrant oil and frankincense, wine and oil, fine flour and wheat, cattle and sheep, horses and chariots, and bodies and souls of men. The fruit that your soul longed for has gone from you, and all the things which are rich and splendid have gone from you, and you shall find them no more at all. The merchants of these things, who became rich by her, will stand at a distance for fear of her torment, weeping and wailing, and saying, `Alas, alas, that great city that was clothed in fine linen, purple, and scarlet, and adorned with gold and precious stones and pearls! (c) For in one hour such great riches came to nothing.'"

a. This confirms that Babylon is the political center of Earth: The kings of Earth weep and lament when their wealth is destroyed when Babylon is destroyed. Apparently, all the nations of Earth are actually client-states of Babylon and their rulers are kept in luxurious power by Babylon.
b. Babylon is also the commercial center of the world; she is the main importer of the world's commodities, making the merchants of the earth wealthy.
c. But the source of their wealth is destroyed in "*one hour.*"

18:17b-19 [The prophecy is fulfilled in John's vision:] (a) *Every shipmaster, all who travel by ship, sailors, and as many as trade on the sea, stood at a distance and cried out when they saw* (b) *the smoke of her burning, saying, "What is like this great city?" They threw dust on their heads and cried out, weeping and wailing, and saying, "Alas, alas, that great city, in which all who had ships on the sea became rich by her wealth! For in* (c) *one hour she is made desolate."*

a. Babylon is a land of major seaports.
b. The sailors see, from a distance, the smoke of Babylon burning. This confirms that Babylon's destruction by fire is a literal event.
c. This is the third time in this chapter that "*one hour*" is mentioned. Apparently, the Lord is making a point: The destruction of Babylon occurs in literally one hour.

18:20-24 (a) *"Rejoice over her, O heaven, and you holy apostles and prophets, for [Yahuah] has avenged you on her!"* (b) *Then a mighty angel took up a stone like a great millstone and threw it into the sea, saying, "Thus with violence the great city Babylon shall be thrown down, and shall not be found anymore. The sound of harpists, musicians, flutists, and trumpeters shall not be heard in you anymore. No craftsman of any craft shall be found in you anymore, and the sound of a millstone shall not be heard in you anymore. The light of a lamp shall not shine in you anymore, and the voice of bridegroom and bride shall not be heard in you anymore. For your merchants were the great men of the earth, for (c) by your sorcery all the nations were deceived. And (d) in her was found the blood of prophets and saints, and of all who were slain on the earth."*

a. Let the celebration over the annihilation of all living things including the human inhabitants of Babylon begin!

b. But now, there is a second destruction! And the dilemma (cf. the commentary on 17:18) as to how Babylon can be destroyed both prior to the midpoint of the Final Seven Years and at the end of the seven years is solved: There are two destructions: (1) the destruction by fire of all natural life in Babylon prior to the midpoint of the seven years, which sets the stage for the ten kings and Antimessiah to take over the world, and (2) the physical destruction of Babylon by a giant millstone-like object, sinking her beneath the waves of the sea, never to be found anymore (cf. Jeremiah 51: 42, 55, 64), here at the end of the seven years. This apparently also alludes to the fact that revived Babylon ("the Revived Roman Empire"), the global kingdom of Antimessiah, of which the modern nation Babylon the Great is the precursor and prototype, is totally destroyed at the end of the Final Seven Years.

c. Satanic spiritual power, as in sorcery (witchcraft), is the reason for Babylon's success, as the headquarters of Satan's horde of evil spirit-beings, in dominating the world religiously, politically, and commercially, even after her destruction by fire. It is revealing that the Greek word translated *"sorcery"* in this verse is *pharmakeia*, from which the English word "pharmacy" is derived. The occult is heavily involved in drug use. Prescribed drugs, drugs in vaccinations, drugs in our food, and illegal drugs are perhaps the main means for opening the doors of our souls to evil Babylonian spiritual influences.

177

d. Of course, Babylon herself did not literally kill all the prophets, Saints, and others murdered on Earth. But figuratively speaking, as the "throne of Satan," the same spirit of the devil (specifically, Ishtar) who animates and energizes Babylon, even before and after her destruction by fire, has been responsible for their deaths throughout history.

The events of Chapters 19 and 20 can only be fully understood in light of the prophetic significance of the Fall "Feasts" (Hebrew: *moed*—appointed times) of Yahuah.

Yom Teruah (the Feast of Trumpets), also called Rosh haShanah (the Head of the New Year) and Yom haDin (the Day of Judgment), is celebrated each year as a rehearsal of the resurrection of the righteous dead at the *"Last Trump"* (cf. 1 Corinthians 15:52), the judgment and separation of Israel into three groups (the nobles or righteous ones, the "intermediates," and the condemned) (cf. Isaiah 44:5), the in-gathering ("catching up") of the righteous ones (cf. 1 Thessalonians 4:16, 17), the wedding of the Messiah, and the coronation of the King.

Then, during the ten "Days of Awe," the *"last plagues"*—the plagues of the Wrath of Yahuah—are poured out on the earth dwellers (cf. 15:1; 16:1), and the faith of the intermediates (nominal Israelites and Yahuah – fearing but unsaved Gentiles) is severely tested.

At Yom Kippur (the Day of Atonement), also called Yom haPeduth (the Day of Redemption), the Shofar haGadol (the Great Trumpet) is blown to gather in those who have, by the mercy of Yahuah, survived the plagues of the bowls of His Wrath. On this day, the King pardons the *"sheep"* of Israel and the nations (those who have remained faithful to Yahuah and have not taken the mark of Antimessiah during the Great Tribulation), allowing them to enter the millennial Messianic Kingdom. Yom Kippur is also, like Yom Teruah, celebrated as a Day of Judgment (Yom haDin) on which the unfaithful *"goats"* are sentenced to *"everlasting fire"* and destroyed (cf. Matthew 25:32-34, 41).

Finally, during Sukkot (the Feast of Tabernacles or Booths), life in the millennial Messianic Kingdom is rehearsed and celebrated.

Chapter 19—The Ultimate Celebration in Heaven, the Marriage of the Lamb, and the Defeat and Destruction of the Messiah's Enemies

19:1-10 (a) *After these things I heard a loud voice of a great multitude in heaven, saying,* (b) *"Alleluia! Salvation and glory and honor and power belong to the Lord our God. For true and righteous are His judgments, because He has judged the great harlot who corrupted the earth with her fornication; and He has avenged on her the blood of His servants shed by her." Again they said, "Alleluia! Her smoke rises up "forever" and ever!* (c) *And the twenty-four elders and the four living*

179

creatures fell down and worshiped [Yahuah] who sat on the throne, saying, "Amen! Alleluia! (d) *Then a voice came from the throne, saying, "Praise our God, all you His servants and those who fear Him, both small and great!" And I heard, as it were,* (e) *the voice of a great multitude, as the sound of many waters and as the sound of mighty thunderings, saying, "Alleluia! For the Lord [Yahuah] Omnipotent reigns! Let us be glad and rejoice and give Him glory, for the marriage of the Lamb has come, and* (f) *His wife has made herself ready." And to her it was granted to be arrayed in fine linen, clean and bright, for the fine linen is the righteous acts of the saints. Then* (g) *he said to me, "Write: `Blessed are those who are called to* (h) *the marriage supper of the Lamb!'" And he said to me, "These are the true sayings of [Yahuah]." And I fell at his feet to worship him. But he said to me, "See that you do not do that! I am* (i) *your fellow servant, and of your brethren who have the testimony of [Yahushua]. Worship [Yahuah]! For* (j) *the testimony of [Yahushua] is the spirit of prophecy."*

a. This is another major shift in focus—from Earth and the annihilation of Babylon to Heaven.
b. The final, total destruction of Babylon, burying her beneath the waves of the sea (Jeremiah 51:42), **really** sets off a celebration in Heaven, because not only are her evil human inhabitants gone, but the physical kingdom of Satan—the "headquarters" for his army of demons/ evil spirits/ fallen angels—is totally eradicated.
c. The celebration consists of praising and worshiping the Lord for ridding Earth of Babylon, avenging the murders of Yahuah's People, and for taking back His reign over Earth.
d. The 24 elders and the four living creatures worship Yahuah.
e. A voice from the throne, apparently Yahuah's, prompts more praise and worship, to which the multitude, apparently of Saints and angels, responds.
f. Notice that the Bride of the Messiah is given garments of fine linen (righteousness), but she has put them on herself. Again, true life in the Messiah is an active rather than a passive religion in which we must choose, by His grace, to *"put on [the Messiah] . . . our righteousness"* (Romans 13:4; Jeremiah 23:6).
g. John's personal angel (cf. 1:1).
h. In ancient Israeli weddings, after the groom took his betrothed to her new home, the actual marriage ceremony, the consummation of the marriage, and the marriage supper (usually a week-long celebration) occurred. So, in Heaven, the events involved in the mar-

riage of the Lamb to His Bride (and His coronation as King) will happen during the ten Days of Awe on Earth.

i. The sentence structure here is a little confusing. The angel is not telling John that he is his human brother or brother in the Messiah; he is telling him that he is John's and John's brethren's fellow servant of the Lord.

j. This is an interesting insight into the roles of those who testify to the truth that Yahushua is Lord: they are actually prophesying. So, when Scripture speaks of the persecution of or killing the prophets, it is not speaking of persecuting or killing only those who foretell the future, but also those who preach the Gospel of Yahushua the Messiah, who are speaking by the same spirit of prophecy as did the BCE prophets or any other prophets of the Lord.

19:11-13 Now I saw heaven opened, and behold, (a) a white horse. And He who sat on him was called (b) Faithful and True, and (c) in righteousness He judges and makes war. His eyes were like a flame of fire, and on His head were many crowns. He had (d) a name written that no one knew except Himself. (e) He was clothed with a robe dipped in blood, and His name is called (f) The Word of [Yahuah].

a. This section reveals a thorough identification of the One who rides the white horse out of Heaven—the One who was mimicked by the false messiah when he went out to conquer the world (6:2).

b. This is a title of the One (the Messiah) who dictated the letters to the seven churches to John (Revelation 3:14).

c. In the end, He is no longer the Lamb; He is the One who righteously judges and makes war.

d. Messiah, Son of Yahuah the Father, Lamb of Yahuah, King of Kings, Lord of Lords, Prince of Peace, Everlasting Father, Almighty God, and many others are descriptive titles, but He has a mysterious, wonderful name that no one on Earth knows (cf. Judges 13:18). It seems that John saw the name written but did not "know" (fully comprehend) it. The children of Israel believed that if the Lord's secret name was spoken, the person who spoke that name would die, because the full essence of the Lord, which no one can bear to comprehend, is expressed in His name.

e. This reflects His role as the sacrificial Lamb of Yahuah whose blood was shed to wash away our sins (1:5).

f. This is another scriptural title of the Messiah (John 1:1).

181

19:14-21 *And* (a) *the armies in heaven, clothed in fine linen, white and clean, followed Him on white horses. Now* (b) *out of His mouth goes* (c) *a sharp sword, that with it He should strike the nations. And He Himself will rule them with a rod of iron.* (d) *He Himself treads the winepress of the fierceness and wrath of Almighty [Yahuah]. And* (e) *He has on His robe and on His thigh a name written: KING OF KINGS AND LORD OF LORDS. Then I saw* (f) *an angel standing in the sun; and he cried with a loud voice, saying to all the birds that fly in the midst of heaven, "Come and gather together for the supper of the great God, that you may eat the flesh of kings, the flesh of captains, the flesh of mighty men, the flesh of horses and of those who sit on them, and the flesh of* (g) *all people, free and slave, both small and great." And I saw* (h) *the beast, the kings of the earth, and their armies, gathered together to make war against Him who sat on the horse and against His army. Then* (i) *the beast was captured, and with him the false prophet who worked signs in his presence, by which he deceived those who received the mark of the beast and those who worshiped his image. These two were cast alive into the lake of fire burning with brimstone.* (j) *And the rest were killed with the sword which proceeded from the mouth of Him who sat on the horse. And all the birds were filled with their flesh.*

a. The armies of Heaven include both the glorified Saints and angels (Matthew 13:41; 16:27; Mark 8:38; 2 Thessalonians 1:7; Revelation 15:6; 17:14; 19;8, 14)—following the King of Kings to Earth on Yom Kippur.
b. There is incredible power in the Word of the Lord, because He *is* the Word. He spoke the cosmos into existence (Psalm 33:6; Hebrews 11:3). His Word is incisive and powerful enough to divide soul and spirit and accurately discern the thoughts and intents of the heart (Hebrews 4:12). And now, all that He has to do is to speak, and his enemies will be vanquished.
c. This seems like a contradiction: How will He strike the nations with a sword, an instrument of death, yet rule them with a rod of iron? A key to the solution is in understanding that the Hebrew term *goy* (plural: *goyim*), translated *"nation"* in the *Bible*, can refer to either Gentile or Hebrew nations, depending on the context.[14]

---

[14]For a complete exposition of the term *goyim* as used in the *Bible*, go to "Appendix 3—Who are the People of Yahuah?"

So, 19:15 could mean that the Lord will destroy the unsaved Gentile nations but spare the Jews and the Gentiles who, after the Rapture, will not take the mark of Antimessiah and who will inhabit the millennial kingdom of the Messiah. And according to *Tanakh* prophecies, that is exactly what will happen. For example, the Lord says, *"My determination is to gather the* [unsaved Gentile] *nations to My assembly of kingdoms, to pour on them My indignation, all My fierce anger;* **all the earth** *shall be devoured with the fire of My jealousy"* (Zephaniah 3:8). However, Micah 5:3 indicates that a remnant of the tribes of Israel dispersed among the nations of the world will return to the land of Israel and be reunited with their brethren who are already in the land. Also, Scripture indicates that Yahuah will have mercy on some from the nations who gather against Jerusalem at the end of the Final Seven Years (cf. Zechariah 14:16), and bring them into the millennial kingdom. The latter will apparently be those Yahuah-fearing Gentiles who do not take the mark of the beast, because all who take the mark will be destroyed by the Wrath of Yahuah (14:9-10). So, it will apparently be the Jews who do not take the mark of the beast and who flee into the wilderness and are hidden and protected there by Yahuah during the Final Seven Years, plus the Gentiles who survive, by the grace of the Lord, the Wrath of Yahuah after the Rapture who will make up the nations who inhabit the earth during the Millennium. This "separation of the sheep from the goats" will occur on Yom Kippur (the Day of Atonement), also known as Yom haPeduth (the Day of Redemption). The spiritual descendants of Abraham—the Followers of Yahushua (cf. Romans 4:15-16)—who are caught up in the Rapture ten days earlier, on Yom Teruah (the Feast of Trumpets) will be in their glorified, resurrection bodies inhabiting New Jerusalem with the Lord during the Millennium. The unsaved Gentile nations (the "earth dwellers") will have been totally destroyed. For more details, see the commentary on Chapters 20 and 21.

d. Cf. 14:19

e. The significance of His name being written on His robe and His thigh is not clear. In the *Bible*, sons are said to come from their fathers' loins (the waist/thigh area) which would be visible on a man who is riding a horse. So, perhaps the indication is that in contrast to His unspeakable divine name is his human title: King of Kings and Lord of Lords.

183

f. Perhaps the angel is standing in the sun (light) to make himself highly visible as he summons the birds to consume the flesh of the earth dwellers destroyed by the Lord. (Notice that this is practically a quote from Ezekiel 39:17, indicating that this is one of the prophesied Gog-Magog wars.) This may also be symbolic of angels (cf. 8:13; 14:6) who are reapers gathering the "grapes of wrath" (the souls of the lost) to be cast into the fire at the end of the Millennium (cf. the commentary on 14:13-19).

g. Notice that all classes of earth dwellers—all who receive the mark of the beast and worship his image—are killed.

h. This appears to be the battle of "Armageddon" (cf. the commentary on 16:16).

i. Antimessiah and the false prophet are not even given the respite of physical death before the Final Judgment; they are immediately cast alive into the lake of fire.

j. The *"goats"* and other earth dwellers are destroyed and the *"birds that fly in the midst of heaven"* obey what the angel who stands in the sun commands them to do.

Chapter 20—The Binding of Satan, the Millennial Kingdom of Yahuah on Earth, and the Final Judgment

20:1-3 Then I saw (a) *an angel coming down from heaven, having the key to the bottomless pit and a great chain in his hand. He laid hold of the dragon, that serpent of old, who is the devil and Satan, and bound him for* (b) *a thousand years; and he cast him into the bottomless pit, and shut him up, and set a seal on him,* (c) *so that he should deceive the nations no more till the thousand years were finished. But after these things he must be released for a little while.*

a. Note that this angel is not Yahuah the Father, Yahuah the Son, Yahuah the Holy Spirit, Michael the archangel, or even a *"mighty"* angel. He is just an ordinary angel, showing how powerless the devil really is apart from the enabling and permissive will of the Lord.
b. There is no reason to think that this is not a literal thousand years. Some allegorically interpret it as a time period in the past or the present, but there has never been a time period without evil ruling the world. And with the terrible and worsening spiritual state of the world, it is impossible to see that the thousand years, when the forces of Satan have been defeated and Satan is imprisoned, is the present time.
c. During the Millennium, none of the nations of the world will be deceived into worshiping false gods, which is the basic tactic of Satan.

20:4-6 And I saw thrones, and (a) *they sat on them, and judgment was committed to them. Then I saw* (b) *the souls of those who had been beheaded for their witness to [Yahushua] and for the word of [Yahuah], who had not worshiped the beast or his image, and had not received his mark on their foreheads or on their hands. And they lived and reigned with [the Messiah] for a thousand years. But* (c) *the rest of the dead did not live again until the thousand years were finished.* (d) *This is the first resurrection. Blessed and holy is he who has part in the first resurrection. Over such* (e) *the second death has no power, but* (f) *they shall be priests of [Yahuah] and of [the Messiah], and shall reign with Him a thousand years.*

a. *"They"* are the redeemed and glorified Followers of Yahushua (cf. 2 Timothy 2:12; Revelation 2:26, 27). Yahushua told His apostles

185

that His Followers would sit on thrones judging the tribes of Israel. They were specifically told, *". . . in the regeneration* [the Millennium], *when the Son of Man sits on the throne of His glory, you who have followed Me will also sit on twelve thrones, judging the twelve tribes of Israel"* (Matthew 19:28). Is that not exactly the scenario that John sees here, at the beginning of the Millennium? As was often prophesied (Isaiah 11-12; 65:17-25; 66:22-24; et al.), the millennial kingdom will be the regenerated, Eden-like world in which one will be considered very young who dies at the age of 100 (Isaiah 65:20). In fact, some may live throughout the Millennium. So, during the 1,000 years, the earth will be populated with a huge multitude of the physical descendants of Israel, exactly as was promised to Abraham, Isaac, and Jacob (Exodus 32:13), including a *"multitude of nations"* who are the descendants of Ephraim (Genesis 48:19). In other words, the nations of the world during the Millennium will be descendants of Jews who believe in the coming Messiah, but who do not recognize that He is Yahushua before they see Him coming in the clouds to gather His Elect, plus the descendants of those Yahuah-fearing Gentiles who survive the Final Seven Years. And the King of Kings, with the glorified and raptured Saints, will rule all Earth from David's throne in New Jerusalem (cf. Isaiah 9:6-7; 2 Timothy 2:12).

b. Among the glorified Saints who live and reign with the Messiah from Jerusalem during the Millennium are the martyrs whom John sees come to life. Some say that this group is comprised only of those who are martyred during the Final Seven Years (cf. 6:9), but the following statements:

> *This is the first resurrection. Blessed and holy is he who has part in the first resurrection. Over such the second death has no power, but they shall be priests of [Yahuah] and of [the Messiah], and shall reign with Him a thousand years,*

clearly indicate that this group is comprised of all the resurrected Redeemed (including the martyrs) of all ages. Also, this appears to be the fulfillment of Daniel 7:9-10, 22, which states,

> *I was watching; and the same horn* [Antimessiah] *was making war against the saints, and prevailing against them, until the Ancient of Days came, and a judgment was made in favor of the saints of the Most High, and the time came for the saints to possess the kingdom . . . I watched till thrones were put in place, and the Ancient of*

186

Days was seated . . . A thousand thousands ministered to Him; Ten thousand times ten thousand stood before Him.

So apparently, among other responsibilities which include judging angels (1 Corinthians 6:3), the resurrected and glorified Saints will, as promised (2 Timothy 2:12), reign with the Lord over all the nations of the earth (the expanded tribes of Israel plus nations formed by descendants of the Gentiles who are allowed to enter the Millennium). And, as promised (5:10), these kings and priests of Yahuah (1:6) will rule, as He does, with a rod of iron (2:27). That's because, although Satan is chained up in the bottomless pit, man's sin nature will not have been eradicated, resulting in death for some (cf. Isaiah 65:20). So, in order to maintain perfect peace, rule with a rod of iron over all is necessary.

c. These are those who are lost, in Hades awaiting the Final Judgment

d. The *"first resurrection"* will include all those who are raptured when the Great Tribulation is cut short on the last day of the Final Seven Years, by the sounding of the Last Trumpet on Yom Teruah, when the Lord Yahushua returns to *"catch away"* the Redeemed before the final Wrath of Yahuah falls. (See the commentary on 11:14-19c; Cf. also 1 Thessalonians 4:16, 17.) But it also includes those martyrs who, at the beginning of the Millennium, John sees resurrected. Do not be confused by the statement that John sees the souls of the martyrs come to life. Remember, Revelation is more like a mural than a strict time-line chart. From Heaven's point of view, it is all part of the same resurrection, just as Yahushua's second coming spans all the events from the Rapture through the establishment of His Kingdom on Earth. The resurrection of **all** those who have died in the Messiah throughout history is a necessary precursor to reigning with the Lord during the Millennium.

e. The Second Death is "eternal" separation from Yahuah, the source of life, following the Final Judgment.

f. The repetition of *"they"* from Verse 4 confirms that both groups—those who John saw sitting on thrones and those who had been beheaded for their witness to Yahushua and the Word of Yahuah—were involved in the first resurrection. They are the redeemed and glorified Saints of both the *Tanakh* and the *B'rit Hadashah* (the Followers of Yahushua the Messiah), who will rule with the Lord during the Millennium.

187

20:7-10 *Now when the thousand years have expired, Satan will be released from his prison and* (a) *will go out to deceive the nations which are in the four corners of the earth,* (b) *Gog and Magog, to gather them together to battle, whose number is as the sand of the sea. They went up on the breadth of the earth and surrounded the camp of the saints and the beloved city. And fire came down from [Yahuah] out of heaven and devoured them.* (a) *The devil, who deceived them, was cast into the lake of fire and brimstone where the beast and the false prophet are. And they will be tormented day and night "forever" and ever.*

a. The people of those saved and protected by Yahuah following the Rapture, who now cover the earth, have had 1,000 years of perfectly-enforced peace in a perfect, Eden-like paradise. So, how could the devil possibly deceive them? What could he offer them that is better than what they already have? How could he entice them to follow him and to rebel against the Lord who, for 1,000 years, has met their every need? . . . in exactly the same way he enticed Adam and Eve to sin against Yahuah: by appealing to their vanity and pride: *"You will be like* [Yahuah]" (Genesis 3:5)—the same vanity and pride that got Lucifer expelled from Heaven in the beginning (cf. Isaiah 14:12-14)—the same incorrigible sin that will be the downfall of anyone, including any of Yahuah's chosen People, who refuse to totally submit to the One True God and who rebel against Him.

b. In Scripture, Gog appears to be the fallen archangel or *"prince of the power of the air"* (Ezekiel 38:2; Ephesians 2:2) who leads nations under his power (Magog) against Yahuah's People. Ezekiel 38 and 39 tell us about a war of Gog and Magog, the prototype of the war at the end of the Millennium, which will apparently occur at the beginning of the Final Seven Years (cf. Ezekiel 39:9) and will be one of the events (the other being the annihilation of Babylon by fire) that sets the stage for the rise of Antimessiah. Another occurrence of the War of Gog and Magog will be at the end of the Final Seven Years when armies from all nations come against Israel (compare Ezekiel 39:17-20 with Revelation 19:17-18). But the Gog-Magog war at the end of the Millennium involves the peoples of the whole earth (which, as was mentioned before, in *"the restoration,"* may consist of one, huge continent). Those of all nations who have been deceived by the devil come against the *"camp of the saints"* (Israel and the Gentiles who have joined Israel under

188

the New Covenant—cf. Zechariah 8:23; Jeremiah 31:33—who live outside the city) and *"the beloved city"* (New Jerusalem). But, as Sodom and Gomorrah and Babylon were destroyed, fire will come down from Heaven and destroy the rebels. In other words, the people of the "nations" during the Millennium will be given another opportunity to remain faithful to Yahuah. But again, although they dwell in a perfect world ruled over directly by their Messiah, many of them will be deceived into following Satan in rebellion against the Lord, and perish.

c. Satan, like Antimessiah and the false prophet before him, is finally finished—cast into the lake of fire.

20:11-15 *Then I saw* (a) *a great white throne and Him who sat on it, from whose face* (b) *the earth and the heaven fled away. And there was found no place for them. And I saw* (c) *the dead, small and great, standing before [Yahuah], and* (d) *books were opened. And another book was opened, which is the Book of Life. And* (e) *the dead were judged according to their works, by the things which were written in the books.* (f) *The sea gave up the dead who were in it, and Death and Hades delivered up the dead who were in them. And they were judged, each one according to his works. Then* (g) *Death and Hades were cast into the lake of fire. This is the second death. And* (h) *anyone not found written in the Book of Life was cast into the lake of fire.*

a. This is the scene of the Final Judgment, when the dead of all ages—before and during the Millennium—who are included in the *"second resurrection"* appear before the Great White Throne of judgment. The One who sits on the throne is the Messiah (Yahuah the Son], to whom the Father has committed all judgment (John 5:22). He will personally judge those who have rejected His Father and Him throughout history.

b. As happened to the islands and the mountains of 16:20 and to Babylon (18:21), the earth and heaven (the cosmos) disappear (cease to exist) (cf. also 2 Peter 3:7, 10-12).

c. These are not the Redeemed who are no longer dead but were brought to life in the first resurrection. This begs the question, however: "Where are those Elect of Yahuah who were not in their glorified bodies but who lived and remained faithful to the Lord during the Millennium?" This commentator does not know; all that he can do is to speculate that they are transfigured and given their new, glorified bodies when the earth and heavens pass away, as was Yahushua in the garden before his crucifixion (Matthew 17:2) and as, undoubtedly, was Elijah when he ascended into Heaven without tasting death (2 Kings 2:9).

d. There are apparently several books maintained by Yahuah, including the books of Yahuah's remembrance of the tribulations of His People and of those who fear Him (Psalm 56:8; Malachi 3:16), the book of Yahuah's creation (Psalm 139:16), the book of the law (Galatians 3:10), the books of people's works (20:12), and the Book of Life.

e. The dead are judged by their works rather than by their faith alone, for *"Faith without works is dead"* (James 2:20). Head knowledge or just saying, "I believe," will not get one saved. It may be inserted here that the Redeemed will also appear before the Lord in the Final Judgment (2 Corinthians 5:10), not to be judged negatively (John 5:24), but to be rewarded for their good works done by the grace of Yahuah through faith (Ephesians 2:8-10) and for their fruitless works to be burned (1 Corinthians 3:13-15), purifying them for "eternity" in the presence of the Lord.

f. Why the sea is listed and Death and Hades are listed separately as places from where the dead come is not clear. Apparently *"sea,"* being singular and mentioned here after the description of the annihilation of earth and heaven, is figurative for the mass of unregenerate humanity (cf. 13:1) and is listed along with Death and Hades to emphasize the comprehensive nature of the second resurrection. Here, the sequence of events seems somewhat out of order: the judgment of the dead is seen prior to the second resurrection. But John is apparently not listing the events in strict chronological order, but from Heaven's point of view, as if he were looking at a mural—as they occur in relation to the central focus of his vision—the Great White Throne of judgment.

g. Perhaps Death and Hades are personified here to emphasize that there will be no more death or place for the unrighteous dead in the Kingdom of Heaven. Or perhaps, as was suggested in the commentary on 6:8, Death and Hades are fallen angels who subject souls to Death and Hades.

h. Anyone whose name had either never been written in the Book of Life (*"vessels of wrath prepared for destruction"* – Romans 9:22) or one whose name had been blotted out of the Book of Life (cf. 3:5).

190

Chapter 21—The New Heaven, the New Earth, and New Jerusalem

Now, we have another time-sequence dilemma. The vast majority of *Bible* expositors state that the new heavens, the new earth, and New Jerusalem of Chapters 21 and 22 appear in eternity, following the Millennium. But 21:27 seems to indicate the presence on the new earth of those whose names are not written in the Lamb's Book of Life and who are not allowed to enter New Jerusalem. Could it be, in the same way Chapters 17 and 18 are parenthetical chapters giving more details about modern, prophetic Babylon, that Chapters 21 and 22 are also parenthetical chapters giving more details about the millennial kingdom? In fact, Isaiah, prophesying about 900 years before Revelation was written, indicated exactly that scenario. He foretold that there will be *"new heavens and a new earth"* (Isaiah 65:17; 66:22) with a newly-created Jerusalem (Isaiah 65:18). And this is in the context of and precedes his description of the Millennium, during which,

I will rejoice in Jerusalem, and joy in My people; The voice of weeping shall no longer be heard in her, nor the voice of crying. No more shall an infant from there live but a few days, nor an old man who has not fulfilled his days; For the child shall die one hundred years old, but the sinner being one hundred years old shall be accursed. They shall build houses and inhabit them; they shall plant vineyards and eat their fruit. They shall not build and another inhabit; They shall not plant and another eat; For as the days of a tree, so shall be the days of My people, And My elect shall long enjoy the work of their hands. They shall not labor in vain, nor bring forth children for trouble; For they shall be the descendants of the blessed of the LORD, And their offspring with them. It shall come to pass that before they call, I will answer; and while they are still speaking, I will hear. The wolf and the lamb shall feed together, the lion shall eat straw like the ox, And dust shall be the serpent's food. They shall not hurt nor destroy in all My holy mountain," Says the LORD (Isaiah 65:19-25). *"And, it shall come to pass* [in the new heavens and the new earth] *that from one New Moon to another, and from one Sabbath to another, all flesh shall come to worship before Me," says the LORD. "And they shall go forth and look upon the corpses of the men who have transgressed against me, for their worm does not die, and their fire is not quenched. They shall be an abhorrence to all flesh.* (Isaiah 66:23-24)

All of this—death, the presence of sinners, childbirth, new moons and Sabbaths, looking on the corpses of the dead with horror, and so forth—does not sound like the (true) eternal state following the Millennium and the Final Judgment, does it? Let us see if the Lord will further clarify the sequence of events as we go through Chapter 21 verse by verse:

21:1 *Now I saw* (a) *a new heaven and a new earth, for the first heaven and the first earth had passed away. Also there was* (b) *no more sea.*

a.   "Heaven" in the Bible is not a monolithic term. It may refer to the sky (the earth's atmosphere), space (beyond the earth's atmosphere but within Earth's solar system), outer space (beyond Earth's solar system where the Oort Cloud of comets, stars other than Earth's Sun, and other galaxies and celestial objects exist), or the dwelling place of the Most High God (beyond His Creation). *"Heaven"* in the present context, since it is singular, seems to refer to the sky (the earth's atmosphere) and all it contains. On first impression, it certainly seems that the new heaven and new earth are "brand new," having totally replaced the heaven and the earth that were destroyed at the Final Judgment. But have they? The Greek word translated *"new"* here is *kainos,* which can mean a renewal, refreshing, or refurbishing of something that already existed, as in *"new [kainos] covenant"* (Hebrews 8:13). The Mosaic Law (*Torah*), on which the Old Covenant was based, was **not** done away with (for example, the Ten Commandments are still intact, and Yahushua said, *"...till heaven and earth pass away, one jot or one tittle will by no means pass from the law [Torah] till all is fulfilled"*—Matthew 5:18). The basic elements of the Law of Yahuah are still intact, the only difference in the two covenants being that in the New Covenant, the Law is written on the heart rather than on *"tablets of stone"* (Hebrews 8:10). In other words, the *Torah* (instruction manual—not just the legal rulings) of Yahuah has not changed. But under what is more correctly called the **Re**newed Covenant, **all** of His People are enabled by His indwelling Spirit to keep it from their hearts rather than having to keep it in an external, legalistic way as under the Old Covenant. In the same way, the basic components of Heaven and Earth will not be totally done away with until the Final Judgment but are just greatly altered and radically restored back to their Edenic state during the Millennium so that they are, in effect, *"new."* By the way, the Greek word that is most often translated "brand new" or "recently born" is *neos,* as in 1 Corinthians 5:7. The difference in the two terms is subtle, and sometimes they are used interchangeably, but the point is that in this verse, *kainos* can, and apparently does, refer to a *re*newal rather than to a total replacement of the first earth and heaven. All the prophecies of the Day of the Lord and His Wrath certainly seem to indicate tremendous changes in the topography of the earth and radical reparations that will have to be made to restore it to its Edenic state during the Millennium. Perhaps the 30-day period foretold by Daniel (Daniel 12:11) that immediately follows the 1260 days of the second half of the Final Seven Years is the time period during which the *re*newed earth and *re*newed heaven are formed. Then, perhaps, during the next 45 days (cf. Daniel 12:12), New Jerusalem will descend to Earth and the Messianic Kingdom will be established. But that is all conjecture.

b.   This verse also, on first impression, makes it seem that the earth and heaven of 20:11 are replaced by the new earth and new heaven because 20:13 states, ". . . *the **sea** gave up the dead*," but 21:1 says there is no more sea. However, as was stated in the commentary on 20:13, apparently, "*sea*" in that verse is symbolic for the masses of unsaved people and does not refer to a literal sea.

21:2-4 Then I, John, saw the holy city, New Jerusalem, coming down out of heaven from [Yahuah], (a) prepared as a bride adorned for her husband. And I heard (b) a loud voice from heaven saying, "Behold, (c) the tabernacle of [Yahuah] is with men, and He will dwell with them, and they shall be His people. [Yahuah] Himself will be with them and be their [Yahuah]. And [Yahuah] will wipe away every tear from their eyes; (d) there shall be no more death, nor sorrow, nor crying. There shall be no more pain, for the former things have passed away."

a.   The New Jerusalem is prepared for a new earth—an appropriate marriage.

b.   We have learned that a voice from Heaven can be the voice of any heavenly being or group of beings—a living creature, the 24 elders, the multitude of redeemed Saints, or an angel—whereas a voice from the throne in Heaven is the voice of the Lord.

c.   The Tabernacle (as opposed to the Temple) was the temporary dwelling place of Yahuah among the tribes of Israel. This may be a clue that the new earth will endure during the Millennium, until the Final Judgment, but is not truly "eternal." The ultimate goal of Yahuah is for His Saints to be One in Him, as Yahuah the Father

193

and Yahuah the Son are One, not just for Him to dwell among them (cf. John 17:21).

d. This is a glimpse of Timeless Eternity (cf. "Appendix 8—How Long is 'Forever' in the *Bible"),* given personally by the Lord Yahuah. These promises are for those redeemed and glorified Saints who dwell in New Jerusalem, but not for those who, during the Millennium, dwell in the nations surrounding New Jerusalem, where there will still be sin, pain, sorrow, weeping, and death, although even that suffering will be very limited compared to pre-millennial history.

21:5-8 *Then* (a) *He who sat on the throne said, "Behold,* (b) *I make all things new." And He said to me, "Write, for these words are true and faithful." And He said to me,* (c) *"It is done! I am the Alpha and the Omega, the Beginning and the End.* (d) *I will give of the fountain of the water of life freely to him who thirsts. He who overcomes shall inherit all things, and I will be his God and he shall be My son.* (e) *But the cowardly, unbelieving, abominable, murderers, sexually immoral, sorcerers, idolaters, and all liars shall have their part in the lake which burns with fire and brimstone, which is the second death."*

a. Here we have an interruption in John's vision of the new heaven, the new earth, and New Jerusalem. The One who sits on the throne, the Alpha and Omega, speaks to John directly.

b. He tells John that He is in the process of making all things new (which is what the Revelation is all about) and tells him to write what he hears, because the words are faithful and true.

c. What is done? . . . Perhaps, with the completion of the events of the Revelation, the reconciliation of His redeemed People and the restoration of all that belongs to Him in Heaven and on Earth to Himself are accomplished (cf. Colossians 1:21; Ephesians 1:10). When Yahushua finished His work of redemption on the cross, He similarly announced, *"It is finished"* (John 19:30). The great accomplishment of the Lord at His first coming was to redeem His People and establish the Kingdom of Heaven in the hearts of those who have accepted Him as Savior and Lord. The great accomplishment at His second coming will be to restore all things on Earth and in Heaven to Himself (Colossians 1:20).

d. And the end result will be adoption as Sons of Yahuah, eternal life for those who thirst for it, and the inheritance of all *"riches of glo-*

ry . . . in [the Messiah Yahushua]" (Ephesians 1:18; Philippians 4:19) by those who overcome.

e.   But separation from Yahuah in the lake of fire is the destiny of those who reject life in the Messiah and continue in the ways of the wicked.

21:9-27   *Then* (a) *one of the seven angels who had the seven bowls filled with the seven last plagues came to me and talked with me, saying, "Come, I will show you the bride, the Lamb's wife." And he carried me away in the Spirit to* (b) *a great and high mountain, and showed me the great city, the holy Jerusalem, descending out of heaven from [Yahuah], having the glory of [Yahuah]. Her* (c) *light was like a most precious stone, like a jasper stone, clear as crystal. Also she had* (d) *a great and high wall with twelve gates, and twelve angels at the gates, and names written on them, which are the names of the twelve tribes of the children of Israel: three gates on the east, three gates on the north, three gates on the south, and three gates on the west. Now* (e) *the wall of the city had twelve foundations, and on them were the names of the twelve apostles of the Lamb. And he who talked with me had* (f) *a gold reed to measure the city, its gates, and its wall. The city is laid out as a square; its length is as great as its breadth. And he measured the city with the reed:* (g) *twelve thousand furlongs. Its length, breadth, and height are equal. Then he measured* (h) *its wall: one hundred and forty-four cubits, according to the measure of a man, that is, of an angel.* (i) *The construction of its wall was of jasper; and the city was pure gold, like clear glass. The foundations of the wall of the city were adorned with all kinds of precious stones: the first foundation was jasper, the second sapphire, the third chalcedony, the fourth emerald, the fifth sardonyx, the sixth sardius, the seventh chrysolite, the eighth beryl, the ninth topaz, the tenth chrysoprase, the eleventh jacinth, and the twelfth amethyst. The twelve gates were twelve pearls: each individual gate was of one pearl. And the street of the city was pure gold, like transparent glass.* (j) *But I saw no temple in it, for the Lord [Yahuah] Almighty and the Lamb are its temple.* (k) *The city had no need of the sun or of the moon to shine in it, for the glory of [Yahuah] illuminated it. The Lamb is its light.* (l) *And the nations of those who are saved shall walk in its light, and the kings of the earth bring their glory and honor into it. Its gates shall not be shut at all by day (there shall be no night there). And they shall bring the glory and the honor of the nations into it.* (m) *But there shall by no means enter it anything that defiles, or causes an abomination or a lie, but only those who are written in the Lamb's Book of Life.*

a. After John's personal conference with the Lord, one of the angels who poured out the bowls of wrath came to him, beckoning him to accompany the angel to a place where John would be shown *"the bride, the Lamb's wife,"* who has been clearly identified in the *Bible* as Yahuah's People, the redeemed Saints of the Lord, including the BCE Saints and the Followers of Yahushua (e.g., Isaiah 62:5; Ephesians 5:23; Revelation 19:7-9).

b. Now, the description gets mystical and highly symbolic. The Bride of Christ, who is also His Redeemed, *is* New Jerusalem. Prophecy seems to indicate that there will be only one huge mountain on the earth (all others will have disappeared—cf. 16:20) during the Millennium, and that will be the mountain of the Lord, Mount Zion (Isaiah 2:3; Ezekiel 17:22-23; 20:40). Apparently, that will be the location to which New Jerusalem descends out of Heaven, for it is from there that the Lord will rule. The description of New Jerusalem is similar to Ezekiel's prophetic description of the city (cf. Ezekiel 40-48).

c. Because human minds cannot begin to fully comprehend New Jerusalem, it is presented in images of the most fantastic, precious, valuable, beautiful objects known on the earth. Her light, reflecting the glory of Yahuah, is like a jasper stone (probably a diamond). Like the jasper stone, the Bride of the Messiah will not be the source of light in New Jerusalem, but will reflect the glory of Yahuah.

d. The twelve gates of the city, three on each side, each attended by an angel, each a having the name of a tribe of Israel written on it, were typified by the twelve tribes of Israel camped around the Tabernacle (Numbers 2). Perhaps this symbolizes that the only entrance into New Jerusalem and the presence of the Lord is through Israel's Messiah.

e. The city walls, which keep out intruders and protect the residents, are built on twelve foundation stones—The Messiah's apostles. Members of the Body of Believers in Yahushua, the Bride of the Messiah, are told that they, as *"living stones, are being built up* [into] *a spiritual house"* (1 Peter 2:5), and also that the Messiah is the *"chief cornerstone"* (1 Peter 2:7). The Body of Believers is built on the foundation of the prophecies and doctrines of the prophets and apostles (1 Peter 2:20). In some wonderful, mystical way,

196

New Jerusalem will literally be the Community of Believers, the Bride of the Messiah.

f. As was mentioned in the commentary on 11:1, measuring the Temple was symbolic of preserving Israel through the Wrath of Yahuah. But that was done with a flimsy cane reed. Now, New Jerusalem is measured with a golden reed, indicating eternal preservation of a highly-valued object—the City or People of Yahuah, the Bride of the Messiah.

g. In Scripture, twelve seems to be the number that represents Yahuah's People: twelve tribes of Israel, twelve apostles; and 1,000 is the number of completion or fullness, as in 144,000 of Israel (12,000 cubed). New Jerusalem, the Bride of the Messiah, is a complete cube, 12,000 furlongs on each side—the perfected, completed City of Yahuah. Literally, the city is approximately 1,500 miles on each side—plenty of room for billions of glorified individuals who are not limited by gravity. But that incidental observation is not important; the symbolism of perfection and completeness is what is important.

h. The height of the wall (which is identified with the leaders of Yahuah's People: its gates with the patriarchs and its foundation stones with the apostles) is the perfect height (as is indicated by the fact that its height is the measure both of a man and an angel) to protect and preserve Yahuah's People. Its height, 144 cubits, is the number of the representatives of ancient Israel (the 12 patriarchs) and the number of the representatives of the Followers of Yahushua (the 12 apostles) multiplied together, which cubes or perfects the number. In other words, it takes both ancient Israel and the Followers of Yahushua perfectly combined to complete the Bride of Christ, New Jerusalem.

i. We will not, for fear of missing the beauty of the forest by focusing on the individual trees, attempt to read meaning into every component of New Jerusalem. If we can just list each component and visualize the incredible combined beauty of those components, perhaps Yahuah will give us an inkling of the awesome, incomprehensible beauty of the actual New Jerusalem: The 144-cubit (216-foot) wall is brilliantly-luminescent, crystal-clear jasper (diamond?); the entire city is gold so pure that it is transparent; the twelve foundations of the wall (the apostles) are adorned with breathtakingly beautiful, precious stones: jasper, sapphire (blue), chalcedony (a greenish emerald), emerald (bright green), sardonyx (red and white), sardius (bright red), chrysolite (golden yellow),

197

beryl (bluish green), topaz (yellowish green), chrysoprasus (apple green), jacinth (blue), and amethyst (violet and purple); each gate is one huge pearl engraved with the name of a tribe of Israel; and the street of the city is pure, transparent gold.

j. This confirms that the new heaven and the new earth, in which Yahuah *"tabernacles"* with His People, are temporary. Mystically again, there is no temple in New Jerusalem, because Yahuah the Father and Yahuah the Son *are*, as One, its Temple. Yahuah no longer dwells in the Saints, who are the temple of the Holy Spirit (1 Corinthians 6:19), but the Saints are *One* in Him (cf. Romans 12:5).

k. The glory of the Lord provides perfect light for New Jerusalem; there are no sun, moon and stars, and hence, no night there.

l. In fact, the light of New Jerusalem, in which the people of the earth shall walk, shall provide light for the whole earth. And the *"kings"* of the earth shall bring their glory into the city. If this is during the Millennium, as it seems to be, the *"nations"* outside the city gates are not-yet-glorified human beings—the nations descended from the Jews plus the nations descended from the Gentiles who survived the Final Seven Years following the Rapture. And walking in the light probably symbolizes walking in the Spirit, as it does for Believers today (cf. John 8:12; Ephesians 5:8; 1 John 1:7; Galatians 5:25), except on a much grander, more general scale. The ones who do not walk in the light will be those of the Gentile nations who have not joined the nations of Israel. During the Millennium, all nations will be ruled by the apostles and other glorified Saints who rule with the Messiah and who will glorify Yahuah by coming into His presence in New Jerusalem and worshiping Him. This is a fulfillment of BCE prophecy, for, as the psalmist declared, *"All nations whom You have made shall come and worship before You, O Lord, and shall glorify Your name"* (Psalm 86:9). What a wonderful world it will be!

m. However, those who are not saved, whose names are not written in the Lamb's Book of Life, will not be allowed to enter New Jerusalem. These, apparently, will be those of the nations who, although allowed to enter the millennial kingdom, do not totally submit themselves to the Lordship of the Messiah and are deceived and reject His Lordship after Satan is released at the end of the Millennium. This seems to confirm that the new heaven, the new earth, and New Jerusalem are the heaven, the earth, and Jerusalem of the millennial kingdom of Yahuah, because in (true) eternity there will be none whose names are not written in the Book of Life in the Kingdom of Heaven.

Chapter 22—More Details about New Jerusalem and the Conclusion of Yahuah's Prophetic Word

22:1-5 And he showed me (a) *a pure river of water of life, clear as crystal, proceeding from the throne of [Yahuah] and of the Lamb.* (b) *In the middle of its street, and on either side of the river, was the tree of life, which bore twelve fruits, each tree yielding its fruit* (c) *every month. The leaves of the tree were for* (d) *the healing of the nations. And there shall be* (e) *no more curse, but* (f) *the throne of [Yahuah] and of the Lamb shall be in it, and His servants shall serve Him.* (g) *They shall see His face, and* (h) *His name shall be on their foreheads. There shall be no night there: They need no lamp nor light of the sun, for the Lord [Yahuah] gives them light. And they shall reign* (i) *"forever" and ever.*

a. Life flows from the throne in New Jerusalem, where Yahuah the Father and the Lamb, in perfect unity, both occupy the throne. Like the walls of jasper and the decorative stone of jasper in the walls' foundation, the water of life is pure and bright, like a perfect diamond (the Greek word, *lampros*, translated *"clear,"* means "shining" or "bright").

b. This sentence is awkwardly translated, and there is no consensus among commentators as to the exact image that it conveys. Perhaps the street is divided, with the river running down the middle and fruit trees on each side of the river. Apparently, the Tree of Life is one kind of tree, but many trees of life are planted along and on both sides of the river of life, each being sustained by the water of the river and each bearing twelve kinds of fruit each month. The important thing is that this is a miraculous, life-giving tree, the fruit of which all the Redeemed in the new earth may eat and live forever. (Adam and Eve neglected to eat of the tree of life in the Garden, choosing instead to eat the forbidden fruit, and brought death on themselves and the whole world—Genesis 2:9; 3:1-6). During the Millennium, people will still have a choice whether or not to partake of the Tree of Life in the midst of Paradise. Those who, like Adam and Eve, neglect it will be deceived by Satan when he is released from the abyss and be separated from Yahuah for eternity.

c. Notice that although there is no day or night, or need for the light of the sun, in New Jerusalem each tree yields its fruit each month. That must be because the river of life and the trees are for the sustenance and the healing of the nations, which are outside New Jerusalem in the millennial kingdom, where day and night and months and seasons still exist (cf. Isaiah 66:23).

d.   Another clue that this is during the Millennium is that the leaves are for the healing of the nations (healing is not necessary if there is no sickness). *"Nations"* (Greek: *ethnos*) refers to ethnic groups, especially to Gentiles, in the *B'rit Hadashah* (e.g., Matthew 4:15). But in some instances it refers to the Jews (e.g., Luke 7:5), redeemed Gentiles and Jews (e.g., 1 Peter 2:9), or to all the nations of the world (e.g., Acts 17:26). It is in reference to all the Redeemed but non-glorified nations of the world that *"nations"* seems to be used here, because, during the Millennium, in the New Jerusalem, the Redeemed will be glorified and have no need of healing, and it will be the non-glorified nations who inhabit the world outside New Jerusalem.

e.   The basic curse that came on Adam and Eve was death (Genesis 3:3). There will be no death in New Jerusalem.

f.   Only in New Jerusalem could the joy of serving Yahuah as slaves (Greek: *duolos*—"bondservants") be identical to the joy of being His children, His Bride, His People, His priests, His kings, and being one with Him. The magnificence and ecstasy of who we are in the Lord will all come together in New Jerusalem!

g.   Human beings have never been able to see the face of Yahuah. But in our glorified bodies, when we are like Him and in His presence, we will be able to see Him face to face (1 John 3:2).

h.   His secret name will be on the foreheads of the Redeemed, eternally identifying them with Him. Perhaps, this name is transferred from the white stone given to them by the Lord (2:17) to their foreheads, and it is also with this name that the 144,000 are sealed (7:3-4; 14:1).

i.   His servants, the Redeemed, shall, as promised (2 Timothy 2:12), reign with Him for all (true) eternity. Over what they will reign— other worlds, heavenly creatures—only Yahuah knows and is not stated, because that is the end of the Revelation of the Lord as far as His present Saints need to be concerned.

Revelation 22:6-9   *Then* (a) *he said to me, "These words are faithful and true."* (b) *And the Lord* [Yahuah] *of the holy prophets sent His angel to show His servants the things which must shortly take place. (c) "Behold, I am coming quickly! Blessed is he who keeps the words of the prophecy of this book."* (d) *Now I, John, saw and heard these things. And when I heard and saw, I fell down to worship before the feet of the angel who showed me these things. Then (e) he said to me, "See that you do not do that. For I am your fellow servant, and of your brethren the prophets, and of those who keep the words of this book. Worship [Yahuah]."*

a. This is apparently still the angel who had just given John a detailed look at the inside of New Jerusalem. He confirms what the Lord has personally told John: that the words of the Revelation are faithful and true (21:5).

b. John testifies that he had not just dreamed up the 40 + visions of the Revelation; an angel of the Lord showed them to him. This sentence is practically a quote of 1:1.

c. This is the Lord Yahushua emphasizing the importance of always being watchful and ready for His second coming, which John, about 60 years before he wrote Revelation, had heard from Yahushua personally (Matthew 24:42, 44).

d. John writes his own words.

e. The angel speaks, telling John that he also is a servant of the Lord and is no more worthy of worship than is any prophet (prophesying is basically the angel's function in giving John the Revelation).

22:10-15 (a) *And he said to me, "Do not seal the words of the prophecy of this book, for the time is at hand. (b) He who is unjust, let him be unjust still; he who is filthy, let him be filthy still; he who is righteous, let him be righteous still; he who is holy, let him be holy still. And behold, I am coming quickly, and My reward is with Me, to give to every one according to his work. I am the Alpha and the Omega, the Beginning and the End, the First and the Last." (c) Blessed are those who do His commandments, that they may have the right to the tree of life, and may enter through the gates into the city. But outside are dogs and sorcerers and sexually immoral and murderers and idolaters, and whoever loves and practices a lie.*

a. The angel continues, telling John **not** to seal up the Revelation— the opposite of what the angel (perhaps the same angel) told Daniel (Daniel 12:9). Why? ". . .*for the time is at hand.*" What? Has it not been almost 2,000 years since the Revelation was written? Yes, but the events foretold in Revelation began to be fulfilled immediately with the persecution of the true Community of Believers in Yahushua and the Jews by Rome and the Roman Catholic Church (a precursor to the Babylon of Chapter 17); the dispersion of the Jews throughout the "wilderness of the world" in 135 AD; the continued attempts of the beast to destroy Yahuah's People the Jews and the Followers of Yahushua down through the centuries; the continual increase of wars, rumors of wars, and natural disasters; and the general increase of lawlessness and following after the god of this world. All these trends and others that are prophesied in the Revelation will culminate during the Final Seven Years, but it was not just a psychological gimmick to keep the Yahushua's Disciples on their toes that the angel told John that *"the time is at hand."* The time was at hand for all the end-of-the-age prophesies to begin to be fulfilled, and it still is at hand, closer than ever. Remember, a thousand years is as one day on Yahuah's mural of history. So, from Heaven's point of view, time, in comparison to eternity, is very short. And that—the eternal perspective—is what the Father in Heaven wants his Children to have. And so Yahushua, to those who understand the brevity of this present life on the earth, declaring that He is Yahuah as He did at the beginning of His Revelation (1:8), repeats again that He is coming quickly. Time is short (cf. 1:1).

b. *"He who is unjust, let him be unjust still; he who is filthy, let him be filthy still; he who is righteous, let him be righteous still; he who is holy, let him be holy still,"* is just a way of saying that for those who refuse to repent and be changed by the Lord, when The End does come and He returns, it will be too late to be saved and to change their ways.

c. Again, it is emphasized that we will be judged according to our works, not just because we say with our mouths that Yahushua is Yahuah (cf. Matthew 7:21). Only those who keep His commandments will be allowed to enter New Jerusalem. And again, this implies that New Jerusalem will exist on the earth during the Millennium, because there will be those in the nations outside the city who are not allowed to enter the city (cf. 21:27).

22:16-21 (a) *"I, [Yahushua], have sent My angel to testify to you these things in the churches. (b) I am the Root and the Offspring of David, the Bright and Morning Star." (c) And the Spirit and the bride say, "Come!" And let him who hears say, "Come!" And let him who thirsts come. Whoever desires, let him take the water of life freely. (d) For I testify to everyone who hears the words of the prophecy of this book: If anyone adds to these things, [Yahuah] will add to him the plagues that are written in this book; and if anyone takes away from the words of the book of this prophecy, [Yahuah] shall take away his part from the Book of Life, from the holy city, and from the things which are written in this book. (e) He who testifies to these things says, "Surely I am coming quickly." Amen. Even so, come, Lord [Yahushua]! (f) The grace of our Lord [Yahushua the Messiah] be with you all. Amen.*

a. Yahushua makes His closing statement, reaffirming that it is through His angel (not John's imagination) that His Revelation is given, and that it is actually His angel who is testifying, making sure the assemblies of Believers get the message.
b. Then, He affirms that He is Yahuah the Son, Israel's Messiah, His Followers' Redeemer. He is, amazingly, both the root (creator/ancestor) and the offspring (descendant) of David (cf. Micah 5:2; John 8:58; Matthew 1:1). *"Root and offspring of David"* strikes a familiar chord with Jews, whereas *"morning star"* is an *B'rit Hadashah* term (2 Peter 1:19; Revelation 2:28). This once again indicates that the Revelation was written for both the Jews and the Gentiles.
c. It is both the Holy Spirit and the Body of Believers in Yahushua who invite the unsaved to come to the Lord for eternal life. And when they do, they also are exhorted to spread the Gospel message.
d. The Revelation is the final Word of prophecy regarding the End of the Age. So, there is a solemn warning, involving "eternal" consequences, not to change it.
e. Finally, reinforcing the sense of urgent expectation, John repeats the Lord's affirmation that He is coming quickly, and adds his emphatic agreement with, *"Amen* [so be it]. *Even so* [according to what You say], *come, Lord [Yahushua]!"*
f. And he closes the Revelation of the Lord with a blessing for the Disciples of Yahushua and a final *"Amen."*

205

Appendix 1—Who is Modern, Prophesied Babylon?

Two Babylons

The *Bible* goes to great lengths to clearly tell us about two different (but similar), literal Babylons: ancient, historical Babylon and modern, prophetic Babylon. There are more verses of Scripture (over 250) that speak of the two Babylons than of any other city or nation on Earth, except for Jerusalem and Israel. Entire chapters of the *Bible* devoted to Babylon include: Isaiah 13, 14, 47, 48; Jeremiah 50, 51 and Revelation 17, 18. Each Babylon is not only identified by a *"great city,"* but by the land, nation or empire in which its great city is located (cf. Jeremiah 50:8, 12, 38); by other nations or territories it dominates politically, economically, militarily, and religiously; and by its treachery against Israel. Two entire chapters plus other passages of the book of Revelation are devoted to modern Babylon. The great exultation of the Redeemed of the Lord before He returns to establish His kingdom on Earth is because of the final (second) destruction of modern Babylon (Revelation 18:21-19:2). So, modern Babylon will be the most important city-state/nation/empire on Earth, other than Israel, during the seven-year period of tribulation and the Wrath of Yahuah foretold in the Revelation. If you are interested in really understanding the events, players, and plot of the book of Revelation, realize that a main key to unlocking that understanding is knowing the identity, activities, and destiny of modern, prophetic, "mystery" Babylon. So, brace yourself, put on your face-up-to-reality hat and let us first take a look at ancient, historical Babylon to see what clues about modern Babylon we can gather.

Ancient Babylon

Actually, there were three ancient Babylons: Babylon the religious center of the Akkadian Empire, Babylon the capital of the first Babylonian Empire, and Babylon the capital of the neo-Babylonian Empire. Aspects of all three ancient Babylons are reflected in *Bible* prophecies concerning modern Babylon.

The *Bible* tells us that, after the Great Flood, Noah's great-grandson Nimrod founded the world's first multi-national, multi-ethnic and multi-cultural empire (cf. Genesis 10:10-12). Coincidentally, thousands of cuneiform (clay) tablets from that same time period (about 2300 BCE) tell us that, in the same location (the "land of Shinar" - Mesopotamia) the Akkadian Empire, which most secular historians acknowledge as the world's first Empire, was founded by Sargon. Close examination of Biblical, Akkadian and Summerian records reveal that Nimrod and Sargon are the same person. Nimrod was his given name and Sargon (which means "True King" or "Legitimate King") in Akkadian was his royal title. According to both the Biblical (Genesis 10:10) and secular records the Kingdom of Akkadia included the religious center that was later named Babylon and the cities of Erich (Uruk) and Accad (Akkad). Also, according to both records, this king invaded and conquered what was then the relatively small, insignificant kingdom of Assyria, built several cities there including Nineveh and Calah, and incorporated it into his growing empire. Thirdly, both the Bible and Akkadian records call this king a *"mighty hunter"* (Genesis 10:9). All Akkadian kings were celebrated as mighty hunters and warriors and were worshiped as deified humans.

To establish himself as a god in the public's perception, Sargon ceremonially married the principal deity of the Summerians and Akkadians, the "Queen of Heaven" Innana (later named Ishtar in Babylon). Scripture states that Nimrod *"began to be a mighty one on the earth"* (Genesis 10:8), which may indicate that he was not only the first empire-building ruler or king, but that he had supernatural satanic powers. His powers certainly were not from the one true God Yahuah, because he practiced a totally idolatrous religious system and attempted to build a tower to heaven—the infamous "Tower of Babel"—reminding us of Satan's enticing statement to Adam and Eve, *"You will be like [Yahuah]"* (Genesis 3:5), and the boast of Lucifer, the (spiritual) king of Babylon (Isaiah 14:4), *"I will ascend into heaven, I will exalt my throne above the stars of [Yahuah]"* (Isaiah 14:13). The title "mighty hunter," spiritually speaking, may mean one who hunts for and destroys the souls of men.

So, virtually all translations (from Hebrew) of the Genesis 10 and 11 account of the history of Nimrod's Babylon are incorrect, and all expositions and teachings based on those translations are incorrect. Nimrod/Sargon was the founder of the Akkadian Empire, not the Babylonian Empire. And the city of Akkad was the capital of the empire, not Babylon. Nimrod/Sargon conquered the Sumerians, who ruled southern Mesopotamia before he arrived, and, to include the Sumerians seamlessly into his empire, although he was a direct descendant of Noah who believed unwavering in the one, true God Yahuah, he adopted the Sumerian religion which included the worship of their gods, especially Innana, the "Queen of Heaven." He then built a city which later came to be called Babylon because the ziggurats (towers) built there to honor and worship the Sumerian/Akkadian deities were called, in Akkadian, *babylons*. (Actually, *babylon* is a Greek variation of the Akkadian word *babilum)*.

Another error based on mistranslations of the original Hebrew Scriptures, which greatly distorts and diminishes our understanding of how Nimrod's Babylon is reflected in prophecies regarding modern Babylon, is the notion that, at the time of the building of the "Tower of Babel," the whole world spoke one language. Archaeological discoveries of the thousands of Sumerian and Akkadian cuneiform tablets and linguistic studies have proven that, by the time Nimrod arrived on the scene, about 500 years after the Flood, many languages were spoken in the world. In Mesopotamia several languages were spoken, including Sumerian, and, after Nimrod arrived, Akkadian was spoken there. Then, Babylonian and Assyrian (dialects that developed from Akkadian) were spoken. The error that the whole world spoke a single language arose from a mistranslation of Genesis 11:1 which states in virtually all versions of the *Bible, "Now the whole earth had one language and one speech."* There are three words in that statement that have been mistranslated down through the centuries. The Hebrew text literally states, *"And the whole **land** [earth] was of one **lip** and of one **word."*** The Hebrew term for "earth" *[erets]* may also mean "land," as in the "land of Israel." And in the context of Genesis 10 and 11, that is apparently how *erets* should be translated, because it is all about the Mesopotamian empire of Nimrod, which certainly did not cover the whole earth. Also, in the ancient Akkadian and Sumerian cultures "one lip" was an idiom that meant "one government" and "one word" was an idiom that meant "one command" as in, "Just say the word and it will be done." So, Genesis 11:1 should be correctly translated, *"And the whole land* [of Mesopotamia/the Akkadian Empire] *was of one government and one commander* [ruler]." In other words, what Nimrod did, in total rebellion against the Lord Yahuah, Whose original intention for human beings was that they would *"have dominion over . . . all the earth"* and Who told Adam and Eve, *"Be fruitful and multiply; fill the earth and subdue it"* (Genesis 1:26, 28), was to attempt to bring all languages, cultures and nations together under his rule as the deified sargon ("true king") of the world. Notice that the Lord nowhere told humans to rule over one another. His later concession to Israel, allowing them to have a human king, was because of their hardness of heart in refusing to submit to Him alone.

Another grievous error in translation that has reinforced the error that the *"whole earth"* spoke one language is naming the ziggurat that the Akkadians were attempting to build to Heaven (probably for worship of their principal deity Innana/Ishtar) the "Tower of Babel." There are only two places in Scripture (Genesis 10:10 and 11:9—the text we are clarifying) where, in translations from the Hebrew, *"Babel"* is identified as a city the Akkadians, under Nimrod, were building. However, there is no such term "Babel" in Hebrew. In every other place in Scripture (280 times) where the Hebrew term translated "Babel" in Genesis 10:10 and 11:9 is used, it is translated *"Babylon."* The original translators of the Hebrew might have thought the Hebrew term was *balal* which means "confusion," and that mistaken translation supported their belief that the Lord stopped the building of the tower and scattered the people of "Babylon" by confusing their language.

Until recently, the sudden collapse of the Akkadian empire in 2154 BCE, within 180 years of its founding, was a mystery to historians. Many Akkadian writings told of the gods raining disasters from the heavens, but historians could not put two and two together. However, archaeological and geological discoveries, especially, in 2001, of the two-mile wide Umm al Binni lake crater in the Amarah region of southern Iraq, only about 125 miles from ancient Akkad and nearby Babylon, plus Akkadian writings like "The Curse of Akkad," have proven that the Akkadian civilization was destroyed suddenly by a comet impacting the earth and exploding with the force of thousands of Hiroshima-size atomic bombs (190 to 750 megatons of TNT). That impact must have totally destroyed "by fire" everything within over 100 miles from the impact. It also rendered the land of much of the empire uninhabitable for a number of years and scattered survivors far and wide.

This scientifically, historically correct explanation of what happened to Nimrod's empire and the city of Babylon throws brilliant light on the Revelation's prophecy of what will happen to modern Babylon. In the same way that Nimrod set himself up as the deified ruler of the world's first empire, the ultimate anti-messiah will declare himself to be *"god"* (2 Thessalonians 2:4) and will establish a (true) global kingdom (cf. Revelation 13:8; 17:17). Nimrod was the first type and foreshadow of the *"beast"* of Revelation (13:4; 17:12). Also, Nimrod/Sargon's Akkadian Empire was the original type of Antimessiah's global empire which will be destroyed in the same way but on a much larger scale than the Akkadian Empire was destroyed.

Also, the annihilation of Babylon will not be an isolated event. Read the commentary on Revelation 6, 7, 8, 9 and 16 to see how **every one** of the trumpet and bowl judgments of the Wrath of Yahuah will involve the impact of comets, Yahuah's *"weapons of indignation"* from the *"storehouse"* of those weapons (the Oort Cloud of billions of comets) located at the *"farthest border"* (surrounding our solar system) (cf. Jeremiah 50:25, 26).

Incidentally, it was about 200 years after the fall of the Akkadian Empire, about 1900 BCE, that Abram (renamed Abraham) left Ur, the ancient capital of Sumer, located in southern Mesopotamia, and moved to Haran, a city in the north. Later, Abraham left Haran and migrated into the land of Canaan (modern-day Israel) under Yahuah's promise that he would become the father of a great nation (cf. Genesis 12).

The second phase of Babylon, when it became a great city-state/kingdom, was ruled by the Amorite dynasty. The most famous Amorite King over Babylonia was Hammurapi (sometimes spelled Hammurabi), who ruled from approximately 1792-1750 BCE. Hammurapi is most famous for his legal judgments, which evolved into the "Code of Hammurapi," from which many of our modern, western laws are derived. The Babylonians had numerous gods which were assimilated from the earlier Sumerian/Akkadian culture which the Babylonians and Assyrians displaced. In fact, basically the same Sumerian religious system with the same gods was in place in Hammurapi's Babylon as during Nimrod's rule hundreds of years earlier. Their chief male god was Marduk the sun god or the god of life and death (whose earlier name was Tammuz). But in Babylon, males and females were seen as equals, and, in fact, the main Babylonian deity, and the god most pertinent to our study, was still the "Queen of Heaven," Ishtar (the Sumerian goddess Inanna, the daughter of the moon god and goddess), the goddess of temple prostitutes (the "Mother of Whores"), also called the "Goddess of Liberty." (Make a note of Ishtar's names; they will be important when we discuss the religion of modern, "mystery" Babylon.) In fact, Sumerian/Babylonian religion may be traced through all the false religions of the world, especially those that impacted Israel. The gods (particularly the goddess Inanna/Ishtar) of Canaan, Egypt, Assyria, Greece, Rome, and, yes, modern Babylon are the same as those of ancient Babylon, just with different names. About 1270 BCE, the brutal, merciless Assyrians (the world's first terrorists) overpowered Babylonia. The Assyrian takeover of the Babylonian Empire also has clear prophetic implications for modern Babylon, as will be explained below. For the next 700 years, the Assyrians dominated the ancient world.

In 626 BCE, a leader named Nabopolassar led Babylonia to regain its independence from Assyria. Under him and his son,

Nebuchanezzar, who took over as King in 604 BCE, the neo-Babylonian empire became one of the greatest city-state-empires in world history. And it is this third phase of Babylon with which Scripture is most concerned, because it was the Babylon of Nebuchadnezzar, starting even before he officially became king, that took the Israelites (the descendants of Abraham), primarily of the tribes of Judah and Benjamin, into 70 years of captivity, beginning in 605 BCE when Daniel, Hananiah, Mishael, Azariah and other members of the royal family of Judah and other children of Israel's southern kingdom (the other ten tribes having been dispersed and many taken captive by the Assyrians about 120 years earlier) were taken to Babylon.

So, to help us understand the many Biblical prophecies concerning both ancient and modern Babylon, let us take a closer look at some of the features of ancient Babylon.

Government and Religion

The Babylon of Nebuchadnezzar and its few other kings who reigned from 626-539 BCE, when it fell to Cyrus, King of Persia, was an absolute monarchy. Although Babylon worshiped the same gods as always (Marduk, Ishtar, and others), its religion became very eclectic as it added Sumerian gods and gods from other parts of the world to its pantheon. Various forms of the occult—witchcraft, divination, sorcery, necromancy, and so forth—as well as eastern mysticism were practiced. And Nebuchadnezzar was a ruthless tyrant who demanded that he also be worshiped. Remember the story of Daniel's three friends, Shadrach, Meshach and Abednego, who refused to worship Babylon's gods or bow down to an image of Nebuchadnezzar (Daniel 3)? Although they were three of Nebuchadnezzar's favorite administrators, he was infuriated and had them thrown into the royal incinerator. So, we might say that Babylon's government was a religious dictatorship in which religion was inextricably intertwined with government. One could be executed either for not submitting to the laws of the land or for not practicing the national religion. We will see that in modern, prophetic, "mystery" Babylon, religion is also in bed with the government.

Economy, Culture, and Citizenry

Babylon was the trade and cultural center of the world. It was called the "Golden City." It had the highest standard of living of any nation on the earth. By the standards of the rest of the world, Babylon's citizens lived in great wealth and luxury. It was the world center

212

for education, the arts, and religion. It was the location of the famous "Hanging Gardens," which, from a distance looked like a lush, green, tropical paradise. It was dotted by temples and ziggurats (religious towers) built for the worship of Babylon's many gods, especially for its main gods, Marduk and Ishtar. Babylon was located on the mighty Euphrates River in southern Mesopotamia, which was not an arid, desert area like it is today. In fact, Babylon was located on the alluvial plain drained by the Tigris and Euphrates rivers, watered by an amazing system of canals built by the Babylonians—boasting probably the most fertile soil in the world, covered by rich crops and other vegetation. It was called the "beautiful land." Babylon was the crossroads of trade for that part of the world. Trade routes passed through Babylon from all points north, east, south and west. Boats sailed up and down the Euphrates, which passed right through the middle of the city of Babylon, from the Persian Gulf in the south into Assyria (modern-day Syria and Turkey) in the north. Because Babylon had been occupied by so many peoples down through the centuries, and because people from so many places passed through Babylon, the citizenry of Babylon was very diverse; it was a real "melting pot." Just like ancient Babylon, modern, prophetic Babylon is the economic, trade, and cultural center of the modern world and also the "melting pot" of the world. Sound familiar?

Morality

Babylon was an extremely licentious, immoral city. As was mentioned above, sex outside of marriage was not only acceptable, but was considered the highest form of religious and spiritual practice. All forms of sexual perversion—homosexuality, bestiality, incest, pedophilia, etc.—were widely practiced. Drunken orgies were common entertainment. Modern Babylon is also very libertarian in its morality.

Defense

Babylon was considered the "invincible city." Built in a square pattern, approximately 15 miles on each side, with wide boulevards running at right angles to each other, north to south and east to west, she was a very large city, but carefully designed for rapid access to all parts of the city. As was mentioned above, the Euphrates River flowed right through the middle of Babylon. And a system of canals from the river provided plenty of water to the whole city for gardens, drinking water, cleaning, and other purposes. So, if under siege, the city could be sustained with water and food indefinitely. Along the river banks on both sides of the city and surrounding the city were two huge walls, 100 feet high and 50 to 60 feet wide (wide enough on top for a chariot pulled by a team of four horses to make a U-turn), with intermittent watch towers and huge, copper-plated gates. Then, other parts of the city, like the King's palace, were also partitioned off by similar walls. So, with soldiers constantly manning the watch towers and patrolling the tops of the walls, Babylon was the most impregnable city in history. Unfortunately, the Babylonians got complacent in their "invincibility" and liked to party. So, one night in 539 BCE, when the Babylonians were in drunken revelry, the army of Cyrus, King of Persia, having dammed up the Euphrates River, stealthily entered the city from the river bed, sneaked into the palace, killed the King, and took over the city without a struggle. The next morning, the citizens of Babylon awoke to find themselves conquered! The *Bible* says that in the same way, modern Babylon, who thinks she is invincible, will be destroyed by a sudden, sneak attack in just one hour. Actually, as we continue, we will see how this prophecy has two fulfillments: the fall of political, economic and military Babylon (like the fall of Hammurapi's Babylon to the Assyrians and the fall of Nebuchadnezzar's Babylon to the Persians) and the total annihilation of Babylon "by fire" (like the burning of the Babylon of Nimrod).

Imperialism

Babylon, under the reign of Nebuchadnezzar, was the most economically, politically, and militarily dominant city-state (nation/empire) in the world. She controlled every nation from Egypt to the Persian Gulf in the South to the Black and Caspian Seas in the north. In the same way, modern Babylon will, and to a large extent already does, rule the world.

Modern, Prophetic, "Mystery" Babylon

Of course, modern, prophetic Babylon is not named in the *Bible* because she was not in existence when the *Bible* was written. But you probably already know who she is, if you read the commentary on Revelation Chapters 17 and 18, don't you? And, if you have read through this page, you are probably starting to get a gnawing feeling that it is obvious, aren't you? When confronted with plain evidence from history, current events, and the *Bible*, the identity of modern Babylon is crystal clear, undeniable, and irrefutable. Then, why do very few Americans acknowledge that Babylon is the United States of America? This commentator has often asked himself that question.

214

Citizens of other nations do not seem so blinded to that reality. I think it is because it is just very, very difficult for us to be objective about something in which we have a very high personal stake, especially if our whole lives we have been taught something different. What do you think?

So please, let me beg you, if you love the Truth and are one of those rare few who are really willing to face up to reality, especially if your eternal destiny and the eternal destiny of your loved ones depends on it (and in this case, it certainly might), please suspend any automatic negative reaction that you might have to the idea that the USA is indeed Babylon long enough to read the rest of this essay. Then, if you want to crucify this writer for his horrible, unpatriotic lies, that is OK, because he has done his best to share with you what he believes Yahuah has shown him, before it is too late and, if he is right, you perish with the rest of the Babylonians.

Historical Evidence

Remember, *Bible* history repeats itself. Modern Babylon must be very similar to ancient Babylon. Think about all the characteristics of ancient Babylon listed above: totalitarian, dictatorial government led by a self-deified ruler; eclectic, idolatrous religion blended with the government; strong sense of national pride and patriotism; luxury and wealth—dominates world economy and trade; by far the most powerful military in the world; powerful defense—seemingly "invincible"; world cultural center; center for world government; the "melting pot" of the world; a very immoral nation, tolerating all kinds of sexual immorality and perversion; a "party" nation, centered on entertainment and revelry; imperialistic—dominating the governments of other nations of the world.

Some may take issue with a few of these characteristics.

For example, is the USA a totalitarian government ruled by a self-deified ruler? Please allow me to suggest that the USA is quickly moving in that direction. President George W. Bush garnered more powers for the top executive than any other President in history. While he was in college, President Bush (as did his father, George H.W. Bush) became a member of Skull and Bones—an organization based on the belief that its members have been "born again" into a state of superhuman spirituality (their own spirit, not the Spirit of the Lord Yahuah). And President Barack Obama, with widespread and intrusive enforcement of the Patriot Act, has continued that trend. In the event of another "national emergency" like that of 9-11-2001, an economic crisis, or World War III, the President could declare national martial law overnight, just as Adolf Hitler did in Germany on November 9, 1938, the date he started having Jews and others who opposed his government killed and thousands of them shipped off to concentration camps. President Obama also practices self-worship, believing that the way one rises above the common and mundane is to develop the god-person within. Plus, in her final form, just before her total destruction "by fire," modern Babylon will be ruled by a totalitarian government with a mandated religion, exactly like ancient Babylon, as will be explained below.

Or, you might object to the suggestion that America is imperialistic. It would probably boggle your mind to know how many nations of the world, including Honduras, Uruguay, Afghanistan, Iraq, several African nations, and many others around the world are just client states of the USA; their economies would immediately collapse if America's multi-national corporations pulled out or stopped importing their goods. Therefore, the USA calls the shots in how those countries are run: Their "elected" leaders are virtual puppet governors controlled by the USA.

The Evidence of American Religion

But, the greatest similarity of all between ancient and modern Babylon is religion. Now many, especially American Christians, will flatly deny that assertion. But please consider the evidence of current events in the light of the history of American religion. Yes please, before you completely close your minds, read what is written here. If it is the Truth, that Truth may set you (spiritually) free from misconceptions about American Christianity.

Virtually all Americans have been taught all of our lives and believe that the United States of America is basically a Christian nation—founded on Christian principles by Christians. In fact, we have been taught, especially in the churches, that America is "God's" Redeemer Nation, and the whole world will be brought to Yahushua ("Jesus") the Messiah ("Christ") through the USA, right? As you will see (if you have the courage and open-mindedness to keep reading) nothing could be farther from the truth. George Washington, Thomas Jefferson, Benjamin Franklin and most of the other Founding Fathers of America claimed to be Christians, but were really Deists. For example, the writings of Thomas Jefferson, the principal author of the Declaration of Independence and the third President of the United States, reveal that he was actually very anti-Christian, denying both the miracles and the divinity of Yahushua. You may ask, "What is a Deist, and what is the difference between a Deist and a true Believer in Yahushua the Messiah?" As you will see, the difference is satanically subtle, but real. A Deist believes in one "God" who created the heavens and the earth and everything that is in them and that He created human beings in His own image—put His good, spiritual nature in us. So far, so good, according to the *Bible*. But then, according to the Deists, "God" left the world pretty much to run on its own, and he left man, who had "God's" spiritual goodness, wisdom, and power within, in charge, to manage and take care of the world. But man blew it; he let sin and corruption into the world. Man lost control. And it has been downhill since that time. But, according to the Deists, man still has "God's" nature; he is still basically good and has the knowledge, wisdom and power, somewhere in his being, to regain dominion of the world. We just needed a god-man, a perfect, sinless man, a messiah and savior, to show us the way back to our godlikeness. And, to Christians, that Messiah and Savior is "Jesus Christ." So, all that Christians need to do is to believe in Yahushua, follow his teachings, and by the wisdom and power of Yahuah's Spirit, which He put in them in The Beginning, bringing them back in touch with their basic, natural goodness, bring the rest of the citizens of the world into actualization of their basic God-likeness, and reestablish Paradise on Earth and their dominion over it.

Sounds true to Scripture, right? So, what is wrong with American Christianity according to the above analysis? Do you see the subtle deceit—the Lie of the devil—in it (cf. Genesis 3:5; 2 Thessalonians 2:4, 11)? If you do not, then you are probably a part of America-Babylon's false religious system. But please, do not stop reading yet. In the next section, exactly what the Lie of the devil is will be explained, and many evidences from the *Bible* for exactly which city-state (nation/empire) is modern, prophetic, "mystery" Babylon will be given. If you can honestly face reality, please keep asking yourself which nation, other than the USA, in the present-day world can come anywhere close to manifesting the characteristics of historical ancient Babylon and the biblical identification of modern Babylon.

Scriptural Evidence

Revelation 17 and 18 are devoted to describing modern Babylon and her destiny. Revelation 17 presents religious Babylon and Revelation 18 presents secular Babylon.

Many insist that modern "mystery" Babylon is the Vatican or Rome. And yes, the Roman Empire and the Roman Catholic Church were the original political and religious prototypes of modern Babylon. The "harlot who rides the beast" (religious, "mystery" Babylon) of Revelation 17, with her robes of purple and scarlet, does bear a remarkable resemblance to the Roman Catholic Church, whose colors are purple and scarlet, and she sits on "seven mountains" (Rome is called the "City of Seven Hills"). But a close examination of the text shows that the conclusion that modern religious Babylon is limited to or consists of the RCC or to Rome is fallacious—she is much, much more than that. The Greek word that is translated *"mountains"* or, in some translations, *"hills"* in Revelation 17:9 is *oros,* which means "mountains" or "large land masses" (like continents or large areas of imperialistic rule), rather than "hills." The Greek word (basically a Latin word borrowed from the Romans that commonly referred to Rome) that is translated "hills" or "mounds" (as in Luke 23:30) is *buonos,* which is **not** used in Revelation 17:9. And if you look at the context of Revelation 17:9, you will see that it is talking about world-dominating kingdoms or empires, which hardly describes the city of Rome. The Roman Catholic Church does have worldwide influence, but it can hardly be said to rule the kingdoms of the world. Also, the religion of ancient Babylon was very eclectic—a mixture of all religions and cults. The Roman Catholic Church has made overtures to other religions, but only to bring them under the influence, and ultimately the control, of the RCC. The RCC is not about to give up its autonomy and belief that it is the one, true Church, and that ultimately all the world's religions will be part of the Catholic Church.

Others believe that modern Babylon will be a revived ancient Babylon, located where Iraq is today. Common sense, looking at the sad state of affairs in Iraq at the present time, should immediately dispel that absurd notion. Besides, which nation is in control, behind the scenes, of Iraq at the present time? Is the USA really interested in helping Iraq rebuild Babylon and regain the world dominance Babylon once had?[15]

Since Iraq, the site of ancient Babylon, does not fit the Scriptural description of modern Babylon, some attempt to shift the location of modern Babylon to Saudi Arabia, stating that Mecca, Islam's main

---

[15]In spite of the USA's deadline to withdraw military forces from there by the end of 2011, she still maintains a very powerful training, advisory,

holy city, is the modern city of Babylon, the nobility of Saudi Arabia live in lavish luxury, immorality in Saudi Arabia is rife, the anti-messiah will arise out of Middle Eastern Islam, the oil wealth of Saudi Arabia controls the nations of the world including the USA, and so forth. Indeed, there are many characteristics Saudi Arabia has in common with modern Babylon and may be a precursor to Babylon the Great. But the argument that Saudi Arabia is, in fact, the final modern Babylon the Great is specious, because many of the over 60 identifying characteristics in the *Bible* of modern Babylon cannot possibly pertain to Saudi Arabia. But, far more than with any other nation on Earth, those characteristics fit the USA perfectly. For example, Babylon is called the "hammer [oppressor] of the world" (Jeremiah 50:23). That description does not remotely fit Saudi Arabia, but, with its military, political and economic dominance of the other nations of the world, America fulfills the prophecy perfectly. Also, just as ancient Babylon was a very idolatrous nation, adopting the gods of the nations over which it held sway, and modern Babylon is prophesied to be very idol-atrous (Jeremiah 50:2, 38), the U.S.A., with its "freedom of religion" mantra, is the melting pot of the religions of the world, just as it is the melting pot of the ethnic groups of the world. However, Saudi Arabia is fanatically monotheistic, tolerating no other gods but Allah. And as to oil wealth, at the present time, Russia is the world's number one oil exporter and Saudi Arabia is second. But, with shale oil deposits that are being developed in North Dakota, Texas and other locations, the USA is projected to be the world's number one oil exporter by 2015.

Others insist that modern Babylon, the kingdom of Satan (cf. Isaiah 14:4), will be a "revived Roman empire"—probably a confederation of European nations—that will rule the religious and secular world as ancient Rome did. Well, that is somewhat confused and limited think-ing; ancient Babylon fell long before the Roman Empire was in exist-ence. Also, modern Babylon will be the world-dominating na-tion/empire at the End of the Age only **until** she is destroyed, then re-placed by the global kingdom of Antimessiah—the ultimate revived Roman Empire which will probably have its headquarters in Turkey—

---

support, and mercenary presence in Iraq. Obviously, the USA intends to maintain controlling influence in that part of the world, because she has just completed and moved into her new, fantastic, sprawling embassy in Iraq—the largest in the world—located just 50 miles from the site of the ancient city of Babylon! Ironic, isn't it?

the location of the capital of the Roman Empire under Constantine, a type of the false messiah (see the commentary on Revelation Chapters 17 and 18 for details).

So, let us see if we can discern who the latter days Babylon the Great is by correctly interpreting Scripture. And as you will see, it is not difficult once we realize and accept the possibility that the USA is indeed modern, prophetic Babylon.

Look again at American religion. We claim to be a "Christian" nation, but are we not awfully tolerant of all the other religions and cults of the world, just like ancient Babylon? Just as America is the melting pot of the races of the world, she is also the melting pot of all the world's religions. And the distinctions between the religions in the USA are getting very blurry. Many groups are being formed for dialogue, action, and even common worship among various religions - Protestants and Catholics Together, Promise Keepers, Buddhism and Christianity, Islam and Christianity, New Age ideas and practices in the Church, Yoga in the Church, Eastern mysticism in the Church, Masonic Luciferianism in the Church, *ad infinitum*. True Christians believe that there is only one way to Yahuah, and that is through Yahushua the Messiah, who is the only human being in history who could truthfully claim to be Yahuah. But more and more nominal (but not true) "Christians" believe that there are many paths to "God" and that all the different religions worship, ultimately, the same god. That is what George Bush said about other religions and Christianity when he was President and what Barack Obama says about other religions and Christianity now that he is President.) True Christians believe that there are basically two "gods" impacting this world. One is the false god, Satan or Lucifer, and the other is the one, true God of Israel, the God of the (true) Followers of Yahushua the Messiah, and that all the other religions of the world are, whether they realize it or not, following Satan. So, to the extent that the American "Christian" Church is uniting with other religions, philosophies, and practices of the world, she is not truly Christian, is she? She is really a false (anti-) Christian church, following the false god of this world.

And that brings us back to the above analysis of American "Christianity." Under which "god" and under in what spirit was America really founded? The Deistic founders of the USA believed that Americans are basically good people, ordained by "God" to establish His kingdom on Earth—by violence if necessary. And that is why we rebelled against Britain and fought the Revolutionary War—not because of some little disagreement over "taxation without representation."

That is why our National Anthem glorifies violent revolution . . . "the bombs bursting in air" (killing people). Oh, what a glorious sight! The real reason we fought the Revolutionary War was for freedom, is that not correct? But freedom from what?—freedom from anyone else telling us what to do or how to spend our money. In other words, we wanted to set up our own little "Christian" kingdom where we could do whatever we please without having to be subservient to anyone else. And there is a lot of evidence that the ultimate goal of the real movers and shakers behind the American Revolution was (and still is) to bring the rest of the world into the American-led New World Order. (Remember President George H. W. Bush talking about the New World Order with its "thousand points of light" in the United Nations General Assembly?)

So, what is wrong with that? What is wrong with fighting for our freedom from unjust treatment by those who rule over us? It is totally UNBIBLICAL and UNCHRISTIAN, that is what. Where did Yahushua tell us to rise up in rebellion to violently fight against those who rule over us, even if they mistreat us? Did He not tell us that if someone in authority forces us to go with him one mile, to go two (Matthew 5:41)? Did not the apostle Peter tell us to do just the opposite of resisting or rebelling against those in authority over us, even if they mistreat us (cf. 1 Peter 2:13-19)? Yet, America was founded on violent rebellion, was it not? And the basic assumption was that we are good, Christian people who do not deserve that kind of treatment and who deserve to be free to take our place as "God's" chosen people in dominion over the earth. The next step in that kind of logic is to "preemptively" invade a small, weak nation like Iraq, who had done nothing to us (except for her president, Saddam Hussein, bad-mouthing America), virtually destroying the whole nation and killing and maiming hundreds of thousands of its citizens—old men, women, and children, besides military personnel. And this was all done, according to President Bush, in the name of Christianity, in the war of good against evil. Again, what is wrong with that kind of atrocious thinking and behavior? It is totally UNBIBLICAL and UNCHRISTIAN, that is what. Where did Yahushua tell us that we Christians are good people who deserve to rebel against those in authority over us and to impose our will on the rest of the world, killing them if they, or even just their leaders, threaten us (but show no signs of attacking us)? No, He did not, because that, my friend, is the Lie of the devil. Did Yahushua not say just the opposite? Did He not say, "No one is good but [Yahuah] alone" (Luke 18:19). Where did He tell us, because we are Christians

221

(or a Christian nation), to attack and destroy and conquer and lord it over others, even if they threaten us? Did He not say that is what the nonbelievers do (cf. Matthew 20:25)?[16]

Did Yahushua not tell us that if we wish to be true Christians, to be everyone's servant (cf. Mark 9:35)? I submit to you that the whole idea that Americans (including Christians who are involved in America's agenda) are basically good (god-like) people who deserve to have dominion over the earth before the Lord returns in person to establish His kingdom is a manifestation of the great Lie of the devil (cf. 2 Thessalonians 2:11). And it is that kind of satanically-deluded thinking that resulted in ancient Babylon's downfall, that resulted in Adolf Hitler's and Nazi Germany's downfall, and will result in the total annihilation of modern Babylon in "one hour" (Revelation 18:10, 19).

The Lie of the devil has always been the same from the beginning, when he told Adam and Eve, *"You shall be as gods"* (Genesis 3:5). Did Yahushua not tell us just the opposite: *"Apart from me, you can do nothing"* (John 15:5)? Apart from Yahushua, we fallible human beings are totally powerless against the spiritual forces that control this world. If Yahushua dwells in us, we have some, limited power over those forces, but the book of Revelation tells us very clearly that the Kingdom of Yahuah—total peace and order—will not be established on Earth until the true Messiah—the Lord Yahushua, King of Kings and Lord of Lords—returns in person to do that (cf. Revelation 19:11-20:4). So, if anyone tells you that the USA—"God's" Redeemer Nation—or the Manifested Sons of "God" or anyone else is going take dominion and establish the Kingdom of Heaven on Earth **before** the return, **in person**, of the Messiah, do not be a fool and believe it! That is the Lie of the devil! Or, if anyone tells you, "That's the Messiah, follow him," do not believe it! That is the anti-Christ (false messiah),

---

[16]Please do not misunderstand me . . . **I am not advocating passivism!** Yahushua was **not** a pacifist. He rebuked in no uncertain terms those religious leaders who perverted the *Torah* (instructions and commandments) of the Lord to suit their own ends, calling them "hypocrites," "serpents," and "whitewashed tombs full of dead men's bones." He violently drove the greedy money-changers who were ripping people off out of the Temple. He did not rebuke Peter, who cut the ear off one who came to arrest Him, because he was carrying a sword or defending his Master; He rebuked Him because he was rebelling against those in authority. In fact, Yahushua told His disciples that, after He was gone, to buy swords (for self-defense, which they didn't need

and that is the Lie of the devil. When the true Messiah returns, no one will have to point Him out; it will be obvious (cf. Matthew 24:27). And then, it will be too late to become His disciple.

So, here are a few quick self-test questions to help you see if you are a false "Christian" or a True Christian –a spiritual citizen of Babylon the Great or of the Kingdom of Heaven: Do you think that you are a basically good person? If you believe in your heart that you or anyone else is, by nature, basically good, then you have believed the Lie and are not a True Christian. Do you believe, as the American Declaration of Independence proclaims, that ". . . all men are endowed by the Creator with certain inalienable rights, and among these are life, liberty, and the pursuit of happiness?" If you do, then you are a phony Christian. The *Bible* teaches that we have no "rights" because all of our so-called **right**eousness is like filthy, stinking rags compared to the true righteousness of the one, true God (cf. Isaiah 64:6). Everything that we have is a gift from Yahuah, not because we deserve it. What we deserve is to go to Hell because of our sinful pride and rebellion against our Lord and His ways. It is only by His amazing grace and mercy that we can lift a finger, take a breath, or live from one day to the next. Do you believe that it is our destiny to establish the Kingdom of Yahuah on this earth **before** He returns in person to do that? If you do, you fit right in with those who are building the anti-Christian Babylonian Empire; you are a false Christian, are deceived by the devil's Lie and are being set up to follow Antimessiah (not the true Messiah) to "eternal" destruction.

So, American religion is much more like Babylonian religion than it is True Christianity. It was founded and still operates more on a spirit of pride and self-sufficiency than true dependence on and faith in Yahuah. And, rather than being just one religion, i.e., True Christianity, modern American-Babylonian religion is an amalgamation of religions serving, often unwittingly, the false god, Satan. That is why

---

while He was with them). So, I am not negating the importance of self defense, defending others, or even serving in the military to defend one's country against evil people (if our motives are pure). What Yahuah 's Word condemns is rebelling against those who already have authority over us rather than patiently trusting and waiting for the Lord to rectify injustices, and imposing our will on others for the purpose of personal gain or to establish our dominance of them (which simple observation with the patriotic blinders off reveals the USA is doing more and more all over the world).

Lucifer is called the (true, spiritual) King of Babylon (Isaiah 14:4). Like Babylon was, the USA is the most religious nation on Earth—the headquarters, as it were, of Satan's false, global, religious system. No other nation has as much worldwide religious influence—sending out missionaries, "apostles," and "prophets" all over the world. No other nation is as hospitable to or tolerant of all forms of religion. Like in Babylon, American religion is extremely nationalistic—to be Christian is to be patriotic. Christians in America, contrary to the teachings of Scripture (cf. 2 Peter 2:20) are very involved in politics. Consider the Religious Right's symbiotic relationship with the Republican Party, for example. Like in Babylon, American religion is very materialistic, sensual, and self-indulgent—the churches are centers for social interaction, good food, fun and games, and entertainment rather than self-sacrificial service to others and Yahuah. They have it backwards: Most church members give a very small part of their income to the ministry and keep the rest for themselves. But did Yahushua not say, *"If anyone wants to follow Me, let him deny himself, and take up his cross daily, and follow Me"* (Luke 9:23)? Then He said, *"Sell what you have, and give to the poor, and you shall have treasures in heaven: and come and follow Me"* (Matthew 19:21). To me that sounds like, "Keep only what is absolutely necessary for yourself and give the rest for ministry of the Gospel and meeting the needs of others"—just the opposite of what is happening in American "Christianity." A couple of days before I wrote this, I read a shocking report from the United Nations, stating that over 17,000 children (not counting adults) are dying from starvation daily around the world—over 6 million per year! Then, I read another report that 99% of the people of the east African nation of Somalia are Muslims, and those of all other religions, especially Christianity, are being aggressively sought out and killed. Yet, what are most "Christians" most concerned about here in America—what we are going to have for dinner, what TV shows we are going to watch, what we are going to do for recreation on the weekend? How utterly disgusted Yahuah must be with American (Laodicean) "Christianity" (See the commentary on Revelation 3:17-19), don't you agree?

Hopefully, you are beginning to see the truth about American religion. Let me mention another item to drive the point home. What is the main symbol of American Freedom? What do the passengers on all ships that sail into New York Harbor see? What welcomes all the peoples of the world to America? What makes Americans' hearts swell with pride when they see it? That is correct; it is the Statue of Liberty.

224

Do you know who designed and built the Statue of Liberty?—the French, specifically a French Freemason, sculptor Frederic Auguste Bartholdi, who wanted to honor a Masonic doctrine that dates back to the time of Nimrod! Bartholdi intentionally clothed Liberty as a classical Roman deity, the goddess Libertas. She wears a palla, a cloak that is fastened on her left shoulder by a clasp. Underneath is a stola, which falls in many folds to her feet. Around her feet is a broken chain, symbolizing freedom from all restraint—religious, political, moral, or otherwise. Libertas, also called the "Queen of Heaven," is a Roman version of Ishtar. By the way, there is a city just up the coast of Long Island from New York City named Babylon. People on ships sailing into New York Harbor from the northeast can see its sign: "Welcome to Babylon." Ironic, is it not? Babylon, New York, was founded and named by poor Jewish immigrants who, because of their circumstances, identified with the Jews of ancient Babylon.

Speaking of Freemasonry, several of the founders, fourteen presidents and many other high government officials throughout the history of the United States of America have been Freemasons—many of them Masons of the highest order (33rd degree). Do you know what the spiritual roots of Freemasonry are? They are basically derived from Babylonian religion and involve the worship of Lucifer. One of the Masonic deities is Isis, the Egyptian name of Ishtar.

The Assyrian Connection

Besides direct comparisons with Ancient Babylon, the identification of the USA as modern Babylon the Great can be proven another way.

It can be argued that pride (blind patriotism) has been the root cause of the fall of every nation and empire throughout history. *("Pride goes before destruction, and a haughty spirit before a fall."*— Proverbs 16:18) Even Yahuah's own nation of people Israel fell to the Assyrians in 722 BCE because of her disobedience of the Lord's command to repent of her idolatry, especially self-idolatry (pride). As Jonathan Cahn has vividly explained in his best selling book *The Harbinger*, after an initial "warning" attack on Israel by the Assyrians, the Lord gave His People a series of nine signs (harbingers) that, if not heeded, would result in total destruction of the northern kingdom of Israel. And, ten years later, because those warning signs not only were not heeded but were arrogantly defied, Israel was attacked, demolished and replaced by those same cruel, merciless Assyrians (the original terrorists).

225

In *The Harbinger*, in a gripping, eye-opening way, Cahn explains how that same prophecy (Isaiah 9:10) applies in exactly the same way to the USA! Exactly the same nine signs of Israel's coming destruction apply to the soon-coming destruction of America. In the same way that in Assyria's first attack on Israel the wall around Samaria, the capital, was breached, the USA's seemingly impenetrable "wall" of air defense was breached by terrorists from the same part of the world (the Near East) and the World Trade Center towers were destroyed on 9-11-2001. And in the same way the leaders of Israel, rather than repenting and turning to the Lord for help, responded to the attack by defiantly proclaiming, "We will rebuild, and we will rebuild stronger!" America's leaders replied to the 9-11 attack with by arrogantly proclaiming, with exactly the same words, "We will rebuild, and we will rebuild stronger!" And, if the Isaiah 9:10 prophecy is followed to its conclusion, in the same way that the government, the economy and the military of the the northern kingdom of Israel were totally destroyed and replaced by the harsh control of the Assyrians, the USA will be destroyed and replaced by a confederation of terrorists and nations from the same part of the world—the location of the ancient Assyrian Empire.

So, are you connecting the dots? You do see that the Assyrian terrorists who attacked, destroyed and replaced Israel were predecessors of exactly the same terrorists who attacked the USA on 9-11-2001, do you not? But now, to correctly comprehend the whole picture, make this connection: Exactly the same terrorists from exactly the same part of the world (modern Turkey and Iran) are prophesied to attack, utterly destroy and replace modern Babylon (Jeremiah 51:27-29).

Incidentally, do you know that the USA's first capital was its "great city," New York City? Immediately after his inauguration as the first President of the United States of America, George Washington went with some leaders of Congress to pray for the newly-formed nation at St. Paul's Chapel in New York City. St. Paul's Chapel, the oldest active church facility in New York City, is, ironically, across the street from the fallen and currently being rebuilt World Trade Center towers—America's greatest monument to her **un**godly spirit of pride and arrogance.

More Scriptural Evidence
Still not convinced that America is Babylon? Well, that is OK, because we have just scratched the surface of Biblical evidences for the identification of modern, prophetic Babylon. Please keep reading.

226

Revelation 18 tells us about modern, prophetic, secular Babylon. But the Babylon of Revelation 18 is the same Babylon as the religious Babylon of Revelation 17 because she has exactly the same name, "Babylon the Great," in both chapters (cf. Revelation 17:5 and 18:2) and she suffers the same fate, destruction by fire, in both chapters (cf. Revelation 17:16 and 18:8).

Actually, there are over 250 verses of Scripture that identify modern, prophetic Babylon. When all of those Scriptures are studied, it is astonishingly clear who modern, prophetic Babylon is. The following quiz is borrowed and slightly modified from the book *America the Babylon—America's Destiny Foretold in Biblical Prophecy* by R. A. Coombes (available through Amazon), who did (before he passed away in 2013) many years of research and study on the identification and destiny of modern, prophetic Babylon.

The Babylon Quiz—Name that City-State/Nation/Empire

The following is a fun quiz to test your knowledge concerning the identifying characteristics of modern, prophetic Babylon. Each question refers to an identification characteristic of "mystery Babylon," with Scripture references given for each. The answers may surprise you.

What City-State/Nation/Empire . . .

Q: Is the location where all the world's leaders come to meet - the headquarters of world government (Revelation 17:18; Jeremiah 51:44)?
A: New York City, USA, is the location for the only world-governing body, i.e., the United Nations, which is dominated (behind the scenes) by the USA.

Q: Is called the "Queen of Kingdoms" - controls the other kingdoms/nations of the world (Revelation 17:2; Isaiah 47:5)?
A: The USA rules the nations of the world through her trade with them in sensual and material goods and services. It is projected that by 2015, America will be the number one oil exporter in the world, making the nations of the world "drunk with the wine of her fornication."

Q: Is the leading center of world commerce - the "engine of wealth" of the world's economy (Revelation 18:11, 15, 16, 19, 22, 23; Isaiah

47:15)?

A: NYC, the home of the World Trade Center, the NY Stock Exchange, the American Stock Exchange, NASDAQ, the New York Commodities and Mercantile Exchanges, the Federal Reserve Bank - the largest bank in the world—as well as the most powerful concentration of American banks. Also correct with this answer is the United States of America, with its numerous great cities of international commerce - Seattle, San Francisco, Los Angeles, Houston, Chicago, Dallas, New York, et al. If the economy of the U.S. collapses, virtually all the economies of the world will collapse.

Q: Is the leading center of imports and exports (Revelation 18:11-13?
A: The ports of New York/Jersey make NYC the leading deep water port city in the Western Hemisphere, especially as the marketplace center and gateway to America, where world prices are most often correlated to NYC/USA prices. The NYC port, together with all the other deep water ports surrounding the nation, make the USA by far the leading import/export nation of the world.

Q: Is a leading center of manufacturing (Revelation 18:22)?
A: NYC has been the leading center of corporate headquarters for manufacturing in the world. Certainly, the USA is the world's industrial giant.

Q: Is the center for world trade in gold, silver, copper, oil, precious gems, cloth/clothing/fashions, lumber, containers, household items, furniture, iron, marble, ivory, spices, cosmetics, health products, wine, grains/foods, livestock, transportation, and services (Revelation 18:11-13)?
A: NYC is the world's foremost city of commodities trading, with these commodities exchanges trading daily: Coffee, Sugar, Tea & Cocoa Exchange; New York Cotton Exchange (also trades orange juice); New York Mercantile Exchange: crude oil, gasoline, natural gas, heating oil, platinum, palladium; New York Mercantile Comex Division: gold, silver, copper. Chicago is also a world leader in commodities trading with the following exchanges: Chicago Board of Trade: wheat, corn, oats, soybeans, soybean oil, soybean meal, also U. S. Treasury notes, and stock indexes; Chicago Mercantile Exchange: cattle, hogs, bacon, wood-lumber, and all major world currencies. World prices for the following "cash" commodities are also set or keyed from the USA. (Source: Wall Street Journal): barley, bran, burlap, butter, broiler

228

chickens, eggs, coconut oil, cottonseed oil, palm oil, lard, tallow, wool, aluminum, lead, mercury, steel, tin, zinc, rubber. Also, Chicago is where the world's currencies are traded and is the location for trading all U. S. Federal Treasury Securities on a 'futures' basis, though initial offerings are derived from the NYC Fed Reserve. Also, Chicago holds futures trading on the Standard & Poor's 500 Index and the Major Market Index, plus stock options trading as well as commodity options trading. New York City is also a leader in the marketing of: diamonds, precious gems, iron, ivory, marble, spices, cosmetics, legal pharmaceutical drugs, professional services especially related to media and the arts. NYC is also the main import city for fine foreign wines from around the world.

Q: Is the center for expertise in marketing, merchandising, public relations, advertising & sales (Revelation 17:2; 18:3, 23; 19:2)?
A: New York's Madison Avenue is the 'nerve center' and informal world headquarters for the world's best and most prestigious advertising, marketing & merchandising companies. Madison Ave. is home to the world's best salesmen those from advertising and the public relations fields, where the whole world learns and follows the latest techniques of how to 'move' or sell goods and services. It is the largest marketing center in the U. S. and the world.

Q: Is noted for its culture and aesthetics (music, art, dance, theater, etc.) (Revelation 18:22)?
A: New York is the key cultural city of the world: Carnegie Hall, Madison Square Garden, Radio City Music Hall, Lincoln Center, Broadway theaters, Greenwich Village, Manhattan's world class restaurants, TV networks, newspapers (NY Times, etc.), magazine and book publishers, Rockefeller Center, world-famous museums & art galleries, Times Square, Manhattan, and the whole City of New York, immortalized in songs and movies. It is also the location of more book publishers, plays, and movies than any other city in the world.

Q: Is noted for its intoxicating High Society, elegant, and sumptuous lifestyle (Revelation 17:2; 18:3, 14; Isaiah 47:1, 8; Jeremiah 51:13)?
A: Park Avenue, penthouse lifestyles of the rich and famous, Trump Towers, the noted lifestyle of New York is glamorous, glitzy, and sumptuous.

229

Q: Is noted for its bright, gaudy, colored lights and nightlife (Revelation 18:14)?

A: NYC is called the "city that never sleeps" as Sinatra's song says about New York, … "I wanna wake up in the city that never sleeps … to find I'm king of the hill, top of the heap … these little town blues keep melting away …" New York offers the glitter of Manhattan, Broadway's lights, and the lights of Times Square, plus the entire nighttime skyline of NYC. Another U. S. city world-famous for its lights and nightlife is Las Vegas, Nevada.

Q: Is noted for its drug consumption and importation (especially illegal) (Revelation 18:23 - Note that the primary meaning of the Greek word pharmakeia, translated "sorceries" in Revelation 18:23, is "the use or administering of drugs.")?

A: NYC is the largest center of legal and illicit drug consumption in the world, especially hard-core drugs, like heroin and cocaine. The USA's lengthy sea coast borders and borders with Canada and Mexico make it especially vulnerable to illicit drug traffic.

Q: Is noted for its architecture, buildings and skyline (Isaiah 13:22)?

A: New York's architecture - its super-tall or mega-story skyscrapers like the World Trade Center (the world's tallest building before it was destroyed), the Empire State Building, Rockefeller Center, the UN building, reach into the sky, similar to the Tower of Babel and the ziggurats of ancient Babylon.

Q: Is noted for being a city/nation of immigrants from all over the world - an international city (Jeremiah 50:37; 51:44)?

A: NYC is a city of immigrants, and always has been. It has been the historic point-of-entry for immigrants and is epitomized by the quote on the Statue of Liberty: "Give me your … huddled masses yearning to be free." NYC is host to the UN. It has "China Town", "Little Italy", "Little Moscow", "Little Bombay", "Little Tokyo", "Little Mexico", "Little Havana", etc. Unlike any other city in the world, every single ethnic group has its own little community in NYC. The USA in general is known as the "melting pot of the world."

Q: Is a cosmopolitan and urban nation (Jeremiah 50:32)?

A: America started as a rural, agricultural nation, but the life of the nation revolves around the cities now.

Q: Is noted for being both hated and envied by the world (Revelation 17:16; 18:9, 11,15, 17, 19)?

A: The city that seems to inspire the most animosity, disgust, and even hatred is New York City. The most denounced country in the world is the United States. "Yankee go Home" has been a popular slogan in many countries around the world for the last generation. Yet, at the same time, the U. S. is the most admired nation for its accomplishments and affluent lifestyle.

Q: Is noted for its waste and wasteful extravagance - overconsumption (Revelation 18:3, 7, 9, 16)?

A: NYC is like no other in consumption - noted for its extravagance. The waste by-product volume is so enormous as to be mind-boggling, practically bringing the city to a stand-still at times. One of the first impressions a visitor gets is the dirtiness of the streets and the city as a whole.

Q: Is noted for spiritual and moral 'dirtiness' and impurity (by implication: wantonness, reveling, involvement in the occult, etc.) (Revelation 17:1-6; 18:2, 4-9, 23; Isaiah 47:8, 9, 12)?

A: NYC is morally and spiritually impure in its sensual, hedonistic lifestyle, pandering to sexual interests - prostitution, pornography, and so forth - drug use, wild "partying," and its occult connections. NYC is the largest occult merchandising center in the world. Besides the immense number of fortune tellers, psychics, and occult shops, there are mail order houses for occult items. There is also an aspect of the occult exemplified by the "Amityville Horror" (Amityville is a town in the NYC metropolitan area, next to Babylon, NY), where there are reportedly "doorways to Hell."

Q: Could be said to worship materialism or things (Revelation 18:6-7)?

A: NYC, like no other city on the earth, epitomizes the worship of materialism. NYC newspapers abound with gossip and news about the wealthy, like the Trumps, the Leona Helmsleys, the Rockefellers, the Kennedy family, the magnates of Wall Street, Madison Avenue, and Broadway, along with movie stars and other famous celebrities and artists. Wall Street is where some of the temples of materialism (called "capitalism") abound. Manhattan is crammed with temples to capitalism of every kind.

231

Q: Reflects the image of hyper-selfishness and pride (Revelation 18:7)?

A: NYC carries an image of hyper-selfishness and rudeness, not only the rich with their extravagant lifestyles, but the common people convey it through everyday rudeness, as exemplified by cab drivers and subway passengers. Also, scenes from sporting events of sports fans pushing and shoving, and arguing, and insulting each other, along with their fickleness toward even the hometown teams and stars.

Q: Promotes itself - is extremely proud and arrogant—to the point of "self-deification" (Revelation 18:7; Isaiah 47:8, 10; Jeremiah 50:31, 32)?

A: NYC - "the Big Apple" . . . again, through songs like Sinatra's "New York, New York", but also through its media, through its publications, through Wall Street, and its show biz. Its leaders worship their own accomplishments in the city, and the city itself, especially the Statue of Liberty, giving a religious-like homage to the statue, to capitalism, and to liberty that the city "gave birth to."

Q: Promulgates and exports Idolatries - is "insanely idolatrous" (Revelation 18:3-7; Isaiah 21:9; Jeremiah 50:38)?

A: The leaders of NYC and the U.S.A., through the media - the networks, newspapers, and magazines - and through Madison Avenue and Wall Street, promulgate the religion of capitalism-materialism (i.e., worship of material riches) more blatantly than does any other city/nation on the earth. Worship of sports heroes and celebrities is also pure idolatry. (Why do you think one of the most popular TV shows is called "American Idol"?)

Q: Is treacherous and deceit-filled in its political and business dealings (Revelation 18:23; Isaiah 21:2)?

A: Wall Street and American business in general is cut-throat. The U.S. government has a long history of deceiving its own people, including but certainly not limited to the effects of scientific experiments involving nuclear radiation upon innocent civilians, the reasons for invading Vietnam, Bosnia, Iraq, etc., scandals like Watergate, sexual affairs in the White House, hiding information about UFOs, detention (torture) facilities for political prisoners, tax loopholes for the wealthy elite, dealing treacherously with other nations (like Israel) ... ad nauseum.

Q: Shares a similar distinction with ancient Babylon as being the host country for the majority of the world's Jewish population (from about 600 BCE, when Israel was taken into captivity, until 400 CE, Babylon had the world's largest Jewish population) (Revelation 18:4; also Jeremiah 50:8, 28; 51: 6, 45; Isaiah 48:20)?

A: NYC has the largest population of Jews in America, and the U. S. is home to more Jewish people than anywhere in the world, except perhaps Israel, most of whose ancestors came to America during the Russian pogroms against the Jews between 1821 and 1905.

Q: Has been a persecutor of Jews and is treacherous in her dealings with the Jews (Jeremiah 50:11)?

A: When Hitler offered to let the Jews leave Germany just before World War II, the USA refused to accept them, in fact, sent a shipload back, where they probably died in the Nazi death camps. There is strong evidence that the American government is dealing treacherously with Israel today - claiming to be her ally, but really using her as a pawn to keep us involved in the Mideast, while setting her up to be destroyed by the surrounding, hostile Muslim nations.

Q: Is the "daughter" of another great superpower nation (Jeremiah 50:12)?

A: The USA was founded by citizens of England, the world's greatest superpower nation at the time - until the 1920s. America is the only superpower nation in history that has been produced by another superpower nation.

Q: What city/state/nation is the lone and last ("hindermost") "superpower" in the world (Revelation 17:18; 18:7; Isaiah 47:5, 8, 10; Jeremiah 50:12)?

A: Since the demise of the Soviet Union in 1989, the USA has been the only, and probably the last, "superpower" nation in the world.

Q: Is considered to be the "world's policeman" - the "hammer of the world" (Jeremiah 50:23)?

A: The USA has over 7,000 military installations and/or bases all over the world, in 63 nations, especially in the world's "hotspots." For example, Iran is completely surrounded by ten U. S. air bases, located in countries bordering Iran. Just stop and consider all the incidents in which the U. S. has used military power to intervene and stop conflict:

233

Bosnia, Somalia, Haiti, Kuwait, Panama, Grenada, Vietnam, Korea, Afghanistan, and Iraq come to mind.

Q: Has no fear and little reason to fear invasion of its home soil by foreign armies (Isaiah 18:1-2; 47:7-8)?
A: The USA has, including its Star Wars technology and massive air defense, its "stealth technology" and "black ops" project, by far the most powerful, seemingly impenetrable national defense in the world. Protected by two oceans and a gulf, America is isolated geographically from the turmoil of Europe, Asia, and Africa. It would be seemingly impossible to launch a naval/amphibious invasion against America by any or all nations combined. The world's combined naval strength could not transport enough armed units to successfully invade America. With the demise of the Soviet Union, the main concern at the present time is the possibility of terrorist action (by which Scripture indicates America will be destroyed).

Q: Has carried over and incorporated many aspects of the old Babylonian religion, particularly in regard to art symbols and figures (Jeremiah 50:2, 38)?
A: NYC is the world's only city whose image is so closely linked to Babylonian religion. The Statue of Liberty and NYC are inseparably linked, and such a union is unprecedented in world history. Not even in Rome or Greece could a city boast of such an identification with such a profound or dominant figure as that of "Liberty." No other city has had such an imposing statue of a woman with an ideal or philosophy to uphold or to offer to the world. Meanwhile, Revelation 17:5 refers to the woman as "The Mother of Harlots" (practitioners of false religion). The Statue of Liberty may very well be said to be the main American idol. Other examples of Babylonian-type symbols used in America include the statue of freedom on the Capitol Dome in Washington D. C., the symbols on the currency, such as the pyramid with the 'eye' at its top, the 'Apollo' (the Greek name of an ancient Babylonian god) space program, many of the Masonic symbols spread throughout the land, including those at the Denver Airport.

Q: Is noted for the natural created beauty of its land (Isaiah 13:19)?
A: "America the Beautiful" … for spacious skies, for amber waves of grain, for purple mountains majesty, from sea to shining sea …The Shenandoah Valley, The Mississippi River, the Rocky Mountains, the Grand Canyon, Old Faithful, Redwood Forests, the Great Lakes, etc.

Q: Is noted for being highly and overly optimistic, confident of its success, with a "can-do" attitude, especially about its future (Isaiah 47:7-10)?
A: America has always been the nation of optimism - a John Wayne type of "can-do" attitude.

Q: Is considered by the world to have had a unique and remarkable beginning, different from all the other nations before it, has been awe-inspiring since its birth with regards to its ingenuity, resourcefulness, and power, and is still awe-inspiring - considered powerful and oppressive - to the world today (Isaiah 18:2)?
A: No nation other than America has had such a unique beginning, overcoming, against all odds, her own parent nation (Great Britain), the most powerful nation on the earth at the time; then quickly establishing herself as a mighty nation with a unique, representative form of government.

Q: Is noted as a land of rebels, not only in its birth, but now in its judgment for rebellion against Yahuah (Jeremiah 50:24; 51:1)?
A: The U. S. started out as a land of rebels. There was the rebellion for independence, and the rebellion of the South against the North, causing the Civil War, the student rebellion against the Vietnam War, etc. Indeed, stubbornness and rebellion are practically considered virtues in America.

Q: Is noted for its cultural insanity (Jeremiah 50:38)?
A: The U. S. and NYC, Hollywood, Los Angeles, San Francisco, and much more. You pick the topic: abortion, movies, TV, music, pornography, child abuse, cloning, drugs, murders, gangs, divorce, celebrity and hero worship . . . ad infinitum - a culture gone crazy.

Q: Is noted for its being a land of many fresh waters, with a broad river in its middle and divided by many rivers (i.e., abundant, clean, fresh water for drinking, which is unique in that most nations have poor water supplies) (Jeremiah 51:13, 36)?
A: The USA is blessed with the far more fresh water sources than any other nation on the earth - tremendous numbers of rivers, including the Mississippi, which divides the country as did the Euphrates in Babylon, and other large rivers, which divide the rest of the country; hundreds of fresh water lakes, including the Great Lakes, plus abundant underground aquifers for most of the nation.

The above quiz is not exhaustive—there are other identification characteristics of modern Babylon listed in Scripture (over 60 in all). But hopefully you can tell that when the time arrives for modern, prophetic, "*mystery*" Babylon to play her part on the world stage, Yahuah does not want anyone who studies and believes His Word to have any doubt about who she is; Scripture is crystal clear about that. Don't you agree? Babylon, claiming to be a good, Christian nation, is actually the ultimate false (anti-) Christian nation—the most evil, "beast" nation in the history of the world, whose true ruler is Satan himself. And can there be any doubt at all in anyone's mind who has even a tenuous grip on reality that modern Babylonia is indeed the United States of America, with her "great city," New York City? If you cannot accept that clear, Biblical Truth by now, then you might as well stop reading this essay and go on about your business, because it is doing you no good. The only question is not whether Bob is right or wrong; the question is whether or not you believe the *Bible*. Right?

But, if you can now see that America is Babylon, and you want to know the destiny (in the very near future) of America-Babylon, please keep reading.

What is Modern Babylon's Destiny?

Again, Yahuah does not want us to be in doubt. He tells us exactly what is going to happen to prophesied Babylon, approximately when, and what He wants His people to do about it. I will share with you enough of what the *Bible* says about America-Babylon's destiny to help you understand her future.

So how, specifically, will the destruction of Babylon occur? Now that we understand what really happened to Nimrod's empire and the Akkadian city of Babylon, as well as how the first Babylonian empire of Hammurapi and the neo-Babylonian empire of Nebuchadnezzar fell, and if we believe that the fall of those three empires were precursors to the fall of modern Babylon the Great, the answer is obvious, is it not?

In the same way that the first Babylonian Empire was conquered by the Assyrians and the neo-Babylonian Empire was conquered very quickly without resistance by the Medo-Persians, Scripture indicates that modern Babylon will first fall very rapidly to her enemies— terrorists and a confederation of nations led by Turkey and Iran (descendants of the ancient Assyrians, Medes and Persians) (cf. Isaiah 13:17; Jeremiah 50:29-30; 51:2-5, 11; 27-31). The attack will come from within and without the borders of the USA. Since Muslims have, for many years, been allowed relatively free entry into the US, it is

236

easy to see that hundreds of terrorist cells might be festering within America's borders. And if hundreds—or thousands—of bombs, including suitcase-size nuclear devices, are simultaneously detonated in major population centers of the USA, including New York City and Washington D.C., the resulting chaos will be unimaginable, because virtually all of America's national defense is focused on preventing attacks from **outside** the nation. Americans who resist the terrorists will be sitting ducks for armed, trained and coordinated terrorists to mow them down. (Millions of Americans, especially college students, who have been indoctrinated to favor the Islamists will offer no resistance to the terrorists and, in fact, will join them in their takeover of the USA.) Also, since there will be no clear direction from a paralyzed and chaotic Washington in the case of such an attack, America's foreign military installations will be vulnerable to simultaneously executed missile attacks. And Babylon-America might very well be overthrown by the same people who conquered both ancient Babylonian Empires! If that happens, the USA will truly become in every way (politically and religiously, as well as spiritually) modern Babylon the Great. Also, this may be the event that begins the Final Seven Years, because the whole world, which is dependent on America's economy, will also be thrown into chaos, giving rise to the Antimessiah going forth to conquer the world (cf. the commentary on Revelation 6:1).

But also, as is noted in the commentary on the destruction of Nimrod's empire, Scripture indicates that all life in Babylon-America will suddenly, in *"one hour"* of *"one day"* be *"utterly burned with fire"* (Revelation 18:8,10). R. A. Coombes, noted above as the author of *America the Babylon*, believes the destruction of Babylon in one hour by fire may come directly from Yahuah, in the same way He destroyed Sodom and Gomorrah. In fact, both the prophets Isaiah and Jeremiah compare the destruction of Babylon to the destruction of Sodom and Gomorrah (Isaiah 13:19; Jeremiah 49:18; 50:40). Coombes notes numerous Scriptures (Isaiah 13:3, 5; Jeremiah 51:48, 53; et al.) that may refer to the attack against Babylon as being carried out by "angels" from "heaven." However, the same Greek word *(aggelos)* that is translated *"angels"* is also translated *"messengers"* in Scripture. And Jeffrey Goodman, in his eye-opening book *The Comets of God* notes that the ancient Akkadians considered comets, comet fragments, meteorites and asteroids that impacted the earth "messengers" from "heaven" (far outer space). And he explains that a comet less than a mile in diameter exploding in the atmosphere above an area the size of the U.S.A. will immediately annihilate *"by fire"* all living plants, animals and humans

237

in America. But, regardless of how it happens, according to both the *Tanakh* and the *B'rit Hadashah*, Babylon-America will be annihilated suddenly and quickly by fire.

When will this happen? Again, there are differing opinions. As stated above, this commentator believes that the political, economic and military fall of America will be the event that precipitates global chaos at the beginning of the Final Seven Years when the anti-messiah goes forth to conquer the world (see the explanation of the probable identification of the anti-messiah in Footnote 9, the commentary on Revelation 17). Then, the total annihilation of all life in Babylon-America by fire will occur at the midpoint of the seven years, just before the "beast" (the anti-messiah) declares himself to be god and is given his global *"kingdom"* (singular), the Revived Roman Empire (cf. the commentary on Revelation 17:16-17). Then finally, Babylon the Great, the headquarters of Satan's horde of evil spirit-beings, will, at the end of the Final Seven Years, be totally physically annihilated, never to rise again (cf. the commentary on Revelation 18:21).

But, regardless of exactly when the annihilation of Babylon-America occurs, the events of world history and current global events, in the light of *Bible* prophecy, seem to be pointing to the reality that it is very near—right at the door. Are you ready? Current events in the light of *Bible* prophecy seem to indicate that the most appropriate question for Americans (as well as the rest of the world) is not, "How can I survive the coming holocaust?" but, "Am I prepared leave this present life and enter the World to Come?"

Meanwhile, for a wealth of information about what is really going on, behind the scenes, in American politics and religion, I highly recommend Steve Shearer's articles at www.antipasministries.com. Although his conclusions about the sequence and timing of events of the Final Seven Years and the role of the "Church" during that time are not accurate according to Scripture, Steve has remarkable insight, from a Biblical point of view, as to what is happening in America that is rapidly bringing the nation closer to The End.

And for more about what it means to be a True Christian and how to be saved from the soon-coming Day of the Lord, or to learn more about Last Trump Ministries and how you can be involved, please visit www.RevelationUnderstoodCommentary.com. Or if you have questions, suggestions, comments, or just want to visit concerning anything you have read in this commentary, please contact Watchman Bob at WatchmanBob@gmail.com.

Appendix 2—Be Saved from the Wrath of Yahuah!

Most Bible expositors either teach that Believers in Yahushua will be caught up ("raptured") to Heaven before the events of the Great Tribulation and the Day and the Wrath of Yahuah commence, or that they will be supernaturally protected from those events. However, both of those views result from a carnal, worldly-minded focus and misunderstandings of Biblical terms and the sequence of End of the Age events.

As has been explained throughout this commentary, the Great Tribulation, the Day of the Lord and the Wrath of the Lord are not synonymous terms. Many *Bible* expositors and teachers label the entire Final Seven Years as "the tribulation" and make no distinction between that period of time and its events and the Day (and the Wrath) of the Lord. But an honest examination of the text reveals that The Great Tribulation (cf. Matthew 24:21; Revelation 7:14) is totally different from the Day of the Lord. The Great Tribulation is the wrath of Satan (12:12) being poured out on all who oppose him and begins at the midpoint of the Final Seven Years when his incarnation, Antimessiah declares himself to be "god" (cf. the commentary on 7:13-14c). However, the Day of the Lord begins later, during the last half of the Final Seven Years, when the Wrath of the Lord—the plagues of the trumpet and bowl judgments—begin to be poured out on the followers of the anti-messiah (cf. the commentary on 6:15-17).

Nowhere in Scripture are the Followers of Yahushua (the "Church") promised exemption from any of the physical suffering, tribulations, persecutions and death that are the lot of all human beings as long as we are in our corrupt, human flesh and subject to sin. Our complete exemption from suffering will occur only when we are in our new, glorified bodies in the presence of our Redeemer in His millennial kingdom. Yahushua Himself told his disciples that they would suffer persecution and tribulation (cf. Matthew 24:21; Mark 10:30). And the apostle Paul frequently spoke of his infirmities, reproaches, needs, persecutions, distresses and so forth (e.g., 2 Corinthians 12:10).

There are two extremes in interpreting what the Bible states about suffering. One is the "word of faith," "health, wealth and prosperity," "name it and claim it," "believe it and receive it" doctrine that no suffering in this life is necessary for the Believer whose faith is intact. The other is that true Believers in the Messiah will escape to Heaven in the Rapture before the real suffering of the Great Tribulation and the

Wrath of the Lord begin. Both views are flawed, unscriptural and potentially tragic, resulting in the destruction of the faith of those who cling to either doctrine when they find themselves in the midst of the wrath of either Satan (the Great Tribulation) or the Lord (the Day of the Lord).

So, let us look briefly at what it really means to be saved from the Wrath of Yahuah.

What is the Day of the Yahuah?

In the *Bible*, the Day of Yahuah is a very prominent and important prophetic theme. The explicit term, *"Day of [Yahuah],"* occurs over 20 times in Scripture. It is used in both the *Tanakh* and the *B'rit Hadashah*. It is described by eight BCE prophets, mentioned by three *B'rit Hadashah* writers, and alluded to many other times as *"that day,"* *"the Day of Christ,"* and by other terms. Here is the prophet Zephaniah's description of that Day:

> *The great Day [Yahuah] is near, near and coming very quickly. Hear the sound of the Day of [Yahuah]! When it's here, even a warrior will cry bitterly. That Day is a Day of fury, a Day of trouble and distress, a Day of waste and desolation, a Day of darkness and gloom, a Day of clouds and thick fog, a Day of the trumpet and battle-cry against the fortified cities and against the high towers* [on the city walls].

> *I will bring such distress on people that they will grope their way like the blind, because they have sinned against [Yahuah]. Their blood will be poured out like dust and their bowels like dung. Neither their silver nor their gold will be able to save them. On the Day of [Yahuah's] fury, the whole land will be destroyed in the fire of His jealously, for He will make an end, a horrible end, of all those living in the land.* (Zephaniah 1:14-18)

As prophesied in the Revelation (6:12-14), the Day of Yahuah will be announced by the most awesome catastrophes in world history (except for the Great Flood), including cataclysmic worldwide natural and/or human-caused disasters. Then it will include the period of time of a few years during which the initial plagues of Yahuah's judgments announced by the seven trumpets is poured out on those who have rejected and rebelled against Him. Then, at the blast of the seventh and *"last trumpet"* on Yom Teruah at the end of the Final Seven Years, the resurrection of the Righteous will occur and the Messiah Yahushua will return and *"catch away"* the Redeemed of Yahuah to Heaven

240

(Mark 13:26-27; 1 Corinthians 15:52; 1 Thessalonians 4:14-17). Next, while the marriage and wedding feast of the Lamb and His Bride are being celebrated in Heaven (19:7-9), the *"last plagues"* of the seventh bowl judgement of Yahuah (cf. 11:18; 15:1) will be poured out on Earth (16:1). Then, on Yom Kippur, the newly-crowned King of kings and Lord of lords (the Messiah Yahushua) will descend with the armies of Heaven (the glorified Saints and angels) to destroy His enemies at the battle of "Armageddon," cast Antimessiah and the false prophet into the Lake of Fire, and cleanse the earth of all unregenerate earth dwellers (19:11-21). Then, after binding and imprisoning Satan, the Messiah will bring His People Israel out of the *"wilderness"* into which they have fled from the persecution of the anti-messiah and establish the glorious millennial Kingdom of Yahuah on Earth (Isaiah 11:12; Zechariah 14:1-11; Revelation 12:6, 14). At this time, the heavens and earth will be renewed and New Jerusalem will descend from Heaven (cf. Isaiah 65:17, 18; Revelation 21:1) , the tribes of Israel will occupy the Land (Ezekiel 40-48), and the surrounding nations will be formed by Gentiles on whom Yahuah had mercy and allowed to enter His millennial kingdom (Zechariah 14:16). Finally, the Day of Yahuah will end with the Final Judgment when the Redeemed of Yahuah will be ushered into eternity in His glorious presence and the damned (including Satan) will be cast into the Lake of Fire (20:11-15).

So basically, the Day of Yahuah will begin with the biggest showdown in world history—a period of time (not a literal 24-hour day) during which the Lord Yahuah will take back the wonderful, perfect Creation that Satan usurped from Him 6,000 years ago. The Lord will first set Satan up—giving his incarnation, Antimessiah, a short time after proclaiming himself to be "God" to (in his deluded mind) establish his dominion on Earth. But then, through a series of ever-intensifying, supernatural disasters, culminating in the seventh bowl of Yahuah's Wrath being poured out at the end of the seven years, Antimessiah's global kingdom will be totally demolished.

But, the point is, we don't want to be on Earth during the time when the *"last plagues"* of Yahuah's Wrath are being poured out here! It is going to be a wonderful, glorious time from the perspective of those who are already in Heaven, as we celebrate with all the heavenly hosts the destruction of the Lord Yahuah's enemies and the redemption of His Creation, but a horrible, horrible time, like the world has never before seen, for those still on Earth. The Remnant of Yahuah's physical People the Jews, who have not given in to the incredible deception or agonizing oppression of that time, and some Yahuah-fearing Gentiles, who have not taken the mark of the beast, will be supernaturally protected and saved, but all others who have been suckered or pressured into following Antimessiah as their (false) messiah will find themselves in unimaginably horrible, hopeless straits.

When will the Day of Yahuah occur?

As with other future End-Times events, the timing and sequence of the Day Yahuah is a matter of great debate among *Bible* scholars and prophecy teachers. A few things are clear in Scripture: (1) there will be a seven-year period of time in the near future—a time called in the *Bible* the *"Birth Pains of the Messiah"* or the *"Time of Jacob's Trouble"*—when the history of the world, as you and I have known it all our lives, will be brought to a terrifyingly tumultuous close, (2) the last half of that seven years, immediately following the midpoint, will be a time of "Great Tribulation"—a time when the wrath of Satan (cf. 12:12) will be poured out on all who oppose him, especially Believers in Yahushua as the true Messiah who are on Earth at that time (Yahuah's People the Jews who are looking forward in faith to the coming Messiah but have not yet recognized that He is Yahushua will be hidden and protected in the *"wilderness"* during the Great Tribulation—12:14), and (3) the last part of that seven years will be overshadowed by the Day of Yahuah, during which the judgments and the Wrath of Yahuah (cf. Revelation 6:17) will be progressively poured out on all who oppose Him, including Antimessiah.

Virtually all scholars and teachers who believe in the literal seven-year scenario agree about the Great Tribulation (the wrath of Satan), the Day of Yahuah, and the Wrath of Yahuah being part of it. The disagreement is over the timing and sequence of events within the seven years. Joseph Good (www.hatikva.org), for example, believes that the Day of Yahuah, the Great Tribulation, and the Wrath of Yahuah all run concurrently throughout the seven years. The prewrath rapture people—Robert Van Kampen [deceased], Marvin Rosenthal, Charles Cooper, et al. (cf. www.prewrathrapture.com)—believe that the Great Tribulation comprises a short period of time immediately following the midpoint of the seven years, after which the Day of Yahuah, which includes the Wrath of Yahuah, will occur during the last year or two of the seven. S. R. Shearer (www.antipasministries.com) believes that the tribulation comprises the entire seven years, with the Day of Yahuah being a literal 24-hour day that occurs on the last day of the seven years.

This commentator has been studying the Scripture and all these teachings for many years, and tends, to an extent, to go along with the prewrath view because it seems to be the most natural, literal, common-sense interpretation which best harmonizes all the prophetic Scripture. However, if one holds to a literal prophetic fulfillment of the Spring and Fall feasts of Yahuah, then, just as the Messiah's first coming, death and resurrection, and the pouring out of His Spirit were exactly, to the day and hour, foreshadowed by the Spring Feasts, His second coming, the resurrection and rapture of His Bride, the pouring out of the last plagues of the Wrath of Yahuah (the plagues of the seventh bowl of wrath following the sounding of the seventh and final trumpet), the "sheep and goat" judgment, and the establishment of His millennial kingdom must all occur within the 15-day period of the Fall feasts following the sounding of the seventh and final trumpet blast.

But, guess what?—when it comes down to where "the rubber meets the road"—to how I need to be living my life in the present moment—I do not know and I do not care about the exact timing and sequence of these events. All that I know and care about is that **they will occur**, and I need to be doing my best to be warning everyone I can to be prepared, regardless of when in the sequence of events, they occur. There also will be other specific events during the seven years that people need to be warned about or prepared for, whether they occur at the beginning, middle, or end of the seven years. The timing of some events (e.g., Antimessiah standing in the Temple declaring himself to be "God" at the midpoint of the seven years) are clearly specified. So, I believe that Yahuah has made clear, at least to those who study prophetic Scripture diligently and sincerely want to know the Truth, the sequence and timing of certain events. The sequence and timing of other events—the annihilation of Babylon, the beginning point of the Day of Yahuah, and so forth—are not so clear. And all that the endless debate over controversial times and sequences accomplish is to distract us from living each day in total self-denial for the good of others and the glory of Yahuah, and so, I believe, are nothing more than devices of Satan to distract us from the work of Yahuah on Earth at the present time. I doubt that the untold millions around the world who are in agonizing suffering, starving to death, freezing to death, being oppressed or persecuted, or being killed every day are very concerned about when the rapture will occur or when their oppressors (and Yahuah's enemies) will be destroyed, do you? They just need to know that **it will happen**, and that **it will happen soon**, and what they need to do about it. They need salvation and hope, not debatable details.

And there are several indications that the implications of the events of the Final Seven Years pertain just as much to the Jews as to the Followers of Yahushua. For example, the seven years are called *"the Time of Jacob's* [Israel's] *Trouble"* (Jeremiah 30:7). And this will be especially true during the Great Tribulation. Because Revelation gives the details of how the *Tanakh* prophecies will be fulfilled, when these things do occur just as was prophesied by Israel's prophets and by Yahushua to His Disciples and in the Revelation, their eyes will be opened to see that He is the Messiah for whom they have been looking. And that is why it is just as important to preach the Gospel according to the Revelation to the Jews as to the Gentiles: They may not immediately accept it, but when these events unfold, their eyes will be opened to the Truth, and they will be saved (Romans 11:26)!

But meanwhile, are **you** ready for all these wonderful or terrifying (depending on your point of view) *". . . things which must shortly come to pass"* (Revelation 1:1)?

Where will you be on the Day of Yahuah?

The *Bible* indicates that the Believers in Yahushua, whether or not they enter the seven years, will not have to endure at least the *"last plagues"* of the Wrath of Yahuah. Also, there are some indications that only the unsaved earth dwellers who have taken the mark of the beast will be affected by the trumpet and bowl plagues (cf. 9:4, 20). It tells us that the Redeemed will be *"caught up"* (from the Latin, *rapio*) in our newly-acquired, glorified bodies, to meet the Messiah in the sky, then taken to a place he has prepared for us (in Heaven) (cf. 1 Corinthians 15:52; 1 Thessalonians 4:17; John 14:2-3) before Yahuah's Wrath is poured out (cf. 1 Thessalonians 5:9).

Nevertheless, it is difficult to see, if Believers are present on Earth at all during the last half of the Final Seven Years, how they can avoid being affected by the plagues of the Lord that affect virtually the whole earth. One possible solution is that the Rapture will occur during the Great Tribulation but just before the plagues of the Day and the Wrath of the Lord begin to be poured out. So this commentator will not be dogmatic about when, in the sequence of events, the Rapture will occur. For more on the timing of the Rapture, read "Appendix 6—When is the Rapture?"

But, regardless of whether or not the Saints are present during the Day of the Lord, they **will** have to patiently endure the Great Tribulation if they are present during that time (cf. the commentary on 12:7-17g; 13:6-10b; 14:6-13d; and 16:15). And **if** they endure whatever trials and tribulations come their way (cf. 2 Timothy 2:12), overcome whatever obstacles Satan places in their path, and keep doing what Yahuah has given them to do until The End, they will be saved (cf. Revelation 2:26).

Of course, I am not teaching a work-your-way-to-Heaven salvation here. Good works and grace are **not** mutually exclusive (contrary to what many Christians believe and teach). I acknowledge that it is only by Yahuah's grace and Spirit that we can do anything right and keep the commandments of the *Torah*. But I just wanted to point out that endurance and good works (by Yahuah's enabling Spirit) are necessary confirmations of a saving faith (cf. James 2:17). In other words, if the Holy Spirit does not dwell in us, enabling us to live a good life and do good works, then our "faith" is phony and will not get us to Heaven. Just because we believe in our heads that Yahushua is the Lord does not make us eligible for citizenship in the Kingdom of Heaven. Only if Yahuah the Holy Spirit dwells in us, enabling us to ". . . *deny* [ourselves], *take up* [our] *cross*[es] daily, *and follow* [Him]" with our whole heart, soul, strength, time, and all of our possessions, can we be sure of escaping the Wrath of Yahuah, and ultimately, "eternity" in Hell.

As I've mentioned on other pages of this commentary, most American "Christians" are deceived. They have a strong tendency to think that they are OK with the Lord when they are not. How about you? Have you really surrendered your life—"lock, stock, and barrel"—to the Lord, in the name of Yahushua the Messiah, and do you know that the Holy Spirit is in you, enabling you to do everything that you do? If you are not sure, you'd better make sure, before you find yourself right in the midst of the worst nightmare (but real) that you have ever conceived—the awesome, terrible Wrath of Yahuah.

If you have any doubt about where you stand with the Lord Yahuah, please let me encourage you to read "Appendix 4—The Subtle Demise of True Christianity."

Meanwhile, if you have any questions, comments, or suggestions about anything you've read so far, if you want someone to pray with or for you, if you just want to discuss these things, or if you would like to get involved in Last Trump Ministries, please visit our website at www.RevelationUnderstoodCommentary.com or contact me at: WatchmanBob@gmail.com.

Appendix 3—Who are the People of Yahuah?

The Christians say they are "God's" People. The Jews say that they are the People of Yahuah. The Muslims say they are Allah's people. Other religious groups say they are the people of "God." And within these groups there are many sub-groups—all making exclusive claim to being the people of "God." Many of these groups are at one another's throats. Jews and Christians are antagonistic toward one another; Jews and Christians war against Muslims and vice versa; Christians and Muslims persecute Jews; Shiite Muslims fight Sunni Muslims; Jews exclude Christians from the "Commonwealth of Israel" (Ephesians 2:12); Protestants war with the Catholics; Charismatics war with the Fundamentalists; various sects, denominations, and churches within Christianity fight one another; even congregations within a church are antagonistic toward one another; various sects of Judaism conflict with one another.

And this divisive conflict is sad, because Yahushua, who gave His life that the **whole world** might be saved (John 3:16; 1 Timothy 2:6), prayed, just before He finished His mission here on Earth, that all ". . . *who believe in Me . . . might be **one**, as You, Father, are in Me, and I in You; that they also may be **one** in Us . . .*" (John 17:21).

So, who are, really, the "Chosen Ones," the "Redeemed of the Lord," the "Elect," the People of Yahuah whom He longs to be united in Him and He in them? If we will just get our egos and misconceptions out of the way long enough to look at Scripture comprehensively and objectively—getting the big picture of Yahuah's wonderful plan to restore His **entire** Creation in Heaven and on Earth to Himself (cf. Colossians 1:16-20), as well as the details of that plan—we will see with crystal clarity who His People are. And you are invited to do exactly that with me right now.

In the Beginning

To find out who Yahuah's People are, we have to start at the beginning, understanding the Lord's original plan for His Creation. In the beginning Yahuah created the universe and all that is in it (Genesis 1:1-25). Then, His crowning achievement was the creation of human beings—Adam and Eve—who were perfectly united with one another and with Yahuah (cf. Genesis 1:27; 2:24). So, Adam and Eve were the first People of Yahuah. And it was Yahuah's will that they eat of the Tree of Life (Genesis 2:9, 16) and live in perfect harmony with Him, one another, and His Creation forever. And Yahuah wanted Adam and Eve to be categorically different from all other created beings or animals in Heaven or on Earth. So, He created them in His own image (Genesis 1:27). And since the essence of Yahuah is love (1 John 4:16), He created human beings, unlike any other creatures in Heaven or on Earth, with His capacity for pure, unselfish love. And it is the love of Yahuah that unites us with Him and with one another (1 John 4:16).

But, in order to love unselfishly, we need to be able to choose **not** to love, don't we? For how can we say that someone loves us if they have no choice but to love us? So, among all the beings Yahuah created, human beings are the only ones He created with free will—the capacity to choose between right and wrong, good and evil, to love or not to love Yahuah and one another. Some may argue that Lucifer, the brightest angel, chose to rebel against Yahuah. But, as we will see, Lucifer really had no choice—he was created by Yahuah to rebel against his Creator. So fasten your seatbelts; some of this may really stretch your understanding of Yahuah. But if you will hang on and go along for the ride, you will see that a true, Scriptural understanding of Yahuah's plan for the restoration of His **whole** Creation is nothing less than astonishing in its wisdom and magnificence.

So, the Lord gave Adam and Eve a choice. He planted the Tree of the Knowledge of Good **and** Evil in the Garden and told Adam and Eve **not** to eat of that tree—that the day they ate of that tree they would die (Genesis 2:17). It has never been Yahuah's will, although He created it, for His People to have an intimate knowledge of evil. Yes, you are reading correctly: In the same way that Yahuah created Lucifer to rebel against Him and become Satan, and in the same way that He created the deadly Tree of the Knowledge of Good and Evil, He created what was in the fruit of that tree—evil itself. Yes, this is a little too much for our puny human minds to comprehend, but remember what the apostle Paul told those who questioned Yahuah's choosing to favor some and "hate" others:

> *What if [Yahuah], wanting to show His wrath and to make His power known, endured with much longsuffering the vessels of wrath **prepared for destruction**?* (Romans 9:22)

In other words, who are we to question Yahuah, whose ways are infinitely above ours? What if, like Paul pointed out, Yahuah created evil and the evil one and put them into the world, later to be destroyed, but meanwhile to give humans the choice between good and evil, so that we could, in His image, manifest our Creator's goodness and love. In the end, it will all make sense and we will have a perfect understanding of Yahuah's ways.[17]

But meanwhile, please notice what happened. Adam and Eve made the wrong choice; they chose to believe the Serpent's (Satan in disguise) lie that they would **not** die if they ate of the Tree of the Knowledge of Good and Evil (Genesis 3:4). And, as Yahuah had warned, that day they died and were banished from His presence. No, they did not die physically—they had children and lived many more years, but they died (were separated from Yahuah) spiritually. In other words, they were no longer one with Yahuah and with one another in His Spirit of pure, unselfish goodness and love. And, at that point in time, they ceased being His People; they became children of the devil, controlled by the spirit of evil.

So, what makes someone a Person of Yahuah?

Let's take a close look at what happened to Adam and Eve. When we understand why they fell out of favor with Yahuah and ceased being His People, we will understand who, down through history, have been the People of Yahuah.

Adam and Eve forfeited their relationship with Yahuah because they were disobedient. He told them not to eat of the Tree of the Knowledge of Good and Evil, and they ate of it. It's that simple, right? Wrong. Their disobedience was just a symptom of a deeper, spiritual deficit—lack of faith. They **believed** the serpent rather than **believing** Yahuah. And so they gave in to their impulses and the lies of the devil, and joined him in His rebellion against Yahuah. A loving relationship with anyone—a spouse, a friend . . . or with Yahuah—is based on trust, isn't it? If we don't trust (have faith in) that person, or Yahuah, we have no real relationship with him or her, do we? So, when we look at the People of Yahuah down through history, we see that **the key qualification for being one of Yahuah's People is faith in Him.**

The People of Yahuah in the Bible

Here is a chronological list of some of the other People of Yahuah named in the *Bible* together with Scriptures that tell why they were Yahuah's People:

---

[17]Yahuah's ultimate plan is to restore His entire creation, including the fallen angels, to Himself. For more about that, read "Appendix 8—How Long is 'Forever' in the *Bible*?"

Abel – Genesis 4:1-4; Hebrews 11:4
Enoch – Genesis 5:24; Hebrews 11:5
Noah – Genesis 6-9; Hebrews 11:7
Abraham – Genesis 15:6; Romans 4:3; Hebrews 11:8, 17-19
Sarah – Genesis 21:1-3; Hebrews 11:11
Isaac – Genesis 27:26-40; Hebrews 11:20
Jacob – Genesis 48:1-20; Hebrews 11:21
Joseph – Genesis 50:22-26; Hebrews 11:22
Moses – Exodus 2:11-15; 10:28; 12:21; Hebrews 11:23-28
The Children of Israel – Exodus 14:22-29; Joshua 6:12-20; Hebrews
    11:29-30
Rahab – Joshua 2:1; 6:25; Hebrews 11:31
Deborah – Judges 4:4-16
Ruth – Ruth 1:16
David – 1 Samuel 17:45-47
Elijah – 1 Kings 18:24-38
Esther – Esther 4:16-5:2
Mary – Luke 1:31-38
The Apostles – The book of Acts
Cornelius – Acts 10

Now, what is the one thing that all these People of Yahuah had in common? Was it because they were males? No . . . many of the great People of Yahuah throughout history have been women. Deborah was a judge and prophet of Israel. Was it because they were all Jews? No . . . about half of the people listed above—Abel, Enoch, Noah, Abraham, Sarah, Isaac, Jacob, Rahab, Ruth, and Cornelius—were not Jews (descendants of Jacob). Ruth, a Moabite woman, was an ancestor of Yahushua. Was it because they were "Christians"? No . . . in the above list, only the apostles (after the Messiah's resurrection) and Cornelius were what were called (by the Gentiles) "Christians." Was it because they were good, righteous people? No . . . they were all sinful humans, just like you and me. Abraham and all the Patriarchs were adulterers and polygamists. Abraham, out of fear of what Pharaoh would do to him if he knew Sarah was his wife, lied to Pharaoh, telling him Sarah was his sister, and turned her over to Pharaoh. The Children of Israel were constantly whining and complaining about their circumstances, rebelling against Yahuah, and worshiping other gods. David, the "apple of Yahuah's eye," was an adulterer and murderer. Rahab was a Gentile prostitute. So, it is not our own goodness and righteousness that make us People of Yahuah, is it?

Obviously, the one factor that makes a person one of Yahuah's People is **faith**, isn't it? . . . a faith that keeps us coming back to Yahuah in repentance although we frequently fail Him, trusting Him to work everything out in the end. All the above references in the book of Hebrews state, "By faith" Abel, Enoch, Noah, Abraham, Sarah, Isaac, Jacob, Joseph, Moses, the children of Israel, and Rahab did this and that great thing. Abraham is the prototype of Yahuah's People. And it was in faith that this great man of Yahuah, who was very comfortable and prosperous in Mesopotamia, the place where he was born and raised, gathered up his possessions and left, not even knowing where he was going, simply because the Lord told him that if he would do so, He would make his descendants a great nation (Genesis 12:1, 2). And it was in faith that Abraham was willing to obediently offer his son as a sacrifice to Yahuah (Genesis 22:9-10). And it was simply because of his faith, not because of his obedience or lack of sin, that Yahuah considered Abraham righteous (Genesis 15:6; Romans 4:3).

Yes, the People of Yahuah are obedient, but that is only through their faith. Often, when they are not acting out of faith, they are disobedient. But if they are truly the People of Yahuah, they will keep repenting of their sins, turning back to Him in faith for forgiveness, and trusting Him to save them in the end. And it is not just going through the motions of obedience that makes one a Child of Yahuah. Cain obeyed Yahuah in offering a sacrifice, but it was not done in faith, so it was rejected (Hebrews 11:4). King Saul offered sacrifices to Yahuah, but not in faith, so his sacrifices were rejected and so was Saul (1 Samuel 13:9-13). The *Bible* states, "Whatever is not from faith is sin" (Romans 14:23). We can attend every service and function of the Assembly of the Saints, sing praises to Yahuah with our hands raised, give away all of our possessions, do great things in the name of Yahushua, pray fervently, and still not be His People. Only those who do His will **in faith** are Yahuah's People (cf. Matthew 7:21).

The People of Yahuah Today

So who are Yahuah's People in the world today? They are the same as His People throughout history—those who have trusted Him with their lives and follow Him wherever He leads. And, because there are thousands of "gods" being worshiped in the world, the one, true God, the God of Abraham, Isaac, Jacob, and the Children of Israel, has made Who He is very clear and specific by manifesting Himself as a human being—Yahushua the Messiah. To believe in Yahushua, the

251

only person in history who could legitimately claim to be both Yahuah and human, is to believe in Yahuah (cf. John 14:9-15).

The People of Yahuah have always interacted with and looked forward to the Messiah coming to take back dominion of the world from Satan. Yahuah the Son has been personally involved with His People throughout history. For example, Abraham met and gave a tenth of the spoils of war (an act of worship) to the Messiah in the person of Melchisedec, the mysterious king of Salem who had no mother nor father, no descendants, no beginning nor end, and who was also called the "King of Righteousness" and the "King of Peace" (Hebrews 7:1-4). And Genesis 18:1 states that, on another occasion, the Lord appeared to Abraham in the form of three men. Then, hundreds of years later, Yahushua confirmed that He had been present with Abraham, and that Abraham had rejoiced to (in faith) see the coming of His day (John 8:56). Yahuah's ancient People, the descendants of Israel, have always looked forward to the coming of the Messiah to rule from the throne of David (e.g., Isaiah 9:6, 7). In fact, He has interacted personally with Hebrews throughout their history. Examples include appearing to Joshua (Joshua 5:13-15) and to Zechariah (Zechariah 1:8; 2:5). Most of the Jews have just not yet realized that the Messiah is Yahushua.

Then, the apostle Paul, in his letter to the believers in Rome, explains very clearly who the People of Yahuah are: They are all those who are the spiritual descendants of Abraham through faith in the coming Messiah—Jews or Gentiles (cf. Romans 4). As was pointed out in the commentary on Revelation 19, the term translated "nation" (Hebrew: *goy*, plural *goyim*) in the *Bible* can refer to any of three groups— the physical descendants of Abraham, Isaac, and Jacob (Israel), the spiritual descendants of Abraham (those who look forward in faith to the coming Messiah), or the unsaved Gentile nations, depending on the context. Generally, the singular *(goy)* refers to the physical nation of Israel while the plural *(goyim)* refers to either the spiritual descendants of Abraham (including the tribes/nations who will inhabit the millennial kingdom) or to the unsaved Gentile nations of the world. As examples: Genesis 12:2 refers to the physical descendants of Abraham (a *"great nation [goy]"*), identified as the *"holy nation [goy]"* Israel in Exodus 19:6. In Genesis 18:18, *goy* and *goyim* refer to the Hebrew and Gentile nations, respectively—*goy* refers to Israel and *goyim* refers to *"all the* [Gentile] *nations of the earth."* Then, the Lord promised Ephraim (the Birthright son of Israel, whose name is used interchangeably with Israel) that his descendants would be a *"multitude* [He-

252

brew: *melow'*—fullness, that which fills] *of nations* [*goyim*]" (Genesis 48:19)—Hebrew nations who will populate the Kingdom of Yahuah during the Millennium. (The descendants of the Northern Kingdom of Israel will be reunited with the tribes of the Southern Kingdom when they return to the Promised Land at the End of the Age [cf. Ezekiel 37:21-22]. Then, together, they will again form the united nation of Israel, the twelve tribes of which (along with the Gentiles who survive the Final Seven Years—cf. Zechariah 14:16) will become the nations of the millennial kingdom of the Messiah). In Romans 11:25, exactly the same phrase is used: *"fullness* [Greek: *pleroma*—fullness, that which fills] *of the Gentiles* [Greek: *ethnos*—nations]," but in that context referring to the spiritual descendants of Abraham—Gentiles who have come to faith in Yahushua as their Messiah—who have been grafted into the Commonwealth of Israel (cf. Romans 11:24; Ephesians 2:12).

Unfortunately, virtually all Gentile translations of the *Bible* and commentaries fail to recognize that *goy(im)* refers to both Hebrew and Gentile nations. This has resulted in much confusion as to how Yahuah is going to deal with Israel vis-à-vis the Gentile nations at the End of the Age, even to the extent of the formation of the false doctrine that Gentile "Christian" nations or churches have replaced Israel as Yahuah's chosen nation and will be the ones who inhabit the Kingdom of Yahuah on Earth during the Millennium. For example, in the context of describing the establishment of the millennial Kingdom of Yahuah, Isaiah 11:10 in the NKJV states,

> *And in that day* [the Day of the Lord] *there shall be a Root of Jesse* [the Messiah]*, Who shall stand as a banner to the people; for the **Gentiles** [goyim]* [falsely implying only non-Jews, including the unsaved] *shall seek Him, and His resting place shall be glorious.*

But please notice that the context of Isaiah 11:10 is a prophecy that the Messiah will return to *"set up a banner for the **nations** [goyim], **and** will assemble the outcasts of **Israel*** [non-Hebrews were never cast out, because they were never Israelites in the first place]*, **and** gather together the dispersed of **Judah*** [a tribe of Israel] *from the four corners of the earth* [Gentiles were never scattered to the four corners of the earth]" (verses 11 and 12). Clearly, in these verses (10-12), the banner is being set up not only for the Yahuah-fearing Gentiles on whom the Lord will have mercy and allow to enter the millennial kingdom of the Messiah, but for the physical descendants of Israel who will come out of the Gentile nations, because, at this point in time (at the end of the

253

Final Seven Years), the faithful Remnant of both the descendants of Ephraim/Israel (the Northern Kingdom) and those of the House of Judah (the Southern Kingdom) who have not yet recognized that Yahushua is the Messiah will be eagerly looking for the Messiah's return, but the time for the unsaved, pagan Gentiles to come to the Lord will have ended—those who are not saved by then will not be seeking Him.

So, Paul points out to the grafted-in (Gentile) Believers that they should not look down their noses at the Jews who rejected the Messiah the first time He came. It was all part of Yahuah's plan to make faith in the Messiah Yahushua available to **everyone**. Paul explains it very graphically, stating that the Jews (those of Israel who look forward in faith to the coming Messiah) are Yahuah's original chosen People (the cultivated olive tree) and the redeemed Gentiles (not the natural, physical descendants of Israel) are branches of the wild olive tree (*"elect according to the foreknowledge of [Yahuah] the Father"*—1 Peter 1:2), grafted, *"contrary to nature"* (Romans 11:24), into the cultivated olive tree. And the wild branches have been grafted in only because the cultivated branches have been (temporarily) cut off. Therefore, the wild branches grafted in through faith in Yahushua should not boast against the cultivated branches that have been cut off, because if Yahuah did not spare the cultivated branches who did not believe in Yahushua when He first came (but who will be grafted back in when they do believe), He will certainly not spare the wild, grafted-in branches if they do not continue in the goodness (through faith) of Yahuah. (Romans 11:17-24)

So, the only difference, at the present time, between the Renewed Covenant Saints (those who have already believed in the Messiah Yahushua) and the Saints still living under the original covenant with Israel is that the Renewed Covenant Saints have (or should have) the *Torah* written on our hearts (Hebrews 10:16) and the fullness of the indwelling Holy Spirit enabling us to live by the *Torah*, not that we are any more the chosen People of Yahuah than are the Jews who believe in the coming Messiah. The doctrine that the cultivated olive tree, composed of those of the twelve tribes of Israel who still believe in Yahuah and look forward in faith to the coming Messiah, although they have not yet recognized that He is Yahushua, are not just as much the People of Yahuah as those who have already accepted Yahushua as their Savior and Messiah, is called Replacement Theology, and is totally unsubstantiated by Scripture.

254

Therefore, there is no Scriptural reason for anti-Semitism, is there? All believers in the coming Messiah, whether or not they have yet recognized that He is Yahushua, are Yahuah's People.[18] And the efforts of Christians, rather than condemning the Jewish people if they don't convert to Christianity, should be directed toward ministering the Truth in love to them, so that when the Messiah Yahushua does return on the last Yom Teruah at the End of this Age (cf. "Appendex 6—When is the 'Rapture'?"), they will recognize Him and be saved.

I realize that this is quite a convoluted explanation, but it is not easy to explain who the People of Yahuah are to those who think of themselves as separate from or superior to others who believe in the coming Messiah. In fact, the vast majority of those who claim to be Christians, in their worldliness, rejection of the "law" (*Torah*) of the Lord, and anti-Semitism, are not truly Yahuah's People—they are members of the apostate church who will follow Antimessiah to destruction (cf. 2 Thessalonians 2:3-4).

Please continue through "Appendix 4—The Subtle Demise of True Christianity"—to find out who among those who call themselves "Christians" are the True People of Yahuah.

---

[18]For the apostle Paul's clear description of how both the Jewish and grafted-in Gentile Believers in the Messiah are Yahuah's People, please read Ephesians Chapter 2.

Appendix 4—The Subtle Demise of True "Christianity"

Note to Messianic Believers: The following essay originally was written especially for my loved ones in the Christian Church, in which I was raised. But it, except the part about anti-Semitism, applies just as much to those of us who embrace the Hebraic roots of our faith. Wherever it says "Christian," just substitute "Follower of the Messiah," and wherever it says "Church," substitute "Assembly of Believers in Yahushua."

The Church's Deadliest Disease

Cancer—America's second deadliest disease (next to heart disease)—dreaded by everyone. AIDS—incurable loss of immunity to disease, deterioration of health, and finally death. But during the past few years I have been made painfully aware of a far more insidious, pervasive, and devastating disease infecting the American Christian Church—an evil, spiritual malady capable of destroying both body and soul if not checked. Why so painful to me? Because I've had to admit that for most of my 65 years on Earth, I too have been infected by this disease, and I am presently striving, by Yahuah's grace, to eradicate it from my own soul. So please understand, dear friend, that I am not pointing an accusative finger at any individual, because I realize that when I do, there are always three fingers pointing back at me. Therefore, if you feel that what is written here is speaking to or about you personally, you'd better pay attention, because that conviction is not coming from me—it's probably Yahuah speaking to you through your own conscience. And it's definitely not wise to ignore the voice ("Word") of Yahuah. If the shoe seems to fit, rather than getting offended at the shoe, no matter how much you do not like that shoe, I pray that you will wear it until you can replace it with a good shoe.

One other point: If you are not a Christian, some of this essay will not apply to you because it is directed primarily to Christians, or at least to those who claim to be Christians. But some parts may hit home with you too, and I pray that you will take those to heart. Your (eternal) life may be at stake.

Three Spiritual Maladies

There are two terrible maladies closely related to and feeding the third, most insidious and pervasive evil—the Church's "deadliest disease."

The first is pride, which often manifests itself in a sense of self-sufficiency or a "we're better than you are" attitude, especially in competitive activities. Pride pervades our whole culture, doesn't it? America is the home of the rugged, independent, "self-made man." Pride is a primary motivation for most Americans' accomplishments. One Sunday, when my wife and I visited a local church in the small farming community in which we lived, we heard the pastor preach an excellent sermon against the evils of pride. But later, we heard the same pastor, who was also the head science teacher at the high school in that community, going on and on about how "proud" he was of his students' accomplishments. Too bad his own sermon wasn't taken more to heart. Isn't pride what the "We're number one," "We're the best," and "We-are-proud-of-you" cheers are all about at sporting contests? And isn't building "self-esteem" (pride) in our children a basic goal of education? I use these examples because I was in education and coaching for 30 years. But doesn't this **un**godly spirit of pride pervade everything we do—our occupations, our accomplishments, and our accumulation of material possessions? Don't we take pride in our jobs, our achievements, our promotions, our homes, the vehicles we drive, our family members . . . *ad infinitum*? [17]

Some may object, "Well, hold on, Bob. That's not the kind of pride we're talking about when we say, 'We are proud of you' [as if there are two kinds of pride—one good and one evil]. We're simply showing our appreciation and support of the ones we love." Oh, really? Then why not say, "I appreciate what you are doing," or, even better, "I thank Yahuah for you," or simply, "Good job," or "I am very pleased with you" (what Father Yahuah told His Son, Yahushua), rather than using a form of that horrible word "pride"? Or don't you know that pride is one of the three basic, fundamental sins (cf. 1 John 2:16) and that Yahushua listed pride right along with other "evil things" that defile a person (Mark 7:20-23)? Perhaps you are not aware that it was pride that got Lucifer (later called Satan) kicked out of Heaven (Isaiah 14:11-14). It got Adam and Eve kicked out of Eden (Genesis 3:5). And pride will get those who are infected by it a hot reservation in Hell, excluded from Heaven (Proverbs 16:18). [19]

What is the Christian alternative to pride? Obviously, it's humility. Scripture states, *"[Yahuah] resists the proud, but He gives grace to*

---

[19]Pride also motivates anti-Semitism. Even though Christians may say that they are pro-Israel and even that the Jews are the People of Yahuah, they

the humble" (Proverbs 3:34).   And how can we tell that someone is humble? Again, that's obvious: The truly humble person always gives credit, honor, and glory to whom credit, honor, and glory are due—and that is not to oneself or to any other human being.   Yahushua said, *"Apart from Me, you can do **nothing"*** (John 15:5).   You see, my friend, unless Yahushua (Yahuah the Son) gives us the will, the opportunity, and the power, we cannot inhale one breath, speak one word, take one step, or even think one thought, much less achieve other "accomplishments," whether we acknowledge Yahuah's omnipotence or arrogantly deny it (cf. Philippians 2:13).   Later, the apostle Paul wrote, *"**Whatever** you do in word or deed, do **all** in the name of the Lord [Yahushua]"* (Colossians 3:17), and again, *"In **whatever** you do, do it so as to bring glory to [Yahuah]"* (1 Corinthians 10:31).   That's both specific and comprehensive, isn't it? Yet, we insist that pride is OK. In fact, in America, pride is considered a virtue, isn't it? That just goes to show how subtle and deceitful the Devil is, and what total control, apart from Yahuah's gracious intervention, he has over our hearts and thought processes.

At a high school activities awards banquet, just before I was fired from that school's staff, I mentioned that in my four years of teaching and coaching there, I had not once heard anyone—any student, any athlete, any teacher, any coach, any school administrator, any parent, any church leader or minister, or any other member of the community— give Yahuah the full credit and glory for the accomplishments being recognized at that banquet.   In fact, the most frequent word heard

---

usually consider Jews second-class citizens in the Kingdom of Yahuah, or not really the People of Yahuah at all.   The apostle Paul wrote the entire eleventh chapter of Romans to refute and warn against that view, explaining that the Jews are the original People of Yahuah who have been temporarily put "on hold"—blinded to the fact that Yahushua is their Messiah—so that the Gentiles who are branches of the "wild olive tree" who come to faith in Yahushua, could be "grafted into" the "natural olive tree" (Israel).   So, the grafted-in Believers in Yahushua should certainly not look down their noses at the Jews, because if the natural branches could be cut off but later grafted back in, how much easier would it be to cut off arrogant, anti-Semitic, anti-Zionist grafted-in branches? (cf. Romans 11:1, 13-25) Paul further explains the relationship between the Jews and the grafted-in Believers by calling them "fellow citizens" in the "commonwealth of Israel" (Ephesians 2:12, 19).   So, it is actually more correct to say that Gentiles who have come to faith in Yahushua are Israelites than it is to say that Jews who have come to faith in Yahushua are Christians.

there was "proud." Now, what's wrong with that picture? Didn't most of the people in the community, including the administrators, teachers, and coaches at the school, claim to be good, church-going Christians? And again, I'm not finger-pointing here, because much of my life, especially during my teaching and coaching career, I too was guilty of keeping credit and glory to myself, rather than praising Yahuah for what He had enabled my classroom kids, athletes, and me to do. All that I wanted to do at that awards ceremony and all that I want to do now is to light a little candle in the darkness of self-adulation (including my own). Acknowledging Yahuah in all that we do, rather than just patting ourselves on the back, is very, very important, with eternal implications, because Yahushua said,

> *Whoever acknowledges Me before others I will acknowledge before my Father in Heaven. But whoever denies Me* [keeps the credit and glory for self] *before others I will deny* [disown] *before my Father in Heaven.* (Matthew 10:32)

Isn't stealing the credit and glory for what Yahuah has done, or even giving it to others to whom it doesn't belong, a form of denying Him?

The second spiritual malady pervasive in the American Christian Church is covetousness (greed). Yahushua said,

> *Do not lay up treasures* [wealth] *on earth, where moths and rust destroy, and burglars break in and steal. Instead, store up for yourselves treasures in Heaven, where neither moths nor rust destroys, and burglars do not break in and steal. For where your treasures are, there your heart is also."* (Matthew 6:19-21)

"Now, wait a minute, Bob," you may again object. "I live in a community with very modest incomes. No one is extravagant. Everyone works together and shares. I certainly am not greedy—I give to the Church and I'm generous with others. I'm just trying to get by." Well, are you willing to test that assertion against Yahuah's Word (and again, I'm speaking primarily to "Christians")? Yahushua said,

> *If anyone wants to follow Me, let him deny himself, take up his cross daily, and keep following Me. For whoever tries to save his own life will destroy it, but whoever destroys his life on My account will save it."* (Luke 9:23-24)

And He told a wealthy young community leader who asked what he needed to do to be saved, *"Sell whatever you have, distribute the pro-*

260

ceeds to the poor, and you will have treasures in Heaven. Then come, follow Me!" (Luke 18:22). So what does Yahushua mean to "deny ourselves"? He means just what He said: Unless we are willing and in fact are in the process of giving up all of our prideful, self-indulgent, worldly pleasures and treasures to follow and serve Him (primarily in bringing others to Him - Matthew 28:19-20), we will have no place in His glorious, soon-coming kingdom with Him. And carrying that cross (the figurative instrument of death to self) is not a comfortable, painless thing to do. And what are *"treasures in Heaven"*? They are certainly not the things we accumulate on Earth, are they? We can't take anything (money, homes, vehicles, land, awards, fame, position, pleasure, unsaved family members, etc.) with us after this short "puff-of-smoke" life on Earth is over (Ecclesiastes 2:18). Let me submit to you that the only treasures we can lay up in Heaven are human souls (our own and those of others whom Yahuah saves through our influence). Proverbs 11:30 states, *"He who saves souls is wise."* And are you familiar with Yahushua's Parable of the Pearl of Great Price? When a merchant found a very valuable pearl, he sold everything he had to purchase it. What is more valuable than a human soul? Get the picture? Saving souls is Yahuah's heavenly savings plan.

So, dear friend, let me ask you a few simple questions. Please answer them honestly, then decide for yourself if you are infected with the covetousness malady.

- Are your awards—your certificates of accomplishment, letter jackets, ribbons, medals, trophies, plaques, pictures in the newspaper and on the wall—treasures on Earth or treasures in Heaven?
- How is most of your time spent—trying to secure your own and/or others' success, comfort, and pleasure on this Earth, or helping those you love secure their place in Heaven?
- On what do you spend most of your money—on yourself and the worldly success, comfort, security, and pleasure of your family and others, or, either directly or indirectly, on the Gospel—getting your loved ones saved from this evil world?
- What do you talk about most of the time—temporal, worldly things, or, either directly or indirectly, the Lord and His great and wonderful plan of salvation?
- When someone compliments you, do you say, "Thank you," and keep the praise to yourself, or do you give the credit and glory to Yahuah?

- And here's a real soul-searcher: What do you think about most of the time—temporal, worldly success, things, pleasure, and relationships, or the Lord and His great and wonderful plan of salvation and how to get your loved ones saved?

Your honest answers to these questions should give you a pretty good idea of whether or not you are storing up treasures on Earth, which is covetousness, or in Heaven. And again, my friend, I have to admit that I have wasted most of my life working foolishly and futilely for worldly success and possessions. But, by the grace of Yahuah, I am changing that focus and direction in my life. I pray that you will join me.

But the third evil, spiritual "disease," which is the child of and is reinforced by pride and covetousness, is the most insidious and the deadliest of all, because most "Christians" are not even aware that it infects them, and when confronted with its existence in them, they tend to deny it. The good news is that, unlike many forms of cancer and AIDS, it is totally curable, **if** they will face up to and admit ("confess") it, reject ("repent of") it, and allow Yahuah to replace it with His alternatives—His Truth and pure, unselfish Love. Yahushua spoke His strongest words of censure against the third evil—the Church's deadliest disease. What did Yahushua call those who claimed to be good, "law-abiding" people, but who were really full of the first two spiritual maladies—pride and covetousness? That is correct; He called them *"hypocrites—white-washed tombs* [beautiful on the outside but full of dead people's bones and all kinds of rottenness on the inside]." (Matthew 23:27) Does that description fit you? Are you claiming to be a good Christian—perhaps even a church leader—but are really full of hateful bigotry—condemning and mistreating those who don't agree with your political, religious, or racial views? Do you claim to be a good Christian, but are really full of pride and covetousness—patting yourself on the back and denying the grace of Yahuah by refusing to give Him the credit for your accomplishments (and encouraging others to do the same), thereby laying up your treasures on Earth? Are you mainly preoccupied with maintaining your own materialistic, self-indulgent lifestyle, and just giving the "tithe" or the leftovers to the needy, the Church, or devote it to the Gospel?

And again, I'm not pointing my finger at any individual. I have been as guilty of all three of these deadly spiritual diseases as anyone, and it's only by Yahuah's wonderful mercy and amazing grace that He has saved me from them and their "eternal" consequences, although I

262

pray daily for Him to continue to eradicate them from my own soul. (True Christianity is not a static state of goodness and holiness—it is a continual process of *"putting off the old person and putting on the new person"* or *"growing in the grace and knowledge of our Lord and Savior, [Yahushua the Messiah]"*). I pray the same for each of you whom the shoe fits, before it is too late. Remember, the blatant sinners were not the ones who were primarily responsible for killing Yahuah's prophets and His Son; those were the hypocrites—the ones who claimed to be good religious people—especially the religious leaders. Are you considered a "good Christian" or even a church leader, but are really, deep in your heart, congratulating yourself and proudly accepting the praises of others? If so, that's pure hypocrisy. Please repent and start giving Yahuah **all** the credit, honor, and glory, and start devoting **all** that you have to the Gospel, before it is too late and you find yourself sharing a place in Hell with the Prince of Pride and Covetousness (Satan).

Are you an *"almost* Christian"?

Yahuah tells Believers to *"Examine yourselves to see whether you are living the life of faith. Test yourselves. Don't you realize that [Yahushua the Messiah] is in you?—unless you fail to pass the test"* (2 Corinthians 13:5). In other words, search your heart, asking yourself and Yahuah if you are a True Christian or are really just a phony hypocrite—what the Puritan preacher, Matthew Mead, called an *"almost* Christian." I've been doing a lot of that soul-searching lately, and I invite those of you who claim to be Christians to join me as we share a few points from Mead's book, *The Almost Christian Observed.* If you don't claim to be a Christian, this part may interest you anyway, because it will help you see who in your community is a True Christian and who to avoid because they are infected with the Church's deadliest disease.

A person may go through all the "steps" of becoming a Christian and even have a highly emotional and spiritual conversion experience in being "saved"—and still be but *almost* a Christian. The *Bible* says that even the demons believe in Yahuah and know that Yahushua is His Son—Yahuah in a human body—and tremble (Mark 1:34; James 2:19). There is a faith that is seated in the understanding but does not touch the spirit and permanently change the heart and the will. A person may believe in his mind every word of the *Bible*, be convicted of, confess, and repent of his sins (see the next section), believe in Yahushua, be baptized, and become a member of a Christian Church, but still be as lost as one who hates Yahushua and never sets foot in a church. His natural mind and conscience may be enlightened by Yahuah's Word, and he may be "saved" to avoid going to Hell or even out of gratitude to Yahuah for his saving grace in sacrificing His Son for us, but if his heart is not transformed by the Holy Spirit, his "conversion" is basically just a selfish device designed to get him the benefits of the Kingdom of Heaven without the totally new and unselfish life in the Messiah. And the new "Christian" is but *almost* a Christian.

A person may hate sin and go far in repenting of sin, overcoming sin in his own life, and opposing sin in others—indeed, be a great crusader against evil—and yet be but *almost* a Christian. Every human being, somewhere in his soul, although it may be seared over by much wrongdoing, has a conscience—a sense of right and wrong, good and evil. Most would agree that rape, murder, stealing, greed, abuse of others, arrogance, selfishness, and other attitudes and actions that the *Bible* calls "sin" are wrong. And they may hate that sin in themselves and others. And they may go far in eliminating sinful attitudes and behavior in themselves and helping others do the same. They may even make those changes in response to the enlightening of Yahuah's Word, the *Bible*. And so they consider themselves and others consider them "Christians." Yet those changes may be but natural and rational—not spiritual. Their natural and rational hearts, attitudes, and behavior are changed in hoping that they will receive the benefits of a sinless life (basically a selfish motive), but their spiritual hearts are untouched by the Holy Spirit of Yahuah. So they remain but *almost* Christians.

A person may be under great, visible changes—may become a "good," moral person and yet be but *almost* a Christian. There is a civil and moral change as well as a spiritual and supernatural change. Many are changed morally, even to the extent that it is said of them that they have become "new" people; but they are, in heart and nature, the same still. A person may be converted from a profane life to a form of godliness, from filthy to clean, wholesome conversation and behavior, and yet the heart is basically the same in one as in the other because it is not permanently renewed by the Holy Spirit. King Saul changed greatly when he met the Lord's prophets, even becoming a prophet himself. Indeed, it was written of him that Yahuah gave him "*another*" heart (1 Samuel 10:9). But in the end, Saul was not saved after all: an evil spirit entered him and the Spirit of Yahuah "*departed from him*" (1 Samuel 16:14). That's because there's a critically important difference between having "another" heart and having a "new"

264

heart. Yahuah can give someone "another" heart to transform his out-ward attitudes and behavior temporarily, or he can give that person a "new" heart transforming him from the inside out eternally. A person whose outward attitudes and behavior are changed but who has not been given a new heart is but an *almost* Christian.

A person may be very religious—a zealous church leader and even a pastor and a pillar of the community—and yet be but *almost* a Christian. Jehu, a king of Israel, served Yahuah and did what He commanded, destroying all the worshipers and priests of the false god Ba'al, and was very zealous in His service, proclaiming, "*Come with me, and see my zeal for the Lord of Hosts!*" (2 Kings 10:16). And yet, in all this, Jehu was a hypocrite, making no effort to live wholehearted-ly according to the Word of Yahuah and refusing to turn from the sins introduced into Israel by King Jeroboam. So a person may be a very religious, zealous, and devoted church member, and yet be but *almost* a True Christian.

A person may go farther yet. He may have a "love" for Yahuah, the People of Yahuah, his friends, and even his enemies, and yet be but *almost* a Christian. There is a natural affection for those who love us and bless us. Some will even go so far, Yahushua said, as to give his life for his friends. But this is basically a selfish "love" which loves only those who return that love, even if it's just a "Thank you" from them. But when Yahuah gives a person a new heart and fills it with His totally unselfish love, which blesses and even lays down one's life for someone, including an enemy, expecting nothing in return, as Yahushua did, then that person is a True Christian. But a person may even go so far as to give his life for his enemies—even to the point of being tortured or burned at the stake—and still be lost. How? Because when he does **anything** primarily for the purpose of getting something in return—perhaps only a reputation as a martyr or the salvation of his own soul—then his love is basically conditional and selfish. So, a per-son may have great "love" and make great sacrifices for others and still be but *almost* a true Christian.

A person may have great spiritual gifts and yet be but *almost* a Christian. Yahuah can use anyone or anything through whom or which to manifest His gifts. He spoke to the pagan prophet Balaam through a donkey (Numbers 22:28). That was a gifted donkey! He then spoke through Balaam to the pagan king Balak a true word of prophecy concerning Israel (Numbers 23:16). But neither the donkey nor Balaam were true believers, were they? So, a person may speak amazing prophecies that come true, do astonishing miracles, heal people, speak in other tongues supernaturally (Antimessiah and the False Prophet will do all these things), and still be but *almost* a Christian.

Now you may ask, "If a person may hate, repent of, and go far in overcoming sin in his life, become a 'good,' moral person, be a zealous and devoted church member, love and make great sacrifices for others, and manifest powerful spiritual gifts from Yahuah in his life, and still be but *almost* a Christian, how in the world may I know that I am a True, saved Christian?" The answer is simple and takes us back to the beginning of this article: "*Whatever you do in word or deed, do all in the name of the Lord [Yahushua]*" (Colossians 3:17), and again, "*In whatever you do, do it so as to bring glory to [Yahuah]*" (1 Corinthians 10:31). If there is the tiniest element of selfishness or pride in anything we think, say, or do as Christians, then that is not True Christianity—that is hypocrisy—the deadliest spiritual disease. Fear of going to Hell may drive us to Yahuah, or gratitude to Yahuah for what He has done for us may draw us to Him (self-interest is what motivates unsaved people), but fear of Hell or hope of Heaven, by themselves, will not keep us saved. When we are truly saved, He gives us a new heart and fills it with His pure, unselfish love, and we are no longer as concerned about the consequences or benefits to ourselves as we are in glorifying Him and blessing others. Yes, of course, in our humanity, we all want to be blessed in this life and saved from the horrible destruction soon to come on this world, but, as Christians ("*new creations in [the Messiah]*"), those basic human desires are no longer our focus and no longer provide the **primary** motivation for our lives. If any impulse other than the pure, unselfish love of Yahuah governs our attitudes or behavior, then we are but *almost* Christians and will perish with the rest of the unbelieving world.

The Bottom Line

So, what is the conclusion—the real difference between a True Christian and a phony, "almost" Christian? It is very simple: The True Christian is a person who has come to the full realization that he is not basically and naturally a good person—that, in fact, apart from the indwelling Spirit of Yahuah, there is absolutely no goodness or righteousness in us (Romans 3:10-12). And whatever goodness is in us or whatever good thing that we do is really the Messiah in us—that, as the apostle Paul affirmed, "*It is no longer I who live, but [the Messiah] lives in me*" (Galatians 2:20). The True Christian is one who has come "to the end of his rope" as far as attempting to live the Christian life in his own goodness or power, repented of his sin in arrogantly

266

attempting to do that, surrendered his life totally to Yahuah in the name of Yahushua the Messiah, and allowed Yahuah the Holy Spirit, to totally take over his life. The phony Christian has never gotten to the point of absolute surrender to Yahuah. He still clings to the delusion of Satan that he is basically a good ("God-like") person (Genesis 3:5) and can live a good, Christian life in his own righteousness and strength, except, maybe, for needing Yahuah's help occasionally when the going gets tough. He lives by the old deluded, self-sufficient dictum: "God helps those who help themselves." He does not understand Yahushua who said, *"Without Me, you can do **nothing***" (John 15:5). And he does not understand nor has he ever experienced the wonderful *"mystery of godliness"* which is *"[the Messiah] in you"* (cf. 1 Timothy 3:16; Colossians 1:25).

The New Covenant

And the reason that most Christians do not understand and have never experienced the Spirit-filled life in the Messiah is because they do not understand the New Covenant which was promised to Yahuah's ancient People Israel (Jeremiah 31:33) and ratified by Yahushua's death on the cross (Matthew 26:28). They think that, when the New Covenant went into effect, the Old Covenant of Yahuah with His People Israel, which was His promise to bless them if they kept His commandments or Law (*Torah*), was replaced by the New Covenant. But what they do not understand is that the Hebrew *Torah* was not comprised of just the legal requirements of the Law of Yahuah, but was all the instructions for living righteous, good, happy, prosperous, successful lives as His People. That is why Yahushua said,

> *Do not think that I came to destroy the Law [Torah] or the Prophets. I did not come to destroy but to fulfill. For assuredly, I say to you, till heaven and earth pass away, one jot or one tittle will by no means pass from the Law [Torah] till all is fulfilled. Whoever therefore breaks one of the least of these commandments, and teaches men so, shall be called least in the kingdom of heaven; but whoever does and teaches them, he shall be called great in the kingdom of heaven.* (Matthew 5:17-19)

And how did Yahushua fulfill the *Torah*? In two ways: (1) He fulfilled the legal requirements of the *Torah* by keeping all of its commandments perfectly, so the Messiah is actually the living personification of the *Torah*, and (2) He fulfilled the prophetic implications of the ceremonial aspects of the *Torah*. For example, the Torah required that blood be shed in animal sacrifices for the sins of the people. The shedding of Yahushua's blood on the cross to atone for the sins of the world fulfilled, once and for all, the prophetic significance of all those animal sacrifices throughout Israel's history. But, as Yahushua stated, the Torah has not been done away with, because its commandments (especially the Ten Commandments) and instructions are still being fulfilled in the lives of the Messiah's Body of People on Earth.

So, if the Old Covenant, which is the promise of Yahuah to bless those who keep the commandments of His *Torah*, is still in effect, what is the New Covenant? The *Bible* tells us exactly what the New Covenant is:

> *But the Holy Spirit also witnesses to us; for after He had said before, "This is the covenant that I will make with them after those days, says the LORD: I will put My laws into their hearts, and in their minds I will write them," then He adds, "Their sins and their lawless deeds I will remember no more."* (Hebrews 10:15-17)

In other words, according to the New Covenant that Yahuah has made with His People the Followers of Yahushua, we are not only no longer required to continually make bloody sacrifices for our own sins (the once-for-all sacrifice of His Son on the cross has taken care of that), but He has put his *Torah*—his instructions for living a happy and successful life in the Messiah—into our hearts and written them on our minds, so that, with the enabling of His indwelling Spirit, we can keep His commandments from our hearts in the Spirit of Yahuah's wonderful love rather than just going through the religious motions, keeping the commandments of the Lord out of duty or in a perfunctory, legalistic way. That is why Yahushua said,

> *He who has My commandments and keeps them, it is he who loves Me. And he who loves Me will be loved by My Father, and I will love him and manifest Myself to him.* (John 14:21)

And that is why it is so important for Christians to embrace their Hebrew roots, which is basically keeping the *Torah* of the Lord Yahuah from our hearts and in His love. When we do that, we discover that, rather than being a burdensome exercise, keeping the Law of the Lord is a wonderful way to live our religious lives—joyfully keeping the commandments of our God out of pure love for Him and others, not because we are afraid of what will happen if we don't obey Him! Thank Yahuah for His wonderful New Covenant!

The Apostate American Church

Sadly, the vast majority of American Christians have neglected the Lord's eternal *Torah*, which is the foundation of life in the Messiah. And in attempting to establish their own righteousness through good works apart from the Lord's *Torah*, kept by His enabling Spirit, they have fallen out of love with their heavenly Father and forfeited His presence and blessings in their lives. It is as the apostle Paul predicted,

> *Now, brethren, concerning the coming of our Lord [Yahushua the Messiah] and our gathering together to Him, we ask you, not to be soon shaken in mind or troubled, either by spirit or by word or by letter, as if from us, as though the day of [the Messiah] had come. Let no one deceive you by any means; for that Day will not come unless the **falling away** comes first, and the man of sin is revealed, the son of perdition, who opposes and exalts himself above all that is called God or that is worshiped, so that he sits as [Yahuah] in the temple of [Yahuah], showing himself that he is [Yahuah].* (2 Thessalonians 2:1-4)

"That day" is the "Day of the Messiah" (the Day of the Lord). And the "falling away" (Greek: *apostasia)*, which must occur before the son of perdition (Antimessiah) is revealed, is what is called the Apostasy of the Community of Believers in Yahushua—falling away from true Christian faith and practice—just going through the religious motions.

So, is American "Christianity" True Christianity? If we take a realistic, honest look at the Church in America, it is blatantly obvious that it bears little resemblance to the first century apostolic "Church" of the Lord Yahushua the Messiah. In fact, American "Christianity" is thoroughly permeated with the sin—the pride, the covetousness, and the hypocrisy—described in this essay. For an overview, please read the discussion of American religion in "Appendix 1—Who is Modern Babylon?"

The Reason for it All

Now, you may be asking yourself, why is Bob writing all this stuff? Does he have an ax to grind—something against Americans or members of the Church? Or is he trying to cover up his own inadequacies as a Christian by judging us? Believe me, my friend, I have done a lot of praying and soul-searching regarding my own motives for putting together this article and this book. But I believe that Yahuah does want me to publish it, and this is why: As a chief offender, I have tasted the sweet relief and joy of Yahuah's forgiveness and His grace in grafting me, a wild branch, into the cultivated olive tree (cf. Romans

11:24), and I want to share that with others! As I have mentioned throughout this essay, no one has been more arrogant, self-centered, and hypocritical than I have been. But Yahuah, through His wonderful grace and mercy, has shown me the way out of that bondage into the exhilarating freedom of His pure, unselfish love. And I believe that He wants me to share that way out of selfishness, pride, and hypocrisy with you, just in case you too want to be free—gloriously, joyfully FREE—to love others unconditionally and to serve and glorify your Lord in everything you do. And what He has shown me is that I first need to fall on my face daily and continually—every time I have a proud or selfish thought—confessing that to Yahuah, repenting of it, and begging Him to replace that sinful impulse with gratitude to Him and His special Yahuah-kind of love for Him and others. And as He enables me to do that more and more, I am finding that, more and more, I am being liberated to enjoy His wonderful presence in my life—His special, spiritual joy, peace, hope, and love. Have you ever done anything—competed in an athletic event, cleaned your house, done your job, helped another person, or anything else—out of pure love for others and the desire to glorify Yahuah, with no thought of what attention or profit (even just a "Thank you") that you were going to get out of it? If you have, then you've had a little taste of the unsurpassed joy that comes from being free from the bondage of selfishness and pride and free to love with the Yahuah-kind of love. And that, my friend, is why I'm writing this book—for, *"He who is free in the Son (Yahushua said) is free indeed!"* (John 8:36) And I want that freedom and that joy for you. I don't want anyone to miss out on the joy of the Lord's salvation.

Meanwhile, I pray that you will take all the things you have read in this commentary to heart, because The End is near, and Yahushua said to His Disciples whom He sent out to share the news of the Kingdom of Heaven,

> *". . . if the people of a town will not welcome you or listen to you, leave it and shake its dust from your feet! Yes, I tell you, it will be more tolerable on the Day of Judgment for the people of Sodom and Gomorrah than for that town!"* (Matthew 10:15)

Then, if you are confident that the Lord's great salvation is yours, The End is just The Beginning for you! Please read "Appendix 7—In The End, there's GOOD NEWS!"—to see what unimaginably fantastic things are in store for you.

Appendix 5—A Flaw in the End-Times Doctrine of the Hebraic Roots Movement

Note: In "Appendix 4—The Subtle Demise of True Christianity"—the tragic results of rejecting or even neglecting the constitution of our faith, the *Torah*, and its author Yahuah was described. However, there is another side of that coin: Many Messianic Believers, in trying so hard to be *Torah*-observant Hebrews, neglect their Renewed Covenant relationship with the Messiah Yahushua and thus ruin their witness both to Jews and to Christians. The following essay explains how our understanding of our life in the Messiah and our relationship to His People applies to our interpretation of End-Times *Bible* prophecy.

I am eternally grateful to Yahuah for opening my eyes to the Hebraic roots of my faith. There is no way that I could fully or correctly interpret prophetic Scripture without some understanding of the language, religion, and culture of the writers of *Bible* prophecy. However, there is a flaw in the doctrine of many Hebraic Roots teachers and Believers that is causing confusion in their understanding of Yahuah's plan for His People at the End of the Age. Few Hebraic Roots teachers seem to acknowledge the clear distinction between Yahuah's plan for His mortal, national People, those of the twelve tribes of Israel who will not recognize that Yahushua is the Messiah **until** He returns at the End of the Age, and His plan for those Jews and Gentiles who **have already** come to faith in the Messiah Yahushua.

Most (not all) Hebraic Roots Believers and teachers think that **all** of Israel, including those grafted into her through faith in Yahushua, will be brought physically out of the Gentile nations back into the Land of Israel at the End of the Age, then, after being reunited as the twelve tribes of the nation of Israel, will inhabit the restored earth in their mortal, physical bodies during the millennial reign of the Messiah Yahushua. However, Scripture clearly reveals that there will be **two** categories of the Redeemed of Yahuah during the Millennium—those who have already trusted in Yahushua as their Savior and Messiah **before** the sounding of the *"Last Trump"* on Yom Teruah (those who are under the Renewed Covenant), and those physical descendants of the twelve tribes of Israel who will not recognize that Yahushua is the Messiah **until** He returns in the clouds on that day (those who, at the present time, are still functioning under Yahuah's original Covenant with Israel). And Yahuah's plan for those two groups of Saints at the

271

End of the Age and during the millennial reign of the Messiah (albeit not throughout eternity) are very different.

Most Hebraic Roots teachers take numerous passages of Scripture out of context, misinterpret them, and misapply them to support their doctrine that **all** of Israel, including the Gentiles grafted in through faith in Yahushua, will be brought physically out of the nations at the End of the Age into the Land and established there as the spiritual **and** physical Kingdom of Yahuah.

An example of a misinterpreted passage is Zechariah 8:23, which states, *"In those days ten men from every language of the nations shall grasp the sleeve of a Jewish man, saying, 'Let us go with you, for we have heard that [Yahuah] is with you.'"* Most Hebraic Roots teachers assert that *"those days"* refers to the End of the Age, when the Lord will gather His People Israel out of the nations into the Land. However, just a cursory examination of the text reveals that this passage is referring to what will happen during the millennial reign of the Messiah, **after** Israel is reestablished in the Land and is surrounded by nations made up of descendants of Yahuah-fearing Gentiles who did not come to faith in Yahushua prior to the Millennium, but who were allowed to enter the millennial Messianic kingdom because they favored and helped the Jews during the Great Tribulation and never took the mark of the beast. During the Millennium, according to the prophecy of Ezekiel 40-48, the twelve tribes of Israel will be reestablished in the Land and will have a favored place in the Land, just as they did in Egypt, in the land of Goshen, when Joseph (a type of the Messiah) was the Prince of Egypt. And, during the Millennium (not during the Final Seven Years and the Great Tribulation at the End of the Age, which is the *"time of Jacob's trouble")*, the surrounding Gentile nations will see that Israel is blessed by Yahuah and will want to share in her prosperity. But, to partake of Israel's prosperity, the Gentiles must observe Sukkot (the Feast of Tabernacles) and the *Torah* of Yahuah. Those who fail to keep the *Torah,* and to go up to Jerusalem year after year to keep the feast days and worship the King, will perish during the thousand years (cf. Zechariah 14:16-19), or will be among those who will be deceived into following Satan when he is released from the bottomless pit at the end of the thousand years, only to be destroyed by fire from Heaven (cf. 20:8, 9).

But this understanding of the End-of-the-Age and the Millennium scenarios begs the question, "If they do not return to the Land of Israel with the twelve tribes, what will happen to those (the Renewed Covenant Saints) who have previously (before the end of the Final Seven

272

Years) accepted Yahushua as the Messiah?" does it not? Again, Scripture is clear to those who have their doctrinal ducks in order and their spiritual eyes open to the Truth: At the end of the Final Seven Years, the wrath of Satan (the *"Great Tribulation"*) will be interrupted (cf. Matthew 24:22) by the awesome events of Yom Teruah (the Feast of Trumpets), when the Messiah will return to gather those who have already believed in Him, catch them up to meet Him in the air, and take them to New Jerusalem (which is still in Heaven), until Yahuah has finished pouring out the *"last plagues"* (15:1) of His wrath on the earth dwellers. Then, after the marriage in Heaven of the Lamb to His Bride (the Body of Believers in Him) and His coronation as King of kings and Lord of lords, the armies of Heaven (including angels and the redeemed, glorified Saints) will return with King Yahushua on Yom Kippur (the Day of Atonement) to destroy His enemies, save the Redeemed of Israel (who had looked on Him whom they had pierced, repented, and accepted Him as their Messiah and King when He returned in the clouds on Yom Teruah), pour out His Spirit on them (Zechariah 12:10), and establish His millennial kingdom on earth. The glorified, Renewed Covenant Saints will then rule with the Messiah over the tribes of Israel and the surrounding nations from their thrones in New Jerusalem (which has descended from Heaven—21:1). (cf. Matthew 19:28; 2 Timothy 2:12; Revelation 2:27; 20:4).

However, contrary to this Scriptural scenario, some of the more popular Hebraic Roots teachers (Bill Cloud, Perry Stone, Jim Staley, et al.), ironically, teach a Hebraic Roots version of Replacement Theology, asserting that those Gentiles who come to faith in Yahushua are actually literal Hebrews of the Northern Kingdom of Israel (the "ten lost tribes") who will be brought back into the Land and reunited with the tribes of the Southern Kingdom (mainly the tribe of Judah) who are already in the Land and who will not come to faith in Yahushua until the Final Seven Years. In other words, according to this doctrine, the "Jews" who do not yet believe that Yahushua is the Messiah are in a different category—they are not yet the People of Yahuah in the same sense that those "Hebrew Gentiles" (an oxymoron) are. This "two-sticks-becoming-one-man" doctrine, which asserts that only the tribes of the Northern Kingdom (consisting of the Hebrew Gentiles) will be brought out of the nations back into the Land, but that the tribes of the Southern Kingdom have never been divorced by Yahuah and exiled from the Land—they have just been temporarily blinded to who He is—is based on erroneous interpretations of Ezekiel 37:16-22, Romans Chapter 11, and Ephesians Chapter 2.

Scripture correctly interpreted, however, proves this doctrine false. A basic reason for its error is in making a false, unscriptural distinction between the House of Ephraim and the House of Judah, stating that the Northern Kingdom was divorced by Yahuah, banished into the Gentile nations of the world and absorbed by those nations, making them "Hebrew Gentiles." But, according to this doctrine, the tribes of the Southern Kingdom, have **never** been divorced by Yahuah and dispersed into the nations, so have not become Gentiles. However, I would submit, that interpretation is incorrect according to sound exegesis. Yes, the Northern Kingdom was divorced by Yahuah because of idolatry, but history tells us that, although as a political entity the Northern Kingdom was destroyed, not all of the ten "northern" tribes were carried away by the Assyrians. Entire tribes remained intact in the land. In fact, although ten tribes rebelled against the *Torah* and practiced idolatry, Simeon was located within the boundaries of the Southern Kingdom, so was not geographically a "northern" tribe at all. Part of the tribe of Dan was also located within the boundaries of the Southern Kingdom. Also, when the Assyrians invaded the Northern Kingdom, multitudes fled to the Southern Kingdom. The population of Jerusalem increased five-fold because of the influx of refugees from the north. And the tribes that were taken away by the Assyrians remained pretty much intact for many years in the lands in which they were relocated. And today, there are groups of people all over the world who are still keeping the *Torah,* or at least remnants of the *Torah,* who either claim to be or genealogical studies have shown them to be descendants of the nine (not ten) northern tribes. And now, DNA studies are further confirming that many of these modern Israelites are indeed descended from or are at least partially descended from various tribes of Israel, including both the "northern" and the southern tribes.

Yes, Hosea 1:6, 7 states that Yahuah will . . . *"utterly take them* [the House of Israel] *away. Yet I will have mercy on the house of Judah . . ."* But obviously, that was a Hebraic hyperbole that meant the House of Ephraim/Israel, as a political and geographical entity, would be destroyed and scattered. It did not mean that the individual Israelites or even the tribes would be absorbed by the nations of the world to the point of totally losing their identities and even becoming Gentiles. Also, although Yahuah had mercy on the House of Judah and did not divorce them **at that time**, they were not blameless before the Lord, were they? Please notice that in Hosea Chapter 3 the focus of the indictment for spiritual adultery generalizes to the whole nation of Israel (the *"children of Israel"*) rather than applying just to the *"House of*

Israel" (Ephraim). And more is said about how the entire nation of Israel was guilty of idolatry from the time they came out of Egypt in 11:1, 2. So, although the book of Hosea addresses primarily the unfaithfulness of the House of Ephraim/Israel and their consequent rejection by Yahuah, and His sparing of the House of Judah because they had not **yet** rebelled against Him as had the House of Israel, about 120 years after the Northern Kingdom was destroyed, the tribes of the Southern Kingdom also rejected the *Torah* and broke the covenant, just as had those of the Northern Kingdom. And just as happened to the House of Ephraim, beginning in about 606 BCE, the House of Judah (which consisted of members not just of the tribe of Judah, but of all 12 tribes) was carried away into captivity into Babylon. Then, please note, 70 years later, only a small remnant returned to the Land of Israel and rebuilt the Temple and Jerusalem. The vast majority remained in Babylon and other places to which they had migrated. And what did those Jews who had returned to the Land do in 29 CE? They totally rejected the Living *Torah*—the Messiah—didn't they? And what happened to them? Just as had happened to the House of Ephraim, they were scattered (in 70 and 135 CE) all over the world. So, exactly as was prophesied (Isa 50:1), **both** houses of Israel were divorced by Yahuah.

So what, really, is the difference between the Northern Kingdom and the Southern Kingdom today? I submit to you that, at the present time, there is ZERO difference—ZILCH! They are **both** members of the cultivated olive tree that have been cut off (Romans 11). They have **both** been scattered all over the world until the Lord gathers them out of the nations back into the land, where, when they see Him return in the clouds immediately following the Final Seven Years, on Yom Teruah at the sounding of the seventh and *"last trumpet"* (1 Corinthians 15:52; Revelation 11:15), will mourn because they will then recognize that their Messiah *is* the *Torah* they have **both** rejected and the one they pierced (Zechariah 12:10; Revelation 1:7) (in a spiritual sense, we have all rejected and pierced the Messiah). So, it will be at **that time**—at the end of seven years (and not before)—that the physical descendants of Israel—all 12 tribes—will repent, accept Yahushua as their Messiah and King, and be saved. There is absolutely no reason to interpret Ezekiel 37:16-22 in any other way than the plain, literal way in which it was written—as referring to the **physical** descendants of Israel—all 12 tribes—being separated and dispersed into the world, then coming back together at the End of the Age. To say that it refers only to the House of Ephraim is a forced, inconsistent interpretation

275

that is disingenuous, to say the least. Please read Ezekiel 37:21-22 carefully and honestly:

> *Surely I will take the **children of Israel** [not just the House of Ephra-im or the House of Judah] from among the nations, wherever they have gone, and will gather them [the children of Israel] from every side and bring them into their own land; and I will make them [the children of Israel] **one nation** in the land, on the mountains of Israel; and one king shall be king over them all [the children of Israel]; they shall no longer be **two nations**, nor shall they ever be divided into **two kingdoms** again.*

And please notice that the terms *"children of Israel," "one nation," "two nations,"* and *"two kingdoms"* all refer to **all 12 tribes** of Israel. The term *"children of Israel"* appears 656 times in the *Bible* (KJV), and it always refers to **all 12 tribes** of Israel—never to just the North-ern or Southern Kingdom.

But the teachers of the Hebrew Gentile doctrine insist that it was only the tribes of the Northern Kingdom, the House of Ephraim/Israel, who were divorced by Yahuah and dispersed among the Gentile na-tions. And, they assert, at the End of the Age, it will be only the He-brew Gentiles who are brought out of the nations back into the Land. And who, specifically, are the Hebrew Gentiles according to this doc-trine? They are those who have already accepted Yahushua as their Savior and Messiah. They are allegedly the branches of the wild olive tree who have been grafted into the natural olive tree, Israel (Romans 11:17), and have been made *"fellow citizens"* in the *"commonwealth"* of Israel (Ephesians 2:12, 19). And, according to this doctrine, this grafting-in process will continue until *"the fullness of the* [Hebrew] *Gentiles has come in"* (Romans 11:25).

In other words, essentially, the terms "Hebrew Gentiles" and "Christians" are synonymous. Both the "Hebrew Gentiles" and the Christians are Believers in Yahushua. And, like most Christians, most of the teachers of the Hebrew Gentile doctrine see themselves as sepa-rate from and therefore, by implication, spiritually superior to those Jews who have not yet accepted Yahushua as their Savior and Lord. The only differences between the "Hebrew Gentiles" and the Chris-tians are that the "Hebrew Gentiles" have (allegedly) embraced their Hebraic roots and believe that they are, literally, descendants of the tribes of the House of Ephraim. No wonder popular Hebraic Roots teachers like Perry Stone, Bill Cloud, and Jim Staley are finding warm acceptance in many Christian churches and their ministries are prospering here in America-Babylon.

However, there are several serious problems with the Hebrew Gentile doctrine:

- In their teachings, those who espouse that doctrine have to do some pretty fancy dancing through the Scriptures to maintain their premise that, **at the present time**, the Northern Kingdom is divorced by Yahuah and have, in fact, become Gentiles, but the Southern Kingdom has not been divorced by the Lord. For example, it is almost comical (if it weren't such a serious error) to see them, in their exposition of Romans 9-11 (which contains the name *"Israel"* 13 times) jumping back and forth between asserting that *"Israel"* refers to the Southern Kingdom in some verses but to the Northern Kingdom in others. Obviously, throughout his letter to the Romans, Paul is using the terms *"Jews"* and *"Israel"* interchangeably to refer to the whole nation—all 12 tribes. (Referring to the whole nation of Israel as *"Jews"* began after the destruction of the Northern Kingdom, and Judah, the royal tribe from whom the Ruler who would sit on David's throne would come and the only remaining intact, identifiable tribe, came to represent the entire nation—cf. Daniel 1:3; 9:7, 11, 20).

- Another example of a forced interpretation, unsupported by Scripture, is their mistranslation and bad exegesis of 1 Peter 1:1, 2:

> *Peter, an apostle of [Yahushua the Messiah], to the* **strangers** *scattered throughout Pontus, Galatia, Cappadocia, Asia, and Bithynia, elect according to the foreknowledge of God the Father, through sanctification of the Spirit, unto obedience and sprinkling of the blood of Jesus Christ: Grace unto you, and peace, be multiplied.*

They state that Peter is writing to the *"lost tribes"* of the Northern Kingdom, who are identified as Gentiles, explaining that the Hebrew word for *"strangers"* is *Goyim* ("Gentiles"). But, that is just flat not true. The Greek word that is normally translated *"Gentiles"* in the *B'rit Hadashah* is *ethnos*. But the word translated *"strangers"* in 1 Peter 1:1 is *parepidimos*, which Strong's (3927) defines as: "one who comes from a foreign country into a city or land to reside there by the side of the natives." In other words, the dispersed ones to whom Peter was writing were indeed descendants of the tribes of Israel, but they had definitely not been absorbed into the nations and become Gentiles.

- A third example of trying to force the interpretation to fit the premise is in stating that in Yahushua's statement to the Canaanite woman, *"I am not sent but unto the lost sheep of the house of Israel"* (Matthew 15:24), He was referring to the northern tribes. But wasn't His personal ministry entirely to the tribes of the Southern Kingdom, which, according to the Hebrew Gentile interpretation, would be excluded by His statement to the Canaanite woman? And in His command to His disciples to take the Gospel to the *"lost sheep of the house of Israel,"* didn't He pointedly tell them **not** to go to the Gentiles, or even to the Samaritans (Matthew 10:5)? How does these teachers' notion that the lost tribes *are* Gentiles jive with that?

- A fourth example of incorrect exegesis is the assertion that the grafting of the (Hebrew) Gentiles into the *"commonwealth"* of Israel is a literal grafting into the physical nation of Israel. However, an honest examination of the text reveals that this graft is not literal but spiritual. The Gentiles are grafted, *"contrary to nature"* (Romans 11:24), into the *"natural"* olive tree (Israel). In other words, those grafted-in Gentiles are not natural, physical Hebrews at all. They are spiritual, not physical, seed of Abraham through faith in the natural seed of Abraham, Yahushua. (Jews who look forward in faith to the coming Messiah but who do not yet recognize that He is Yahushua are the spiritual **and** physical seed of Abraham.) Also, the term *"commonwealth"* does not refer to the literal, physical nation of Israel. Gerhard Kittel's *Theological Dictionary of the New Testament* points out that the Greek word *politeia*, translated "commonwealth" in Ephesians 2:12,

> does not mean civil rights, constitution, or state, [but] rather the pious order of life which, ordained by the Law of Moses, is inherited from the fathers. [With one exception it] is a religious and moral concept rather than a political concept;

278

it denotes the "walk" determined by the Mosaic Law. (Volume 6, p. 526)

Then, David Stern, in his *Jewish New Testament Commentary*, states that *politeia* . . .

> implies an obligation to observe a godly way of life that has its origin in God's relationship with the Jewish people . . . [and] an obligation to relate as family to the Jewish community to whom [the grafted-in Gentiles'] faith has joined them. (p. 582)

In other words, *"fellow citizens"* in the *"commonwealth of Israel"* refers to sharing the familial, spiritual, covenant relationship that Israel has with Yahuah, not to a literal, physical grafting into the nation of Israel. Other indications that Ephesians Chapter 2 is speaking of spiritual and figurative rather than physical and literal realities are the statements that Yahuah has *"raised us up together, and made us sit together in the heavenly places in* [the Messiah Yahushua]" (verse 6) and, the Messiah has abolished the wall of separation between the Jews and Gentiles, creating in Himself *"one new man from the two"* (verses 14 and 15). Then, the apostle Paul confirms that the grafting into Israel is spiritual rather than physical when He states, *"There is neither Jew nor Greek, there is neither slave nor free, there is neither male nor female; for you are all one in* [the Messiah Yahushua]" (Galatians 3:28).

- Another handle onto which the teachers of the Hebrew Gentile doctrine attempt to grab to support their interpretation is the prophetic promise through Jacob that the descendants of his grandson Ephraim would become a *"multitude of nations (Greek: goyim)"* (Genesis 48:19). And they assert that the phrase *"fullness of the* [grafted-in] *Gentiles"* in Romans 11:25 is equivalent to *"multitude of nations."* However, as is explained in detail in "Appendix 3—Who are the People of Yahuah?"—the Hebrew term *goy* (plural: *goyim*) is translated simply *"nation(s),"* and can refer to either Hebrew or Gentile nations, depending on the context. So, the promise to Ephraim looked forward to the multitude of Hebrew (not Gentile) nations—the descendants of Ephraim—during the Millennium.

279

But the phrase *"fullness of the Gentiles"* in Romans 11:25 refers to Gentiles who are (spiritually) grafted into Israel.

So, it would seem that these teachers' distinction between the two houses of Israel is purely arbitrary and contrived, based on misinterpreted Scripture, to support their view that "true Israel" (Romans 9:6) is comprised of those "Hebrew Gentiles" of the Northern Kingdom who have been grafted into the cultivated olive tree, but the Jews of the Southern Kingdom are not quite there yet. And, sadly and ironically, it is at that point that subtle anti-Semitism and Replacement Theology are injected into their teachings.

The present-day, *Torah*-observant Jews (including those physical descendants of both the House of Ephraim and the House of Judah) who believe in Yahuah and look forward in faith to the coming Messiah, although they have not yet recognized that He is Yahushua, are no less the chosen People of Yahuah than were the *Torah*-observant ancient patriarchs and Israelites, beginning with Abraham, who believed in Yahuah and looked forward in faith to the coming Messiah. Or, are the teachers of the Hebrew Gentile doctrine going to insist that Abraham, Moses, Joseph, Elijah and all the other great people of faith in ancient Israel were not "true Israel" and are not, at the present time, saved because they did not accept Yahushua as their Messiah? Yes, many thousands—perhaps millions—of Jews (beginning with those of the House of Judah) of both the Northern and Southern Kingdoms have come to faith in Yahushua, but I submit to you that most of them have not. However, in the end, all of "true Israel" (the physical descendants of Jacob who believe in *Yahuah* and look forward in faith to the coming Messiah, whether or not they have, at the present time, recognized that He is Yahushua), will be saved (Romans 11:26). In the eyes of Yahuah, who sees the whole mural of history from beginning to end, the ones who are saved—past, present, and future—have been chosen from the beginning—*"elect according to the foreknowledge of [Yahuah]"* (1 Peter 1:2). So, who are we to say that only the ones who accept Yahushua as their Messiah **before** He gathers them out of the nations into the Land are His redeemed Elect? Who are we to say that those of physical Israel who will not recognize that their Messiah and King is Yahushua until He returns in the clouds at the end of the Final Seven Years and look on the One they have pierced and mourn (Zechariah 12:10; Revelation 1:7) are not just as much the People of Yahuah as those Renewed Covenant Believers who have already accepted Him as their Messiah and Savior? Because they have been temporarily blinded to who the Messiah is, they have not yet come into the full Renewed Covenant relationship with Him, but as soon as the blinders have been removed when He returns in the clouds on a soon-coming Yom Teruah, the Spirit of Yahuah will fall on them just as it did on the Believers on Shavuot following the Lord Yahushua's resurrection and ascension, and they too will be Renewed Covenant People of Yahuah (cf. Joel 2:28; Zechariah 12:10; Acts 2:3-18).

So, as the apostle Paul warned us (Romans 11:25), let us not, whether we are Messianic or Christian Believers in Yahushua, look down our noses at those Jews who believe in Yahuah and look forward in faith to the coming Messiah, although they have not yet recognized that He is Yahushua. Their blindness to His identity is temporary, and, although they will have a different role in the Messianic Kingdom (in fulfillment of Yahuah's promises to Israel of a physical kingdom on Earth) than have the redeemed and glorified Saints, they are just as much the beloved children of Yahuah. And, in Timeless Eternity following the Millennium (see "Appendix 8—How Long is 'Forever' in the *Bible"*), there will be no distinction between Hebrew and Gentile nations, and there will be no distinction between mortal and glorified Saints; we will all be one in union with the Messiah Yahushua (Galatians 3:28).

For more details and Scriptural support of the above End Times scenario, please read this commentary on the Revelation Chapters 7, 11 and 19-21.

Appendix 6—When is "The Rapture"?

One of the hottest debates in the Community of Believers in Yahushua is the timing of the Rapture in the sequence of End-Times events. The term "rapture" is not in the *Bible*, but the Latin Vulgate translation uses the term *rapio*, which is translated *"caught up"* in 1 Thessalonians 4:17—one of the key passages for the catching away of the Believers. So, the term "Rapture" was coined for that glorious event.

Most of those who don't believe in a literal fulfillment of *Bible* prophecy don't believe in a literal rapture, of course. But remember, this whole book is based on the assumption that the *Bible*, including its prophecies, is subject to a literal, common-sense, face-value under-standing. And, with that understanding, Scripture clearly teaches that a time will come when Yahushua the Messiah will return in the same way that he ascended after his resurrection—in the clouds (Acts 1:9, 11). And there will be no mistaking who He is, because (1) He will be seen coming in "great power and glory," with brilliant brightness, like lightning that flashes from horizon to horizon (Matthew 24: 27, 30), (2) His coming will be heralded by a tremendous trumpet (Hebrew: *shofar*) blast (Matthew 24:31), and (4) those who have trusted Him as their coming Messiah (BCE Believers) or as their present Lord and Savior (CE Believers), whether dead or alive, will instantly be given new, glorified bodies (those Believers who have died will be resurrect-ed at that time) (1 Corinthians 15:52) and will be caught up to meet Him in the air, then be with Him forever (1 Thessalonians 4:16-17). The *Bible* also teaches that when the Believers are resurrected, trans-formed, and gathered to the Messiah, He will take us to a place He has prepared for us in Heaven (John 14:2-3). What an incredibly glorious day that will be! Then (I have been happy to learn), we are not going to just float around in Heaven playing our harps forever. Oh no, that's just the beginning of an eternity filled with joyful activity in Heaven and on Earth! But, I'm getting ahead of myself . . . back to the Rap-ture.

I have also been happy to learn that, besides the direct teaching of the *Bible*, there is another way to understand the events surrounding the Rapture: Everything that Israel did down through her history, in-cluding her festivals and traditions, was prophetic. Why do I use "her" as a pronoun for Israel?—because she is described in the *Tanakh* as the Bride of Yahuah. The whole book of Hosea was written to illustrate the Lord's relationship with his Bride, Israel. Likewise, in the *B'rit Hadashah*, the Body of Believers in Yahushua is presented as the Bride of the Messiah. So, since history repeats itself (Ecclesiates 1:9), it is impossible to understand the *B'rit Hadashah* without understanding the *Tanakh*, and it is impossible to understand what Yahuah is going to do in the future with His Bride, the Body of Believers in Yahushua, without understanding what He has done in the past with His Bride, Israel. Make sense?

As an example of how amazingly prophetic Israel's festivals and traditions are, let's briefly look at the Pesach (Passover) festival and the Festival of the Firstfruits of the Barley Harvest. This is the sequence of events of those two Spring festivals, practiced by Israel since the formation of the nation at Mount Sinai, in approximately 1500 BCE: Every year, on the 10th day of the Month of Aviv (Nisan) on the Jewish calendar (late March or early April on the Gregorian calendar), the Passover lamb was brought into the Tabernacle or Temple area for observation (it must be inspected and found to be unblemished). Then, on 14 Aviv, the lamb was tied to the altar at the 3rd hour (approximately 9:00 A.M.), then killed at the 9th hour (approximately 3:00 P.M.). Then, on the first day of the week following Pesach, the Festival of Firstfruits was celebrated. Now, let's jump ahead approximately 1500 years, to the crucifixion of Yahushua. Historical records and the *Bible* tell us that it "just (coincidentally) happened" that the day He rode into Jerusalem on a donkey and was hailed as the Messiah and King of the Jews was on 10 Aviv, a seventh-day sabbath. Then, for next few days, he sat in the Temple courtyard, being questioned by the religious leaders. Then, on 14 Aviv, at the 3rd hour (at the same moment the Passover lamb was tied to the altar), the Lamb of Yahuah was nailed to the cross (cf. Mark 15:34). Then, at the 9th hour, at the moment the Passover lamb was slain, the Lamb of God died. Then, after being in the grave three nights, He arose on the first day of the following week, the day of the Festival of Firstfruits. 1 Corinthians 15:20 states, ". . . *[the Messiah] has been raised from the dead, the firstfruits of those who have died.*" I don't know about you, but the uncanny "coincidences" of those events send chills down my spine.

Now that we've seen an example of the amazing accuracy and specificity of the prophetic implications of the Jewish festivals and traditions, let's ask, "Which of those festivals or traditions might be prophetic of the Rapture?" And one answer is: the coming of the groom for his bride. The events surrounding a Jewish wedding were also very specific and sequential. The prospective groom would go to his prospective bride's home and pay her father a sum of money or property to "seal the deal." They were then legally betrothed—as good as married—just not yet consummated in their marriage. The groom would then return to his own father's home and build an addition for himself and his bride. Meanwhile, the bride and her bridesmaids would be preparing themselves for the wedding. When the father decided that his son was ready, he would release him to go for his bride. The son would then go get his bride and she (and her bridesmaids) would return to his father's home with him, where the wedding ceremony, the consummation of the marriage, and the marriage feast would be held. There are numerous other details of the Jewish wedding that parallel the coming of the Messiah for his Bride, the Body of Believers in Yahushua, but that's the gist of it. Do you see the amazing parallels here? Do you see the illustration of the redemption of the Believers in the elements of the Jewish marriage? Just as the groom left His father's home to go to his bride's home to pay the price to be betrothed to his bride, Yahushua, the Son of Yahuah, left Heaven to come to Earth to pay the price for our redemption and betrothal to Him. Then, just as the groom returned to his father's home to prepare a place for his bride, Yahushua returned to Heaven to prepare a place for the Believers. Then, just as the groom's father released him to return for his bride, Yahuah the Father will release the Son to return for His Bride. (*"When that day or hour will come, no one knows—not the angels in Heaven, not the Son, only the Father"*—Matthew 24:36.) Then, just as the groom returned to get his bride and take her back to his (and his father's) home, the Son will come to gather His Bride (at the Rapture) and take her to her new home in Heaven. Finally, just as there was a wedding ceremony, celebration, and feast at the home of the groom's father, there will be a wedding ceremony, celebration, and feast in Heaven:

> *Let us rejoice and be glad! Let us give Him glory! For the time has come for the wedding of the Lamb, and His Bride has prepared herself - fine linen, bright and clean has been given her to wear.* ("*Fine linen*" *means the righteous deeds of [Yahuah]'s people.) The angel said to me, "Write: 'How blessed are those who have been invited to the wedding feast of the Lamb!'"* (Revelation 19:7-9, paraphrased)

Yahushua told a parable to His Disciples based on the elements of the Jewish wedding:

The Kingdom of Heaven at that time [the Rapture] *will be like ten bridesmaids who took their lamps and went out to meet the groom. Five of them were foolish and five were sensible. The foolish ones took lamps with them but no oil. But the wise ones took flasks of oil with their lamps. Now the bridegroom was late, so they all went to sleep. But at midnight there was a cry, "Look! the bridegroom. Go out and meet him." The bridesmaids all woke up and prepared their lamps for lighting. The foolish ones said to the sensible ones, "Give us some of your oil, because our lamps are going out." But they replied, "There may not be enough for us and for you; you had better go to those who sell it and buy some for yourselves." But as they were going off to buy, the bridegroom came. Those who were ready went with him to the wedding; and the door was shut. Later, the other bridesmaids came. "Sir! Sir!" they cried, "Let us in!" But he replied, "In truth I tell you, I do not know you."* (Matthew 25:1-12)

Chilling, isn't it?—especially when considered in terms of the Rapture, the Day of the Lord, and "eternity" to follow. The lamp oil is symbolic of the Holy Spirit, who indwells the believers (the bridesmaids) in the Body of Believers in Yahushua (the Bride).[20]

So, exactly when will the Rapture occur? Those who are aware of the "signs of the times" will not be caught unexpectedly or unprepared. Though we may not know the exact year of the Messiah's return, when that year does come we may be able to know within one or two days when it will be. How? As was explained in the introduction to the commentary on Chapter 19, for 3,500 years the Hebrews have been keeping the spring and fall "feasts" (Hebrew: *moed* – appointed times) commanded by the Lord. And, although the Jews were not aware of the prophetic significance of those festivals, as was explained above, although they did not foretell the year of the Messiah's death, burial and resurrection, they were exact—to the day and hour—rehearsals of His sacrifice and victory over the grave. Likewise, the

---

[20]There are numerous other Jewish festivals and traditions that have a prophetic bearing on the events of both the first and second comings of the Messiah. For an excellent, short, easy-to-read explanation of these, I highly recommend Joseph Good's book, *Rosh HaShanah and the Messianic Kingdom To Come*, available through www.hatikva.org. Or get Mark Biltz's DVD set, *Feasts of the Lord*, available through www.elshaddaiministries.us, or Michael Rood's series on the prophetic implications of the feasts, available through www.aroodawakening.tv.

fall feasts are rehearsals of His second coming. So, why would the fall feast that rehearses the resurrection of the righteous and the coming of the Messiah not be just as exact in its prophetic significance? As was explained in the commentary on 7:13-14 and 11:14-19, that day is Yom Teruah, the Feast of Trumpets on the Hebrew calendar. And the Yom Teruah of the resurrection of the Righteous and coming of the Messiah will occur immediately following the last day of the Final Seven Years, when the Last Trump, announcing the final plagues of the Wrath of Yahuah, is blown (cf. 11:15-19; 15:1).

Those who object that Yahushua stated that no one except Yahuah can know the exact day (Matthew 24:36), because that day will come as a *"thief in the night"* (1 Thessalonians 5:2; 2 Peter 3:10), do not understand the context of those statements. Yom Teruah is the only feast day that does not begin on an exact day of the year. That is because it begins when the new moon is sighted in Jerusalem on Tishri 1 of the Hebrew calendar. And, at the time Yahushua made His statement, no one knew the *exact* day or hour, although they did know within one or two days when the Tishri 1 new moon would be sighted.

Yahushua went on to give the example of the head of a household being prepared for a thief who breaks in because he was alert and aware of the signs (Matthew 24:43), but He harshly rebuked those who did not recognize Him at His first coming because they did not recognize the *"signs of the times"* (Matthew 16:3). Then the apostle Paul stated that sudden destruction would come as a thief in the night only on those who are *"in darkness,"* rather than on the *"sons of light and sons of the day"* who are alert and watching (1 Thessalonians 5:2-5). The Messiah's first coming was exactly foretold by Daniel (9:25-26) and other prophets of Israel, and was rehearsed every year by the Feast of Pesach (Passover). In the same way, His second coming, the resurrection, and the Rapture is exactly foretold by Daniel (12:1-2) and other prophets, and has been rehearsed every year by Yom Teruah. So, although the exact day or hour of the Messiah's return cannot be known, especially by those who are "in darkness," it will not take those who are aware of the signs and who are watching and waiting, as commanded, by surprise.

Both the *Tanakh* and the *B'rit Hadashah* seem (to this commentator) to indicate the following sequence of events:

1. After the destruction of Jerusalem and the dispersion of the Jews throughout the world in 70 CE and 135 CE, Jerusalem to

be "trampled" by the Gentiles until "the times of the Gentiles are fulfilled" (still happening)

2. Ever-increasing distress in the world caused by human degradation and debauchery (happening)

3. Ever-increasing natural disasters throughout the world (happening)

4. Ever-increasing persecution and martyrdom of Yahuah's People throughout the world (Jews and Followers of Yahushua have never been more persecuted than they are today.)

5. All of the above events coming to a climax during the "beginnings of sorrows"—the first half of the Final Seven Years

6. Antimessiah desecrating the Temple and declaring himself to be "God" at the midpoint of the seven years

7. The escape of Yahuah's People the Jews into the "wilderness," where they will be protected and sustained for the remainder of the seven years

8. The Great Tribulation (the wrath of Satan) during the last half of the seven years

9. Great cosmic disturbances announcing That Day (the Day of the Lord), including the judgments and Wrath of Yahuah, is about to begin

10. The first six trumpet and bowl judgments

11. The sudden, unexpected return (like a "thief in the night" for those not looking for it) of the Messiah for His Bride, the Body of believers in Yahushua (**the Rapture**) at the sounding of the Last Trump on Yom Teruah

12. The *"last plagues"* of the judgments of Yahuah—the plagues of the seventh trumpet/bowl judgment poured out on Earth during the ten Days of Awe

13. The return of the King of Kings and Lord of Lords on Yom Kippur with the armies of Heaven to destroy His enemies (nominal Jews who are not "true Israel" plus those Gentiles who will not enter the millennial kingdom—the "sheep and goat" judgment), and to establish His millennial kingdom on Earth

14. The "restoration of all things"—the renewed heaven, the renewed earth and New Jerusalem—life in the millennial Messianic Kingdom, as rehearsed throughout Israel's history during the Festival of Sukkot

15. The final destruction of the heavens and the earth

16. The Final Judgment

17. Eternity

Please read the verse-by-verse commentary for Scriptural references and details supporting the above scenario. Regarding the Rapture, pay special attention to the commentary on the Revelation Chapters 7 and 11.

Nevertheless, although we have all these *"signs of the times"* and the yearly rehearsal of the Lord's second coming, the resurrection and the Rapture at Yom Teruah, I refuse to dogmatically argue about the timing of the Rapture or to make it a criterion of fellowship with my brethren in the Messiah. Although to this commentator the above second coming, resurrection and rapture scenario has the most textual support, he does not deny that other interpretations may have validity. For example, the resurrection and rapture of the Believers in Yahushua may be a separate event from the resurrection of those faithful Hebrew saints on Yom Teruah who have died believing in the coming Messiah but have not yet recognizing that He is Yahushua. As has been mentioned in other parts of this commentary, there are some indications in the text that the resurrection and the rapture of the Assembly of Believers in Yahushua (the "Church") may occur earlier during the last half of the seven years, before any of the trumpet and bowl plagues of the Wrath of Yahuah are poured out on the earth dwellers.

There are only a couple of dogmatic statements this commentator will make regarding the timing of the Rapture: (1) There will be **no** "pretribulation rapture." That unfounded doctrine carries tragic consequences for the faith of those who believe it and who will be totally unprepared for "great tribulation, such as has not been since the beginning of the world until this time, no, nor ever shall be" (Matthew 24:21) soon to come. Scripture indicates that Believers in Yahushua will be exempt from the Wrath of Yahuah. (Whether that includes the plagues of the trumpet and bowl judgments or is His wrath executed at the Final Judgment at the end of the Millennium is not clear.) But **nowhere** does the Word suggest that Believers will be exempt from trials and tribulations, including the Great Tribulation (the wrath of Satan). (2) As was stated in "Appendix 2—Be Saved from the Wrath of Yahuah," the Rapture will occur **before** the *"last plagues"* of the judgments of Yahuah are poured out on this earth and its doomed inhabitants, whenever that occurs in relation to the seven years.

The point is that Yahuah's Word (the *Bible*) is the Truth. And these terrible or wonderful (depending on your point of view) events **will** occur. So, regardless of exactly when or in whichever order they occur, I plead with you, don't miss out on the amazing grace and wonderful love of Yahuah! There is hope of avoiding the horrible holocaust soon to come on Earth. Believe the Truth and act on it. The Rapture will occur. As fantastic and "far-out" as everything that I've shared on this website may sound, none of it is a figment of my imagination. All of it, according to Yahuah's sure Word of prophecy, will happen. And Yahushua tells us, as wise bridesmaids, to be prepared at all times for it. Are you? Or will you be the unprepared bridesmaid who is left behind?

If you are not sure, please read "Appendix 4—The Demise of True Christianity"—to make sure that you are a true Believer in the soon-coming Messiah.

Appendix 7—In the End, there is GOOD NEWS!

So far, much of the content that has been shared in this book has been pretty negative, hasn't it?—mankind wallowing in sin, phony "Christianity," the annihilation of Babylon, horrible times to come on the whole world. But, we have to understand what is really happening in the world before we can fully appreciate what I am going to share with you now. And I am really glad that you have come to this page, because now I get to tell you the end of the story. And it is fantastic!—far beyond what you or I have ever imagined. It is even more wonderful than any fantasy-world movie we have ever seen, book we have ever read, or story we have ever heard or imagined, because, according Yahuah's "*sure word of prophecy*" (2 Peter 1:19), the *Bible*, it is absolutely true!

In The Beginning

As I trust is clear by now, to fully understand the present and the future, we must first understand the past. So, let us once again go back to the beginning—to Yahuah's original plan for his creation, particularly man (the *Bible's* generic term for human beings).

In the beginning (of creation) Yahuah created the world (the whole cosmos—universe), all that is in it, and man in His own image (Genesis 1:27). Now, what do you think that means—created in the image of Yahuah? How does that make man different from the rest of Yahuah's creation—plants, animals, and inanimate matter? The *Bible* gives us some clues. It states, "*[Yahuah] is spirit*" (John 4:24). It also states, "*[Yahuah] is love*" (1 John 4:8). And Yahushua said that Yahuah is good (Mark 10:18). So, man was created a good, loving, spiritual being, in the image of Yahuah. "Well, how does that make man any different from my pet dog—a good, loving, spirited animal?" someone might ask. The difference is that, in the core of his being—his spirit—man was created to commune with and, indeed, to be united with the Spirit of Yahuah forever. The *Bible* says that, "*He who is united with the Lord is one spirit with Him.*" (1 Corinthians 6:17) One spirit with Yahuah—that's an amazing reality to try to comprehend, isn't it? But, that's the way it was in the Garden of Eden: Adam and Eve walked with Yahuah and talked with Yahuah, in perfect spiritual union with Him. But, they blew it by sinning against Yahuah and thus separating themselves from Yahuah's life-giving Spirit, bringing immediate spiritual death and eventual physical death on themselves and physical death on every other living thing (cf. Genesis 3:22). Death is simply separation from Yahuah, who is the source of all life. So, although our physical bodies die and decay (cease to exist), our souls (including our spirits) will continue to exist "forever" (either united with Yahuah in eternal life, or separate from Him in "eternal" death), after the rest of creation, including the plants and animals of this present world (which are not spiritual beings), have ceased to exist altogether (cf. Revelation 20:11; 21:1). Also, the goodness and love of Yahuah, which, in union with Him, man was created to manifest, are drastically and categorically different from the "goodness" and "love" of animals. Pet dogs, for example, just act out of instinct in natural affection for and loyalty to their owners. But, we probably won't see a dog voluntarily giving its life to save someone who has abused it or someone it perceives as a threat or an enemy, will we? Yet, isn't that what Yahushua did? Isn't that what we would do if we were united with Yahuah in His love? Wouldn't we, if we had Yahuah's special goodness in our hearts, be kind to someone we saw in need and hurting, even if they had been hateful and cruel to us? See the difference between the totally unselfish Yahuah -kind of love and the "love" and "goodness" of those who are not one with Yahuah, which are no different from the "goodness" and the natural affection of animals?

So, in the beginning, Yahuah created man in His own image—categorically different from and transcending the rest of His creation. He also placed man in a position of benevolent dominion over His creation. Man was given the job of naming all the animals and taking care of the creation (cf. Genesis 1:28)! Now imagine that, if you can: what knowledge! what intelligence! what wisdom! what skill! what power! man must have had to be assigned a perfect, beautiful, wonderful creation to care for! What a fantastic life!

But, tragically, Adam and Eve believed the Lie of the Devil, who told them, "*You shall be as gods*" (Genesis 3:6). In other words, Satan was implying that Adam and Eve could do on their own, apart from Yahuah's Spirit in union with theirs, as "gods" themselves, the superhuman job that Yahuah had given them to do. They also believed that they could get away with doing as they pleased (eat the forbidden fruit), regardless of what Yahuah had said. But what a terrible mistake, because it allowed Satan to get a foothold in Yahuah's creation and immediately take Adam's place as the prince (ruler) of this World (John 12:31)! And it has been downhill for all of Yahuah's creation, including man, since that time; the whole creation has been subject to futility, corruption, and decay (cf. Ecclesiates 2:17); which will continue until Yahuah destroys the present deteriorating world and its inhabitants who oppose Him. And, so far, that's what most of this book has been about.

But, that's not the end of the story; there's incredible Good News! Yahuah's original plan for man has not changed, except that it is even more fantastic now than it was in the beginning! Grasp, if you can, what Yahuah's Word tells us:

Paradise Restored!

Acts 3:19-21 states that Yahuah will send Yahushua the Messiah when it comes time (after the seven years of tribulation and the Wrath of Yahuah) to restore all things to their Edenic state. The period of time when conditions on Earth will again be wonderful beyond our comprehension was foretold numerous times by BCE prophets (Isaiah 65, Jeremiah 23, Joel 2, et al.). It will begin when the Lord returns with the armies of Heaven to destroy the armies of Antimessiah (Revelation 19:11-21). He will then establish His kingdom on the renewed Earth, and will rule over the nations of people who are on Earth at that time (Revelation 19:15), maintaining perfect peace as the "last Adam" (1 Corinthians 15:45) during His millennial reign (Revelation 20).

But, that's just the beginning of the Good News! All those who belong to the Lord Yahushua —who have trusted Him as their Savior and God and are united in spirit with Him—will get to reign with Him, not just on Earth, but over His entire earthly and heavenly creation, including the angels! The Lord Yahushua said, speaking of His faithful Followers,

> To him who wins the victory and does what I want until the goal is reached, I will give him authority over the nations . . . just as I have received authority from my Father. I will also give him the morning star" (meaning Himself—cf. Revelation 22:16). (Revelation 2:26-27)

And the apostle Paul asked his fellow Believers, "*Don't you know that we are to judge angels?*" (1 Corinthians 6:3) To me, that sounds like we Believers in the Lord Yahushua the Messiah are going to be totally indwelled by Him, one with Him, having exactly the same power and authority He has to reign with Him, in Him, and He in us over His creation—with even more power and authority than the first Adam had (over just the Earth) in the beginning. Try to wrap your mind around that!

To more fully appreciate how wonderful it will be to be a child of Yahuah in His Millennial Kingdom, read the following astonishing statement from His Word (paraphrased):

> *It was in keeping with His pleasure and purpose, for His own praise and glory, that [Yahuah] determined before the creation of the universe that through His Son, [Yahushua the Messiah], we would be His spiritual children. In [the Messiah], [Yahuah] our Father chose us in love in advance to be spiritually pure, without defect, in His presence. In union with [the Messiah], through His sacrifice on the cross, we are set free— our sins are forgiven. And in union with Him, commensurate with His grace which the Lord has lavished on us, we were given an inheritance: the Lord has blessed us with every spiritual blessing in Heaven. His ultimate plan, which was a secret until it was revealed by and in [the Messiah], is to place everything in Heaven and on Earth under [the Messiah's] headship. And we, the children of [Yahuah], are to reign with our Lord and [Messiah] over all creation for a thousand years! This is the Lord's will, purpose, and pleasure for our lives.* (Ephesians 1:3-14; Revelation 20:4)

So, there it is, my friend—Yahuah's ultimate purpose for your life. Incomprehensibly wonderful, isn't it? Please, please, please, don't miss out by believing Satan's Lie (*"You shall be as gods."*), by putting any stock in the things of this world, by following a false messiah, or by denying your Lord and Savior before His return. Stay faithful until The End and you will receive your awesome, glorious, "eternal" inheritance in The World to Come! I hope to see you there.

If you are not sure that you have a reservation in the glorious Kingdom of Yahuah, please contact me:

WatchmanBob@gmail.com.

And for even more good news—a glimpse into **Timeless Eternity**, when **all** of Yahuah's Creation, including the fallen heavenly beings and humanity, will be restored to Him, please keep reading, "Appendix 8— How Long is *'Forever'* in the *Bible?*"

Appendix 8—How Long is *"Forever"* in the *Bible*

Have you ever thought that it just doesn't seem fair that people will have to suffer "forever and ever"—for all eternity—in the Lake of Fire because of their sins during this short, "puff of smoke" life on Earth? But, if you truly believe that the *Bible* is Yahuah's inspired Word, you probably immediately censor such thoughts because the doctrines of eternal life and "eternal" punishment are obviously taught by Scripture. In reference to existence after the present earth is destroyed, there are 393 uses of the term *"forever"* and 53 uses of the terms *"eternal"* and *"eternity"* in the *Bible*. But, when we witness to people about the love of Yahuah, they often have trouble reconciling His love with the concept of eternal punishment.

Well, I certainly have no intention of questioning or even doubting Yahuah's Word if that is what it teaches. In fact, I want to qualify the thesis that I present in this essay by stating up-front that **I may be mistaken**, so please do not stake your eternal destiny on what you read here! My purpose is not to influence anyone's response to the Lord, which should be to love, worship, and serve Him with our whole being, no matter what our understanding is of how He executes His judgment of a sinful world, but simply to demonstrate that our understandings of the Lord and His ways are extremely limited, our interpretations of Scripture may be mistaken, and we should always give Him the benefit of the doubt—trusting Him to work all things out for good in the end on behalf of those who love Him (Romans 8:28), for, *"How unsearchable are His judgments and His ways past finding out!"* (Romans 11:33).

And one doctrine regarding which our understanding may be flawed is the doctrine of "eternal" torment. Now, please don't turn me off as teaching some sort of heresy because this is not what you have been taught all your life or what you have read for yourself in the *Bible*. I had exactly the same reaction when I was first exposed to the possibility that the doctrine of eternity in Hell is based on mistranslations of Scripture. But, after much study, thought, and prayer, I am convinced that is exactly the case. So, please hear me out, and I promise that *"You shall know the truth, and the truth shall make you free"* (John 8:32).

The evidence is very simple and clear: the Hebrew and Greek terms translated *"forever,"* *"eternity,"* and all their forms in the *Bible*, did **NOT** mean timeless eternity in the Hebrew and Greek language cultures at the times during which the *Bible* was written. For example, the ancient Greek writer Homer said that the time of one's life (Greek: *aeon* or *aion*) is said to leave him or consume away (Iliad, v. 185; Odyssey, v. 160). But an adjectival variation of exactly the same term is used in Matthew 18:8—*"**everlasting** (Greek: aionios) fire."* But Galatians 1:4 speaks of *"this present, evil **age** (Greek: aion).* So, just from these two verses of Scripture, it can be easily seen that, although *aion* never meant "forever" (in our present understanding of the term) in the surrounding first century cultures, it is translated to mean both finite periods of time and eternity in the *Bible*.

Plus, the BCE Hebrews had a very limited concept of eternity. Based on Scriptures like Ecclesiastes 12:7 (". . . *the spirit will return to* [Yahuah] *who gave it."*), they believed that the disembodied souls of the dead return to Yahuah. But most of their focus was on the present age and the world to come (the Millennium) during which the Messiah would rule from David's throne in Jerusalem. What we today translate *"forever"* (Hebrew: *'olam*) was to them a long, indefinite (but not without end) period of time, as in the *'olam hazeh*—the present world or age—and the *'olam haba*—the world or the age to come. In fact, the term *'olam* also refers to the present physical universe, which will not last into Timeless Eternity (cf. Revelation 20:11). So, verses of Scripture like Isaiah 34:10 . . .

> [*The day of the Lord's vengeance*] *shall not be quenched night or day; its smoke shall ascend 'forever'* [*'olam*]. *From generation to generation* [indicating periods of time] *it shall lie waste; No one shall pass through it 'forever'* [*'olam*] *and 'ever'* [*netsach* – enduring for a long period of time*],

. . . do **not** indicate Timeless Eternity. In the *B'rit Hadashah*, the same thought is repeated:

> *He who receives the mark of the beast . . . shall be tormented with fire and brimstone in the presence of the holy angels and in the presence of the Lamb. And the smoke of their torment ascends forever and ever* [*aion*]. (Revelation 14:10, 11)

It's kind of hard to imagine the smoke of those burning in the Lake of Fire ascending to a perfect Heaven, into the presence of the angels and the Lamb, for all eternity, isn't it?

So, what do all those Scripture passages that refer to *"eternal"* torment or punishment actually mean? The correct understanding of the Greek word for *"torment"* (*basanismos*) may provide a clue. *Strong's Concordance*, definition 929, states that *basanismos* refers to "a testing by the touchstone, which is a black, siliceous stone used to test the purity of gold or silver . . ." In other words, Hell or the Lake of Fire may be a place where the "lost" are refined or their impurities are burned away for a long, indefinite period of time, but not for all eternity.

And this understanding seems to concur with Scripture as a whole, which tells us that, in the end, **ALL** of Yahuah's creation will be restored to Him, pure and undefiled (e.g., Colossians 1:19:

> *For it pleased the Father that in Him* [Yahushua] *all the fullness should dwell, and by Him* [Yahushua] *to reconcile **all things** to Himself* [Yahuah the Father], *by Him* [Yahushua], *whether **things on earth or things in heaven**, having made peace through the blood of his cross.*)

After all, isn't it disturbing to think that the Lord Yahushua the Messiah, through whom "**all** things were made" (John 1:3), and who gave his life as a ransom for **all** mankind (1 Timothy 2:6), would, along with the holy angels, watch people He created being tortured forever in fire?

Then why, if none of the Hebrew and Greek terms that are translated as some form of *"forever"* or *"eternity"* in the *Bible* were used in that way in the surrounding cultures at the time the *Bible* was written, were they translated that way in the *Bible*? The answer is unclear, but I will take a stab at it. Bear in mind that there is no concept of an eternal place of torment in the *Tanakh*. The *Tanakh* term for the (temporary) abode of the unsaved dead (*Sheol*) has no eternal connotations. The *B'rit Hadashah* term equivalent to *Sheol* is the Greek term *Hades*. The concept of a fiery hell (Greek: *geenna* or *gehenna*), was not developed until the Jewish Rabbis came up with it during the first or second century CE, as the following quote from *The New International Dictionary of New Testament Theology* says:

> At the end of the 1st century A.D. or the beginning of the 2nd, the doctrine of a fiery purgatory arose among the Rabbis. All those in whose cases merit and guilt are equally balanced go to *gehenna*. There they are purified and, if they do penance, inherit paradise. Alongside this we find the concept of an eschatological Gehinnom judgment, **limited in time**, after the last judgment. (p. 208, vol. 2).

So apparently, at the time Yahushua was on Earth, the Jewish concept of *geenna* or *gehenna* (Hell) was that it was a place of purification for an indefinite but limited period of time after the judgment.

And apparently, the early "Christian" (Catholic) Church got its concept of Purgatory from the first or second-century Jews! The concept of **eternal** torment must have been added by theologians later, no earlier than the earliest translations of the *B'rit Hadashah* from Greek manuscripts into other languages, beginning with Latin, starting at about the end of the second century CE. In fact, many *Bible* scholars who wrote during the first five or six centuries CE defined the terms *aion* and *aionos* as finite periods of time. For example, the earliest lexicographer, *Hesychius* (*circa* CE 400-600), defined *aion* as: "The life of man, the time of life." And in the sixteenth century the scholar Phavorinus observed that, rather than using earlier definitions of the term *aion*, the famous (Catholic) Council of Constantinople of 543 CE added the concept of eternity "**as** [he said] **it seems to the theologian**" (rather than according to its actual etymologically-derived meaning). So, as noted above, in our present translations of the *Bible*, the terms *aion* and *aionos* have come to denote various periods of time, from brief to extended to eternal.

Perhaps the main passage of Scripture used to support the doctrine of eternal torment is Mark 9:43-48:

> *If your hand causes you to sin, cut it off. It is better for you to enter into life maimed, rather than having two hands, to go to hell, into the fire that shall never be quenched—where* **'Their worm does not die, and the fire is not quenched'** *[a quote from Isaiah 66:24]. And if your foot causes you to sin, cut it off. It is better for you to enter life lame, rather than having two feet, to be cast into hell, into the fire that shall never be quenched—where* **'Their worm does not die, and the fire is not quenched.'** *And if your eye causes you to sin, pluck it out. It is better for you to enter the kingdom of [Yahuah] with one eye, rather than having two eyes, to be cast into hell fire – where* **'Their worm does not die, and the fire is not quenched.'**

To correctly interpret these verses, we must (1) remember that BCE Israel had no concept of eternal punishment and (2) understand Hebrew thought and figures of speech. So, the phrase, (where) *'Their worm does not die, and the fire is not quenched'* from Isaiah cannot refer to eternity. The graphic figure of speech, *"Their worm [maggot] does not die,"* refers to the fact that in Hell, the decaying of the bodies in torment will be a continual process, never ending **until** the process of purification—eating away the corruption—is complete. Likewise, *"the fire is not quenched"* means that it will be a continual process, never ending **until** Yahuah's created beings are restored to Him perfectly purified.

298

But we still don't have the answer to the question "Why?" do we? Why did theologians during the early centuries of the Christian Church add the concept of eternal torment to the Bible? A clue might be that it is an extremely powerful and frightening idea. And most of the early translators of the Scripture were Catholic theologians. And the Roman Catholic Church has become the most powerful and wealthiest religious organization on Earth. How? . . . by terrorizing masses of people through the threats of torture, death, Purgatory, and eternal hell-fire into joining the Church and continually pumping their money and material possessions into the Church through its extensive system of indulgences and gifts. So, the doctrine of eternal torment suits the purposes of church growth and prosperity very well, even if it means the impoverishment of its parishioners. Tragically, the Protestant Reformation did not free its participants from all the Catholic false doctrines, including the doctrine of eternal torment. And today, virtually all Christiandom still subscribes to that pernicious doctrine. One of the most famous sermons in history was the "hell-fire and brimstone" monologue by the New England preacher Jonathan Edwards entitled, "Sinners in the Hands of an Angry God!" which caused hundreds, and since then thousands, to come trembling and weeping to the altar begging to be saved. Although there is more emphasis these days, especially in affluent societies, on the worldly "health, wealth, and prosperity" benefits of Christianity (which is equally contrary to Yahuah's Word), there are still many churches who drive people to church through fear, then, once they are there, keep them there, cowering at the thought of what will happen to them if they leave. And the doctrine of eternal torment is a back-up strategy for some churches who allegedly preach the pure love of Yahuah but cannot offer enough worldly perks to keep their members faithful.

Some may object that to eliminate the doctrine of eternal punishment from the Bible will diminish the power of the Gospel, to whom I would reply simply, "You have no idea of the power of the love of Yahuah, Who *". . . is not willing that **any** should perish, but that **all** will come to repentance"* (2 Peter 3:9) and Who *". . . loved **the world** so much that He gave the life of His only begotten Son, that **whoever** is willing might be saved"* (cf. John 3:16). The fear of being separated from Yahuah and purified in the Lake of Fire for an indeterminate period of time should be plenty of incentive to turn people to the mercy and love of Yahuah without having to threaten them with the **un**-Scriptural, unjust, and inconceivable notion of having to spend all eternity in torment. But, in the end, it is the **love** of Yahuah that saves and keeps a soul saved, not the fear of eternal torment.

And, once we accept the possibility that purging in the Lake of Fire is not for all eternity, many heretofore enigmatic passages of Scripture suddenly come into focus and make perfect sense. For example, 1 Peter 3:18-19 states,

> *For [the Messiah] also suffered once for sins, the just for the unjust, that He might bring us to [Yahuah], being put to death in the flesh but made alive by the Spirit, by whom also He went and preached to the spirits in prison.*

In the *Bible*, *"spirits in prison"* refers to the fallen angels who are kept imprisoned in a place called *"the bottomless pit"* or *"the abyss."* Yahushua stated that, at the present time, He holds the keys to Hades and to Death (Revelation 1:18). In other words, Yahushua decides who goes into Death and Hades and who may be released from those states of the soul, as well as from the abyss—the prison of the fallen angels. From time to time, those evil spirits are released from their prison to do the bidding of Satan and/or Yahuah on the earth (e.g., Revelation 9:1-3). So, what in the world does *"preached to the spirits in prison"* mean, and why would the Messiah do that if those spirits were doomed to an eternity in Hell? The doctrine of purification in the Lake of Fire (rather than eternal torment) might explain why He would, after His crucifixion, go to preach to those spirits. Maybe He told them that He had power over Death, Hades, and the Lake of Fire, and that they would have to spend an indeterminate period of time in the Lake of Fire being purged of their sin—their rebellion against Yahuah. But, when they are finally purified, the whole Creation, including the fallen angels, will be restored to its original, glorious state. (Please note that Colossians 1:20 states that ultimately **all** things on Earth and **in Heaven**, including principalities and powers [spiritual beings] created by the Lord [v. 16], will be restored to Him.)

So, after the Millennium, the total annihilation of heaven and earth, the Final Judgment, the casting of Death, Hades, and all of Yahuah's unregenerate created beings into the Lake of Fire (cf. Revelation 20:10-15) for a long but not eternal time of purification, His entire Creation will be restored to Him in **Timeless Eternity**, which is not described in the *Bible*, except for a few glimpses in the description of the New Jerusalem, where,

*[Yahuah] will wipe away every tear from their eyes; **there shall be no more death**, nor sorrow, nor crying. There shall be no more pain, for the former things have passed away.* (Revelation 21:4)

What a magnificent, glorious plan, and how unsearchable are the ways of the Lord Yahuah Almighty!

About the Author

Watchman Bob was born in Texas in 1945. He grew up in a dedicated, Christian, church-going home and attended the main college affiliated with that church. So, he was thoroughly grounded in church doctrine and *Bible* knowledge.

However, after graduating from college, while serving in the U.S. Navy during the Vietnam War, Bob began to have doubts about some of the doctrines and practices of the church in which he was raised and began to yearn for a more personal, real relationship with "God." But he would never consider leaving the church, because all of his life he had been taught that it was the only true Christian Church, and all those who were not members in good standing were lost.

Remarkably, while in perplexity over these things, Bob received a postcard in the mail, which was an advertisement for a new religious magazine. Bob would normally have trashed mail like that, but felt compelled to subscribe to the magazine. It turned out to be a magazine published by some who had left the church in which Bob was raised! And in about the third issue that he received, there was an article by a man Bob knew who had been a ministerial student at the college they had both attended, but who had left the church and became a minister in another denomination. And in his article, he explained how that the church he had left had the "cart before the horse," so to speak: it emphasized correct doctrine and practice over a personal, spiritual relationship with "God." And, when Bob read that, the lights came on! With that understanding he was enabled break his life-long, legalistic ties to that church.

Then, his quest for True Christianity began. Bob had no doubt about the basics: "Jesus" is "God" incarnate; no one knows the one,

303

true God except through Him; and True Christianity is not just a religion but is a dynamic, growing relationship with the Lord. But the question was: which denomination, church, sect, or group of believers best practices True Christianity? There are thousands of churches or church groups out there. Do most of them, with only minor, unimportant differences, have it right? Or are there only a few? To make a long story short, during the next twenty years, Bob went from church to church: Baptist, Methodist, Seventh Day Adventist, Brethren assemblies, Nazarene, charismatic, Word of Faith . . . . He even visited a Catholic Church. He fellowshipped with them, taught in their schools, read their books, studied their doctrines, and studied the doctrines and practices of many other churches and religions. He studied the Scriptures and prayed that the Lord would show him where he could find True Christianity. But there was always something wrong—something missing—in the churches Bob attended and studied. He could not put his finger on it—wrong emphasis, wrong doctrine . . . something.

Finally, Yahuah the Father spoke to Bob's heart,

> You are looking in the wrong places. You will not find True Christianity in the American churches. They are in bed with the secular world. The emphasis in the churches on fun and games and good food and entertainment is not True Christianity; it is indulging the flesh. Supporting worldly success and comfortable, materialistic life styles is not True Christianity; it is laying up treasures on Earth. Patriotism is not True Christianity; it is capitulating to the secular world. True Christianity is realizing that you are an alien on this planet—just passing through. It is denying yourself, taking up your cross, and following My Son Yahushua. It is just the opposite of the empty form of "Christianity" practiced in America, which consists of giving a tithe of what you have to the Church or to those in need, but keeping most of it for yourself.

Then, Bob learned by experience that the Lord had told him the Truth. When he started to share his convictions about True Christianity in the small "Christian" farming community where he taught high school and coached, he found that he had opened not just a can of worms, but a pit of snakes. The emotional and spiritual climate turned very cold. Then, immediately after making a short speech at an awards ceremony about how we need to be thanking and glorifying "God" for our accomplishments rather than patting ourselves on the back, he was fired from his job and his 30-year career was down the tubes. And as he continued to share the truths and implications of the *Bible*, especially the book of Revelation, with friends and family members, virtually none of them responded positively: Most responded with silence; some had negative comments and made it clear that they wanted to hear no more; some coldly cut off further communications and visits with Bob.

Also, Bob came to the realization that virtually the entire Christian Church, although some of its members insist that they are pro-Israel, consider Jews second-class citizens in the Kingdom of Yahuah when the *Bible* teaches just the opposite—that Gentiles who come to faith in Yahushua are grafted, contrary to their nature, into Yahuah's original, natural, and eternal olive tree Israel (cf. Romans 11:24), making them *"fellow citizens"* in the *"commonwealth of Israel"* (Ephesians 2:12, 19).

So, after over a year of encountering hostility when attempting to minister Yahuah's Word concerning True Christianity to "Christians," plus the awareness of subtle (and often not-so-subtle) anti-Semitism in the Christian Church, the Lord showed Bob that, for the most part, "Christian" America is not open to True Christianity—that America is indeed modern, prophetic Babylon—and that he was, with few exceptions, *"casting his pearls before swine"* in attempting to minister the Truth to Christians.

Therefore, being aware of *"things which must shortly come to pass"* (Revelation 1:1), Bob has dedicated as much time as he can to the study of *Bible* prophecy and current events; seeking out and warning the few (Matthew 7:14) who do have *"eyes that see and ears that hear,"* of the imminent annihilation of modern Babylon, the Great Tribulation, and the Day of Yahuah soon to come; and helping those who are open to the Truth to be on the winning side—the army of the true Messiah. Through his ministry website he is attempting to facilitate the development of a network of likeminded watchmen who will take the Truth to whoever will listen, before it is too late. If you are interested in getting involved, please visit www.RevelationUnderstoodCommentary.com/last-trump.html or contact Bob at WatchmanBob@gmail.com.

The Revelation of Yahushua the Messiah is the result of Watchman Bob's studies and the Scriptural basis of the ministry that the Lord Yahuah has given him.

Thank Yahuah for His Revelation which shows us both *"things which are"* and *"things which must shortly take place!"* And pray for those who, refusing to believe Yahuah's Word, will have no knowledge of what is really happening and what is going to soon happen—until it comes on them like a thief in the night and it is too late for them to do anything about it.

"Come out of her, my people." –Revelation 18:4

Printed in Great Britain
by Amazon.co.uk, Ltd.,
Marston Gate.